The British Army and the Peninsular War Volume 4

The British Army and the Peninsular War
Volume 4

Arroyo Molinos, Tarifa, Ciudad Rodrigo, Badajoz,
Salamanca, Burgos: 1812

J. W. Fortescue

LEONAUR

The British Army and the Peninsular War
Volume 4
Arroyo Molinos, Tarifa, Ciudad Rodrigo, Badajoz, Salamanca, Burgos: 1812
by J. W. Fortescue

FIRST EDITION

First published under the title
A History of the British Army

Leonaur is an imprint of Oakpast Ltd

ISBN: 978-1-78282-573-9 (hardcover)
ISBN: 978-1-78282-574-6 (softcover)

http://www.leonaur.com

Publisher's Notes

Contents

CHAPTER 1

Failure at Badajoz

It was, as already told, on the 17th of May, 1811, that Wellington received between Sabugal and Castello Branco a nervous letter from Beresford, which prompted him to hurry on to the Guadiana with all possible speed.

Arriving at Elvas on the 19th there reached him the marshal's report of the Battle of Albuera, written in so despondent a tone that the commander-in-chief felt bound to send a little note of comfort to his dispirited subordinate. He was not, however, too well pleased, seeing that Sir William had managed to reduce his two British divisions to the strength of one; and, after going over the battlefield on the 21st, he wrote, as we have read, an extremely caustic description of Beresford's proceedings at large. However, he perceived that the enterprise which he had proposed to himself, the siege of Badajoz, was still feasible with the troops which were following him from the Agueda; and, before he had been at Elvas twenty-four hours, he ordered up a fresh battery of artillery from Lisbon to supplement the now attenuated body of gunners that remained with Beresford's army.

It was one of Wellington's great advantages, to use his own words, that no one of the French armies had any communication with any other nor knew anything of its movements, all alike being dependent upon orders from Paris; whereas he, with the whole population friendly to him, knew all that was passing on every side. D'Erlon, as he was aware, had marched away to join Soult in Andalusia, pursuant to the emperor's command, so that the Ninth Corps was for the present out of action. Marmont had retired to Salamanca, having before him the duty of re-equipping and reorganising his army, a task which would probably prevent him from taking the field for several weeks. Bessières was fully occupied with guerillas and other troubles in the

Map of the
SPANISH CAMPAIGN.

English Miles

north; and it was evident from intercepted letters that he was not working kindly with the Army of Portugal. The moment was therefore favourable for taking liberties with the French commanders, and the more so in that Wellington could feel fairly sure that little or no intelligence of his movements would reach them.

Hence he had not hesitated to draw away ten thousand men of his army to the south, to leave the remainder fewer than thirty thousand of all nations—under the command of Spencer on the Agueda, and even to direct the latter, conditionally, to despatch two more brigades to the Guadiana. We can understand that he would gladly have substituted Graham for Spencer, if the former had been at hand; but that desirable exchange, though not far distant, was as yet unaccomplished. However, Wellington left with Spencer very full instructions as to his movements in case Marmont should advance, pointing out that he must retreat by way of Sabugal to Belmonte and the Zezere, contesting every mile of ground, and that Almeida must be blown up. Accordingly, on the Agueda Spencer remained, with an exceptionally good opportunity of displaying his talent, if he had any; but it will be seen that he only justified Wellington's former criticisms upon him. He was fidgety and nervous even to timidity, and earned no distinction except the unflattering name of a "regular old woman." (*Wellington Desp.* To Spencer, 15th, 22nd, 24th May; to Beresford, 19th May; to Howorth, 20th May; to Liverpool, 22nd, 24th May 1811. *Autobiography of Sir Harry Smith,* i.)

Before Badajoz could be invested, however, it was necessary that Soult should retire to a becoming distance. The marshal had begun his retreat, it will be remembered, on the 18th, escorting a huge convoy of wounded by way of Solana and Almendralejo towards Llerena. On the 23rd the British infantry reached Almendralejo, and on that same day the French rear-guard withdrew from Villafranca upon Usagre, and thence to Llerena. On the 25th Soult, wishing to know what force was pursuing him, ordered Latour Maubourg to march back along the road with ten regiments of cavalry and a battery of field-artillery, in all some three thousand men, and to drive in the British cavalry upon its supports.

After moving north-westward for three or four miles Latour Maubourg struck the Spanish advanced parties at Villa Garcia, and chasing them back to Usagre came there upon General Lumley, who had with him the Third Dragoon Guards, Fourth and Fourteenth Dragoons, and Lefebure's troop of horse-artillery, making together with some

10

weak regiments of Spanish and Portuguese cavalry, a force of about twenty-two hundred men, nearly half of whom were British. The ground about Usagre is favourable for an inferior force, and had been thoroughly studied by Lumley. The town lies between two ranges of hills on the south side of a small brook, which runs in a deep ravine and is crossed by a bridge; the approach to which from the south lies through a narrow street, and from the north through an equally narrow defile.

Lumley had carefully noted and sounded the crossing-places above and below this bridge; and, upon the report that the enemy was advancing in some force of all three arms, he sent the Thirteenth Light Dragoons and the Portuguese ahead by these crossing-places, with orders to form line in conjunction with the Spaniards beyond the town. Latour Maubourg thereupon deployed his columns and brought forward his guns, when, having ascertained what they wanted to know, the Allied squadrons fell back slowly, the Spaniards through the middle of the town, the British and Portuguese upon each flank of it. There they took up their stations behind a rising ground to watch the fords; while Lumley with the Third Dragoon Guards and Fourth Dragoons remained in reserve behind the skyline.

The guns of Latour Maubourg continued to fire from the heights about the town as the Allies retired, but without any result; and they were effectively answered by Lefebure's battery, though the British guns were inferior both in calibre and in numbers. Unable to make any headway in this fashion, Latour Maubourg detached General Briche with three weak regiments of light horse to move to his right down the stream, cross it at a ford which had been used by Otway, and turn Lumley's left flank. Briche marched off accordingly, but finding that Otway was waiting for him above the ford, dared not engage him up a steep hillside, and proceeded farther down the water in search of another passage, which he was unable to find. Though these wanderings naturally took much time, Briche omitted to send any report of his doings; wherefore Latour Maubourg, after waiting for over an hour, chose to assume that all was well and ordered the leading brigade of dragoons under General Bron to advance across the bridge.

Bron accordingly moved at a rapid pace through the town under fire of Lefebure's guns, and deployed his leading regiment—the 4th Dragoons—directly it had passed the bridge, quite unconscious that the British Fourth Dragoons were immediately on his front and the Third Dragoon Guards on his left flank. The Third promptly charging upon one flank and the Fourth upon the other overthrew the French 4th; and apparently at the same time the French 20th, which was coming up in support, was caught before it could deploy.

★★★★★★

This seems to be the meaning of Lumley's observation that the French presented two fronts (*Wellington Desp.*, ed. 1852, v. 60-61), the 4th being formed in line to the front, and the 20th coming up in column, and possibly wheeled into line hastily to a flank. Picard (*La Cavalerie dans les Guerres de la Revolution et de l'Empire*, ii.) says that the 4th and 20th were formed in line, the former on the right, the latter on the left. Lapène says that the 4th alone was deployed and the 20th coming up in support.

★★★★★★

Both regiments were driven back in utter rout upon the bridge, but found it blocked by the French 26th which was hurrying over to the rescue; and the Allies, to use Cromwell's phrase, had the execution of their enemies for some minutes as they vainly sought safety in flight up and down the bank.

Latour Maubourg did what he could to save the fugitives by dismounting a regiment and opening fire with carbines, but with little result. The French dragoons at last dropped off their horses and fled to the town on foot; and, when the pursuit ended, one hundred and seventy of them had been killed and wounded, and eighty officers and men captured, (figures given by Picard; Lumley states his prisoners at 78; Cannon's *History of the 3rd D.G.* says that 96 N.C.O. and men were captured, besides officers), besides a great number of horses; whereas the casualties of the Allies did not amount to twenty. Altogether it was a pretty little fight, exceedingly well managed by Lumley who, though no genius with pen, ink, and paper, was capable enough in action.

The ravine at Usagre from that day became the boundary between Soult's army and the Allied forces which covered the leaguer of Badajoz, Wellington being unwilling to delay the siege any longer. The British and Portuguese formed the left of the covering troops, their main body of infantry being at Almendralejo and of cavalry at Ribera; while the bulk of the Spaniards were between Barcarrota and Solana with advanced parties at Bienvenida and Calzadilla. In case of an advance of the enemy from the south the point of concentration was to be, as before, Albuera. (*Wellington Desp.* Memo, of 29th May 1811). Finally on the 27th Beresford left the forces in the field and retired to Lisbon, nominally for the purpose of restoring order and organisation in the Portuguese military departments, really because Wellington had noticed his nervous condition, which for the time unfitted him for independent command. Beresford's successor, Rowland Hill, had meanwhile arrived at Lisbon from England, and was on his way to resume command of the southern detachment of the army as in 1810. On the 31st he arrived at Almendralejo, welcomed by all ranks of the forces and not least by the commander-in-chief.

Wellington during this time proceeded with his preparations for the siege of Badajoz, for which he retained the Third and Seventh Divisions besides Hamilton's and Collins's Portuguese, the whole numbering some fourteen thousand men. The operations were to be conducted against time. Wellington wrote to his brother Henry on the 29th:

If we don't succeed in a few days, we shall not succeed at all, as the seventeen or nineteen battalions and some cavalry of the Ninth Corps are on their march to join Soult, and I think will reach him by the second week in June.

As on the first occasion, therefore, the siege was undertaken with such artillery as was to be found at Elvas, and the principal efforts were directed against the fort of San Cristobal and the castle. One would have thought that Beresford's failure would have sufficed to deter both the commander and the engineers from such false measures; but it did not. Time was the great object, and therefore it was argued that there must be no delay in waiting for the British siege-train, and that the attack must be directed against the strongest points because, if they were taken—a very important condition—the place must fall directly. No account, then, was to be taken of the deficiencies of the antiquated guns at Elvas, nor of the fact, already ascertained by experience, that the soil before San Cristobal was too thin and too close to the rock to permit trenches to be thrown up. The indefatigable Major Dickson was again employed to collect siege-artillery, and, in spite of all that had passed a fortnight before, declared himself sanguine of success. (The Dickson Manuscripts).

The blockade of the fortress had been resumed, as we have seen, on the 18th of May. On the 25th the Seventh Division invested the place on the north bank of the Guadiana; and on the 27th Picton's division, marching from Campo Maior, crossed the river by a ford above the town and joined the besieging force on the south bank. On the night of the 29th ground was broken by reopening Beresford's trenches for a false attack upon Pardaleras; and on the 30th the first parallels were begun at a distance of eight hundred yards from the castle and four hundred yards from San Cristobal.

At the latter point it was found that, though there had been a little soil a fortnight before, there was now none, for Phillipon during his few days of freedom had carted away all that had been thrown up by Beresford. A row of gabions was therefore erected, and every effort was made to bring up earth from the rear; but at daylight the enemy's fire soon knocked over the gabions and picked off several men. Ultimately Wellington was compelled to purchase woolpacks in Elvas, under shelter of which some progress was made on the night of the 1st of June with the construction of the batteries. By the morning of the 3rd four batteries, mounting fourteen pieces, had been completed against San Cristobal, and one battery, mounting twenty pieces, against the castle.

Fire was opened at half-past nine, that against the castle with little accuracy owing to the windage of the guns, and before nightfall two cannon on the north side and two more on the south had been disabled by their own discharges. On the following day the bombardment was renewed with an increased force of twenty-one guns on the side of San Cristobal, when five more pieces succumbed to their own faultiness, irrespective of others damaged by the enemy. On the 5th a new battery of seven heavy guns was brought into action at a range of six hundred and fifty yards against the castle, and some progress was made both there and on the north side; indeed at San Cristobal it was reckoned that another day's battering would produce a sufficient breach. Four more guns, however, were this day rendered unserviceable by their own fire, and it was at last resolved to send for some British iron guns which were expected at Elvas from Lisbon. On the 6th the cannonade of San Cristobal was continued throughout the day, with the result that a practicable breach had been made by nightfall; and it was resolved to deliver an assault some hours later.

Accordingly General Houston organised one hundred and eighty volunteers from the Fifty-First, Eighty-Fifth, and 17th Portuguese into a forlorn hope of two companies, which at midnight ran forward from the trenches. They reached the works with little loss and made their way without difficulty into the ditch; but the French had cleared away the rubbish brought down by the British shot, leaving a sheer ascent of seven feet to the breach, and had blocked the breach itself with overturned carts and *chevaux de frise*. Checked at this point the officers ran round the ditch in the hope of finding some low point where the scarp might be escaladed; but the ladders which they carried with them proved to be everywhere too short; and after losing half their number killed and wounded, the stormers retired. They cannot be blamed for the failure. They had striven against the inevitable, if anything, for too long; and indeed it seems that not only was the assaulting party too weak, but that the entire operation was mismanaged.

On the 7th a new battery was completed against the castle, and the fire visibly enlarged the breach; but the hill, on which the building stands, being of clay would not crumble away, but peeled off in perpendicular sections and remained inaccessible. Moreover the French, no matter how hot the British fire, were always careful to remove any accumulation of rubbish that might facilitate the ascent. By this time Wellington was beginning to despair of success. D'Erlon's Corps was reported to be due at Cordova on the 6th; while Marmont, as will presently be explained in detail, had moved southward from the Tormes on the 3rd. (*Wellington Desp.* To Liverpool, 6th June; to Spencer, 7th June 1811). Unless, therefore, the place could be captured by the 10th the siege must be raised. A heavy fire was maintained on the 8th and 9th; but the Castle was still pronounced unassailable, though San Cristobal had been nearly silenced and much damaged. Two breaches had now been made, and it was decided to deliver a second assault at nine o'clock on the evening of the 9th, so as to allow the less time for their repair and for displacing the fallen ruins at their foot.

Houston accordingly formed a fresh storming party, four hundred and fifty strong, from the Fifty-First, Eighty-Fifth, Chasseurs Britanniques, Brunswick-Oels, and 17th Portuguese, half of them being told off for the actual assault and the remainder detached to make diversions at various points and to keep up a fire of musketry against the parapet. Sixteen ladders of sufficient length were provided; and the forlorn hope was led, as in the previous storm, by Lieutenant Dyas of the Fifty-First.

At the appointed time the column rushed forward, and its commander, Major M'Geechy, and the guiding engineer were both of them killed before the ditch was reached. The rest jumped down into the ditch and made for the breaches, but, finding them still high overhead, planted their ladders. Every man who attempted to ascend was shot down or bayoneted as soon as he reached the top, while the garrison overwhelmed the main column at the foot of the breach with hand grenades, bags of powder, and every description of missile. At last, after an hour's vain struggle to accomplish an impossible task, the column fell back with a loss one hundred and thirty-nine killed and wounded—seven-tenths of the number that had taken part in the assault. Wellington after this failure wrote:

> In fact we have not made a practicable breach either in San Cristobal or in the body of the place. (*Wellington Desp.* To C. Stuart, 10th June 1811).

In other words, such attacks as those of the 6th and 9th signified simple sacrifices of brave men and should never have been delivered at all.

On the morning of the 10th the fire against the castle was resumed with great effect, for the iron guns had by this time arrived from Lisbon. In fact the breach was made actually practicable; but none the less Wellington at noon gave orders to raise the siege. In the course of the morning an intercepted letter from Soult to Marmont had been brought in, which pointed clearly to a junction between the armies of Andalusia and of Portugal within a very few days in Estremadura, and stated that in any case Soult himself would march northward about the 9th or 10th. Simultaneously came intelligence from the north which left no doubt but that Marmont was moving southward and might arrive at Merida on the 15th.

It was still possible for Wellington to continue the cannonade for a day or two; but the only result would have been to deplete the ammunition of Elvas to a dangerous extent for no possible profit. Breaches from four to six hundred yards from the nearest trench might suffice for the storm of an Indian stronghold, but not for that of a modern fortress defended by good regular troops under the command of officers distinguished equally for courage and resource. Moreover the prolongation of the siege, while a hostile army was approaching within perilous proximity, might compel the hazard of a general action upon disadvantageous terms. There was therefore nothing to be done but to abandon the entire enterprise.

This was particularly galling to Wellington, for he had lost four hundred and eighty-five of all ranks, killed, wounded, or prisoners, in the course of the siege, and he also knew that Badajoz contained food for less than another fortnight at longest. Indeed Phillipon had actually put the garrison upon half-rations; and, since he could not hope even so to hold out for more than ten days, he had laid plans for the desperate venture of cutting his way through the beleaguering lines to Merida. Nevertheless the operations were creditable neither to the

British commander nor to his engineers. It is true that the lack of trained sappers and the defects of the Portuguese guns were matters for which they could not be held responsible; nor, I think, can Wellington be blamed that his own siege-train was not upon the spot. He had in those very days ordered it to be sent to Oporto and thence up the Douro; but, believing, as he did, throughout the first four months of 1810, that he might be directed to embark the army at any moment, it is not surprising that he declined earlier to encumber himself with a mass of heavy guns.

★★★★★★

Wrottesly, *Life of Burgoyne*, i. Napier (iv.), ignoring the fact that the siege-train had lain on board ship at Lisbon for at least two years, thinks Wellington open to censure for not asking that it might be sent from England. His ignorance upon such a point is very remarkable

★★★★★★

At the same time, it is unquestionable that every rule for the siege of a fortress was violated by the British, and especially in selection of the wrong points for attack. The engineers blamed Beresford greatly for neglecting their advice during his first short siege, but that same advice was accepted by Wellington with most unsatisfactory consequences; and indeed the general is said to have exclaimed that in any future operation of the kind he would be his own engineer. At Burgos, as we shall see in due time, he fulfilled this threat and tried East Indian methods with disastrous results; so that it may be questioned whether his intervention at Badajoz would have been a change for the better. Upon the whole, it seems likely that the engineers stuck to their faulty plans chiefly out of pique, because Beresford had not, as they thought, given them a fair trial; and that Wellington accepted them from sheer inexperience of this particular branch of the art military. It may be said indeed that the French were as superior to the British in the science of poliorcetics, as were the British to the French in the organisation of transport and supply; and for precisely the same reasons. (Wrottesley, i.)

To turn now to the movements of the enemy, it will be remembered that Marmont had led the Army of Portugal back to Salamanca on the 13th of May. The previous narrative has sufficed to show the condition in which he took it over from Massena, and the drastic measures which were necessary to restore it to discipline and efficiency. Napoleon himself had not been blind to its shortcomings, and, as a

17

first step towards ending the insubordination of officers, had author-
ised the marshal to substitute organisation in divisions for the previous
organisation into army corps, and to send home any general officers
who did not commend themselves to him. Marmont took advantage of this permission at once. He announced that any general who
wished might go home; and the offer was promptly accepted by Junot,
Loison, Marchand, Mermet, and other of the divisional leaders. He
then distributed his force into six divisions and promoted brigadiers
to command them, keeping only Reynier among the older officers, in
case he should be obliged to divide his force.

This done, he completed his battalions to a uniform strength of
seven hundred men, and sent home the empty cadres which he had
depleted in the process. Then turning to the cavalry and artillery he
drafted out the horses unfit for immediate service, and found that
Montbrun's division of six regiments could produce only eight hundred animals, Lamotte's light brigade only two hundred and fifty, and
the artillery a bare four hundred. Within a fortnight he contrived to
obtain horses sufficient for twenty-five hundred cavalry and for thirty-
six guns, but no more; and he was compelled to order a vast number of
dismounted men to march into France. In fine, the effective strength
of the Army of Portugal at the end of May was reduced to twenty-
eight thousand soldiers, several thousand more being scattered about
in various depots and hospitals, from which it was extremely unlikely
that the local commanders, who were always in want of troops to repress the guerillas, would ever permit them to rejoin their regiments.

With so small a force Marmont recognised that offensive movements were impossible for him except in combination with the army
either of the North or of Andalusia; and, the emperor having given him
no instructions except to work for the general interest of the French
forces in the Peninsula, he conceived from the first that his right station, in order to fulfil that end, would be on the Tagus. It so happened
that Soult, before starting for the relief of Badajoz, had written to Massena to say that, if he failed in this object with his own army, he might
be compelled to ask help from the Army of Portugal. This letter was
delivered to Marmont, who responded cordially that, if necessary, he
was prepared to bring his entire corps to his colleague's assistance.

But before Marmont could march he required money, transport,
and the assurance that Bessières would look to the safety of Salamanca
in his absence. The Duke of Istria, however, did not receive his appeals
in a friendly spirit. He declared, probably with truth, that he had no

money to give, and, certainly with untruth, that he could not spare a man for Salamanca. But though niggardly of troops and treasure he was very liberal with advice, urging many reasons to dissuade Marmont from moving to the assistance of Soult. He alleged his colleague's want of transport, cavalry and artillery-teams, the difficulty of supplies, the sufficiency of Soult's army unaided, every plea in fact that could possibly be advanced for the retention of the Army of Portugal in the north. All was to no purpose. Marmont, unlike the majority of Napoleon's Marshals, was a gentleman by birth and by instinct, and was not to be deterred from doing his duty loyally towards his master. (*Mémoirs de Marmont*, iv.)

By the 1st of June the marshal's preparations were completed; and on that day and the next Reynier moved southward with five divisions of infantry and a thousand horse towards the pass of Baños, while Marmont himself with another division and the whole of his light cavalry advanced to Ciudad Rodrigo, and on the 5th threw into it a convoy of provisions. So confidently was this demonstration made that Spencer, with a far superior force of infantry, did not attempt to check him; and on the 6th, when Marmont marched away from Ciudad Rodrigo in two columns upon Espeja and Gallegos, the British commander drew back the Light Division first to Nave de Haver and later to Alfaiates, covering the movement with the Royal Dragoons and one squadron of the Fourteenth.

Slade, who was in command of the cavalry, contrived as usual to blunder in his dispositions, and would have had his rear-guard cut off at the marsh of Nave de Haver, had not a part of the Royals and Fourteenth extricated it by a well-timed charge. It is more than probable that Spencer would have continued his retreat to the Zezere if he had been left to himself; but fortunately Colonel Pakenham and Colonel Waters pointed out that the enemy's movements were more ostentatious than threatening, and that probably they were only intended to screen the march of the main body to the Tagus.

Spencer accordingly halted his forces for the night at Alfaiates and Souto, but he reported next day, June 7, incorrectly, that twenty-one thousand French with thirty-four guns had advanced from Salamanca on the road to Ciudad Rodrigo. Soon afterwards, however, he obtained certain intelligence that a very large column of the enemy was in the pass of Baños; and presently Marmont himself wheeled off to the pass of Perales and was seen no more. It was therefore manifestly Spencer's duty to move southward parallel with Marmont, and to join

Wellington in Alemtejo. (*Wellington Desp*. v., Napier iv.)

It cannot be said that Spencer distinguished himself at this crisis. His hurried and precipitate retreat before a force of less than half his numbers was very nearly disgraceful; and even more discreditable was the unseemly haste with which he ordered Pack to blow up what remained of the fortifications of Almeida and destroy such stores as were in it. Wellington had only advised this measure in case the abandonment of Almeida should be absolutely necessary; and it was very evident that the place had been sacrificed under the influence of panic when it was in no danger whatever. The commander-in-chief was extremely annoyed, and, when writing to Spencer on the subject, was at no pains to conceal his sentiments. (*Wellington Desp*. To Spencer, 11th June 1811). It had never occurred to Sir Brent, who was not a great genius, that the fortress could be useful as a depot for the battering-train when the time should come to besiege Ciudad Rodrigo; probably indeed he believed that the British were more likely to evacuate the Peninsula than to recover the strongholds upon the Spanish frontier.

Meanwhile the march of the Allies southward was continued over the Coa to Penamacor, thence by Castello Branco to Villa Velha, where the Tagus was crossed on the bridge of boats, and on to Niza and Portalegre, Anson's cavalry covering the van and Slade's the rear. The heat was so intense that it was necessary to move chiefly by night, and even so hundreds of stragglers were left exhausted by the roadside. But none the less by the 13th Anson and the Light Division were at Niza; the First Division at Villa Velha; the Sixth Division at Castello Branco; and Slade's cavalry about Salvaterra, watching the road which enters Portugal by Zarza la Mayor. On that day Wellington summoned the head of the column to Portalegre, to which place the troops moved down in succession; Slade's brigade, the last of all, reaching it on the 20th. Meanwhile he had kept his own troops around Badajoz while the siege-train was being transported back to Elvas, maintaining the blockade till the last moment in case some fortunate accident should delay the coming of the relieving force.

On the night of the 14th arrived intelligence that Marmont's foremost troops had reached Truxillo; and on the same day Soult's cavalry was reported to be at Santa Marta. Accordingly on the 17th Wellington passed the whole of his force over the Guadiana by fords, while Blake, pursuant to an arrangement already concluded, crossed the river likewise at Juromenha bound for the Condado de Niebla, Wellington having undertaken to feed his army during the march through Portugal. Thus all the British troops were concentrating timely in the valley of the Caia to meet the enemy in front; while Blake was stealing round to threaten Seville in their rear.

On the French side Marmont's march had from the nature of the case been longer and more severe than that of Spencer; and consequently his advanced guard, moving by Bejar and Plasencia, did not reach Almaraz until the 11th. Considerable delay in the passage of the Tagus was caused by the failure of the commandant at Madrid to send pontoons and provisions, as Marmont had requested him. However, the army eventually crossed the river by a flying bridge, and proceeding by Truxillo and Miajadas reached Merida on the 18th. Soult in the meantime had on the 13th been joined at Usagre by d'Erlon's corps which, moving from Valladolid by Madrid and Toledo, had consumed a full month on their march to reach him.

D'Erlon's troops, which consisted of fourth battalions and extra squadrons, were drafted as far as possible into the regiments to which they belonged; though some five thousand men, belonging to regiments of Victor's corps, were still organised as a provisional division. Thus the gaps made by the slaughter at Albuera were filled up, and Soult's army was raised to about twenty-eight thousand effective men, too weak a force to engage Wellington unaided. Breaking up, therefore, from Llerena on the 12th the Duke of Dalmatia marched north-westward by Los Santos, Villafranca, and Almendralejo, which last place he reached on the 16th; on the 17th his advanced cavalry came in touch with that of Marmont at Merida; and on the 18th the junction of the two armies was finally accomplished.

The meeting between the two marshals was most cordial, Soult being delighted to find at last a colleague who would work for the common good instead of playing only for his own hand, and Marmont equally enchanted with the consciousness of his own virtue. (*"Certes, il y avait de la générosité a moi."* Mémoires du Duc de Raguse, iv.). With nearly sixty thousand men between them they hastened to advance against Wellington, whom their latest information represented to be still at Albuera; and it was not until the evening of the 19th that they discovered that he had recrossed the Guadiana and was gone. On the 20th, the very day on which Phillipon's provisions came to an end, they entered Badajoz; and, after ascertaining on the morrow that Olivenza had been evacuated by the Allies, they decided to cross the Guadiana and either to bring their enemy to action or, if he should have retired before them, to lay siege to Elvas.

Wellington wrote to his brother Henry on the 21st:—

Matters are in a very critical state just now, but I think I shall carry them through.

Against the sixty thousand men of his adversaries the British commander could match some fifty-four thousand of his own, thirty-seven thousand of them British; and though these were not all of them on the spot—for he had kept the Fifth Division and a brigade of Portuguese cavalry in Lower Beira until the last of Marmont's troops should have passed the Tagus—yet with this exception all were between Arronches and Elvas.

Wellington had no wish to risk an action unless in order to provision Elvas; but, in case one should be forced upon him, he had chosen a position upon a ridge of heights between the Rivers Caia and Gebora, facing south-east. His left was to rest on the latter river by the little fortified town of Oguella, in rear of which a forest six miles in extent practically prohibited any turning movement except by a very long circuit through Alburquerque and Castello de Vide. From thence the line ran for between four and five miles to Campo Maior, the fortifications of which had been repaired and furnished with heavy guns, while the weak points in the intermediate ground had been entrenched; and lastly from Campo Maior as a centre the right was prolonged to the bridge of the Caia.

But though this was apparently the ground on which Wellington would have preferred to receive attack, it was in the enemy's power to turn it by the right in an open space of about ten miles between Campo Maior and Elvas, so that the British commander was prepared to defend this space also. (I deduce this from Wellington's dispositions and from the fact that Burgoyne, Wrottesley's *Life of Sir J. Burgoyne*, i., mentions no position except that between the Caia and Gebora). Here the ground was considerably stronger than on the left; while Elvas, perched high upon its granite peak, made the right flank unassailable. Wellington therefore, while occupying his left in some strength, showed no troops upon his right.

Oguella was garrisoned by two companies of Portuguese; between it and Campo Maior lay the Third and Seventh Divisions under Picton; and between Campo Maior and the Caia were the Second and Fourth Divisions and Hamilton's Portuguese under Hill, their camp being hidden away in the woods opposite Torre de Mouro. The Light

Division was at Reguengo, nearly seven miles northwest of Cam Maior, ready to support either Picton or Hill. The First, Sixth, and Fifth Divisions were echeloned along the road which leads from Arronches to Elvas; the Guards' brigade being the foremost at Santa Eulalia, from whence a good cross-road leads by the ford at Torre de Mouro to Campo Maior.

★★★★★★

The Fifth Division did not arrive at Arronches till the 24th. Napier states that the First Division was held in reserve at Portalegre to parry any turning movement by Alburquerque; but Mr. Oman (iv.) shows that this is incorrect. It is evident that Wellington had no idea of keeping a division so far off as to be unable to take part in a general action, as Napier suggests.

Stothert calls the place Santa Olaya, a mistake for Santa Olalla which would be the Spanish form of Eulalia. Mr. Oman is mistaken in describing it as near Elvas, for it is all but nine miles from it as the crow flies. I presume that the remaining brigades were in rear of the Guards, though according to the *Journal of an Officer of the King's German Legion*, (also republished by Leonaur), Low's brigade of the K.G.L. was there also.

★★★★★★

Midway between Santa Eulalia and Elvas, at Quinta de São João, were Wellington's headquarters, at a point where five different roads met from north, south, and east; so that he was not only at hand to dispose the First, Fifth, and Sixth Divisions between the Caia and Elvas, but could gallop away with ease to any quarter of the position. Of the cavalry, Long's brigade of the Eleventh Dragoons (which had recently arrived from England), and the 1st and 2nd Hussars of the Legion, (2 weak squadrons only of the 2nd Hussars), were extended to the right, and Madden's Portuguese cavalry on the left, with De Grey's, Slade's, and Anson's brigades in reserve, the first about Campo Maior, the two last about Arronches. There was a good road along the reverse side of the position from end to end; and the old Moorish watch-towers, which crown every summit on this part of the Portuguese frontier, made admirable signal-stations to pass intelligence from flank to flank. Finally, although Wellington could see clearly every movement of the enemy, the great mass of his troops was hidden away and was invisible from any point that could be reached by Soult.

On the 23rd Soult and Marmont made a reconnaissance in force on the north bank of the Guadiana, Godinot's division advancing at the same time from Olivenza to the south bank over against Juromenha.

★★★★★★

There is a curious discordance among the authorities as to the date of this reconnaissance. Wellington, Soult, and Tomkinson state it as the 23rd; Stolzenberg (*Schwertfeger*, ii.), who was seriously engaged in the course of it, and Leach state it as the 22nd; and Napier as the 21st. Oman has followed Stolzenberg; but the agreement of the two commanders-in-chief would seem to be sufficient warrant to fix the date as the 23rd. Still I am bound to add that, though Wellington's despatch in the printed collection gives the day as the 23rd, the *Gazette* gives it as the 22nd.

★★★★★★

On the British right and centre Bron with one brigade and Latour Maubourg with fourteen squadrons of horse forded the river, the former some way below Elvas, the latter nearly opposite to it; while on the left Montbrun with two brigades crossed by the bridge of Badajoz and pushed forward towards Campo Maior. Bron, of course, encountered no troops; and Montbrun, after driving in the Allied cavalry, was brought to a stand by the sight of the British infantry, which he estimated correctly at two divisions. Latour Maubourg encountered by chance the 2nd German Hussars and the Eleventh British Dragoons which, partly through inexperience (for both were new to the Peninsula) and partly through the faulty dispositions of Long, had thrown out picquets of unnecessarily large numbers.

The result was that the Hussars resisted too long at the fords, had to fight hard to secure their retreat, and only escaped at the last with the loss of some twenty-five of all ranks, and eleven horses killed, wounded, and taken. Turning to his right, Latour Maubourg came upon the rear of a squadron of the Eleventh, which he threatened to cut off from Elvas. Captain Lutyens, who was in command, mistaking the French for the Portuguese, did not perceive his danger till too late, and, though he charged through the first French line, was overwhelmed by the second. Thus the entire squadron, with the exception of one officer, fell, alive or dead, into the enemy's hands; and ninety men of Long's brigade were sacrificed to the ignorance of their officers. (Soult, in his report to Berthier, *Wellington Desp.* v., of course states the number of prisoners at 163, besides killed and wounded). Wellington, much annoyed, read Long a little lecture which cannot have been agreeable to him, and, in reporting the circumstance to

24

Liverpool, was careful to point out the difference between regiments trained and untrained by active service.

The old regiments of cavalry throughout all their service and all their losses put together have not lost so many men as the 2nd Hussars and Eleventh Dragoons, and the Thirteenth Light Dragoons, the former in a few days, the latter in a few months. However, we must make the new as good as the old. (*Wellington Desp.* To Liverpool, 27th June 1811).

★★★★★★

Note:—Meanwhile Wellington treasured up the incident in his memory as an argument against imitation of the French uniform in any particular. "Lutyens and his picquet," he wrote five months later, "were taken because the 3rd hussars (he meant the 3rd Portuguese) had the same caps as the French *chasseurs à cheval.*" *Wellington Desp.* To Torrens, 6th Nov. 1811.

★★★★★★

The reconnaissance of the 23rd proved to the French marshals that Wellington was in force upon the Caia and intended to stay there; but they were little the wiser as to his position or his numbers, for they imagined that the Spanish troops were still with him, and reckoned his force at sixty thousand men. Both of them in their despatches lamented the fact that he declined a general action, which would mean a decisive victory for the French; whereas Wellington at the moment was bewailing the necessity for risking a battle at a time when it was undesirable for him to fight. (Marmont and Soult to Berthier, 21st and 22nd June 1811. Belmas, i. *Wellington Desp.* To Liverpool, 25th June 1811).

Marmont and Soult knew well enough in their hearts that they could force on an engagement without difficulty if they wished it; and it must be admitted that they had every reason to wish it, for, in order to concentrate sixty thousand men at Badajoz, they had been compelled to denude Leon and Andalusia of all troops except garrisons, and to leave those garrisons at the mercy of the Spanish armies of Murcia and Galicia and of the far more formidable guerrilla-bands. Nevertheless the recollection of their recent defeats was so fresh that they shrank from the trial; and, instead of combating the common enemy, they took to quarrelling among themselves.

On the 24th Soult informed Marmont that his letters from Andalusia represented Seville to be in great danger from the insurgent levies of

Ronda, and that he must return thither at once with his army, leaving his colleague to watch over the safety of Badajoz. Soult's fears, it must be explained, were not inspired by any action of Blake's, though he had just heard a report of that officer's march to the Condado de Niebla, but by a general revival of insurrectionary activity consequent upon the weakening of the Andalusian garrisons.

Marmont, a stranger to Spain and highly contemptuous of partisan warfare, considered his anxiety to be ridiculous; and, being forewarned by Junot of the selfishness of Soult, he could only see in the proposal an insidious design to sacrifice alike himself, the Army of Portugal, and Badajoz. He therefore declined to entertain it unless the Fifth Corps and the whole of Latour Maubourg's cavalry division—some fifteen thousand men—were left with him; threatening that, if Soult should draw off the whole of his troops, he would at once repass the Tagus with the Army of Portugal. This compromise Soult was compelled to accept; and thus in less than a week after their exchange of compliments upon the junction of their armies, the two commanders had determined to part company upon terms of mutual suspicion. (*Mémoires du Duc de Raguse*, iv.)

However, for the present the entire French Army remained in its old position, making reconnaissances which kept Wellington very much on the alert, though occupied principally, as he said, by the business of procuring subsistence. On the 27th information came in that Godinot had blown up the fortifications at Olivenza and marched to Valverde, and two days later it was ascertained that he had taken the main road to Seville. Soult, as a matter of fact, had on the 28th started for Seville with the divisions both of Godinot and of Conroux, and with three regiments of cavalry; but it was a fortnight before Wellington ascertained positively, through an intercepted letter from Marmont to Berthier, that more than one division had accompanied him. (*Wellington Desp.* To Liverpool, 11th July 1811).

Yet the departure of even one division showed that the period of peril was past; though, so long as Marmont remained in the vicinity, Wellington was bound to remain likewise, in order to ensure the safety of Elvas; and Marmont, for his part, could not move until he had revictualled Badajoz. Until the 15th of July, therefore, the two hostile armies watched each other from opposite sides of the Guadiana, the French during the interval gathering together six months' provisions for the fortress.

Then d'Erlon, who was now in command of the Fifth Corps,

withdrew his troops to Zafra, Los Santos, and Merida; while Marmont, leaving one division and his light cavalry at Truxillo, fell back from the exhausted region of Northern Estremadura to the valley of the Tagus and the Vera de Plasencia. With one division in the province of Avila, another at Plasencia, headquarters at Naval Moral, and strong bridge-heads at Almaraz and on the Tietar, he judged himself well situated to concentrate for action either in Estremadura or Old Castile.

Wellington did not long outstay him. There was no object in clinging to the unhealthy valleys of the Caia and the Guadiana since all chance of recovering Badajoz had vanished. Accordingly on the 18th he issued orders for the troops to go into cantonments, from Castello Branco in the north to Estremoz in the south, headquarters being transferred: on the 24th from Quinta de São João to Portalegre. Hamilton's Portuguese, the Second Division with Long's and De Grey's brigades of cavalry, and the brigades of Portuguese horse of Otway and Barbaçena alone remained in the vicinity of Elvas at Villa Viçosa and other villages farther to the north, under the very competent command of General Hill. Thus the immediate outcome of the elaborate movements of both French and English to the Guadiana was a deadlock. But it was not for nothing that Wellington had drawn the bulk of the French field-armies to that point; and we must now see what had been going forward in other parts of the Peninsula.

When Wellington led first a part and latterly the whole of his army southward to the Guadiana he necessarily engaged the attention of the French Army of Portugal and of the South with his own troops. But there was yet another French force, the Army of the North under Bessières, for which he was obliged also to find employment lest it should penetrate into Portugal on his left flank and rear, and, with the aid of Soult and Marmont, perhaps force him back to Lisbon. From the very first, ever since the deputies of Asturias had appealed to England for help, the British Ministers had specially interested themselves in the northern provinces of Spain; and in September 1810 they had established a special agent, General Walker, at Coruña to distribute arms, give advice to the generals and insurrectionary leaders, and furnish intelligence to London.

The Army of Galicia, as we have seen, had never been very efficient or well organised; and it was in far from good condition when Walker arrived. Asturias, on the other hand, had always shown spirit and activity under such leaders as Porlier; and towards the end of April 1811, Liverpool, upon Walker's suggestion, submitted to Wellington a proposal for seizing and fortifying the port of Santoña in Biscay, as a haven from which the British ships of war could cut off all marine communication between France and Asturias, and as a depot from which the insurrection in the north might be nourished and directed. The British Government was perhaps the more inclined to favour the project owing to correct information that Napoleon had ordered Santoña to be fortified for his own purposes; but Wellington deprecated the employment of British troops in any such enterprise. He had already matured a scheme for a Spanish diversion in the north, and, though he was prepared to allow the occupation of Santoña to form a part of it, he could find work enough for the British soldiers in the Peninsula without locking them up in a fort on the Atlantic. (*Wellington Desp.* Liverpool to Wellington, 28th April; Wellington to Liverpool, 26th May 1811. *Corres. de Napoléon*).

The force of Bessières in the north amounted to four divisions, namely, that of Bonnet, hitherto always employed in Asturias; that of Serras which, with headquarters at Benavente, watched the frontier of Galicia; and those of the Young Guard under Generals Roguet and Dumoustier, which were cantoned in the provinces of Palencia, Valladolid, and Burgos. In addition, there were two brigades of cavalry and some odd battalions, bringing the total of the whole up to sixty thousand men; but it was quite evident that these were none too many to keep in subjection an area of some forty thousand square miles, much of it very difficult country and haunted by some of the ablest of the guerrilla leaders. It was only with the greatest reluctance that Bessières consented to take over temporarily from Marmont the protection of the north of Leon; and his first step, after the march of the Army of Portugal southward, was to order Bonnet to evacuate Asturias and march his entire division to Leon. Napoleon on hearing of this step condemned it with more than his usual vigour; but, as shall now be seen, when Bonnet reached Leon on the 17th of June, he came none too soon for the safety of Bessières.

Pursuant to Wellington's directions General Santocildes on the 12th of June brought forward nearly eight thousand men of the Army of Galicia to Astorga; while simultaneously General Cabrera led another division of twenty-five hundred men from Puebla de Senabria upon La Bañeza. A third division of Asturians should have acted with them; but half of it was detained to occupy Oviedo, and only one brigade under General Castañon was sent round by a circuitous route to join Santocildes. On reaching Astorga on the 19th of June the latter officer found that the weak French garrison had retired to Leon after blowing up part of the works; but presently Serras advanced from Benavente to meet him, while Bonnet detached two battalions under General Valletaux to second Serras.

That general was brought to a standstill by Cabrera near La Bañeza; and Valletaux, rashly attacking the bulk of the troops of Santocildes at Benavides, was assailed on his right flank by Castañon who arrived opportunely upon the field from Asturias and was repulsed with a loss of over three hundred men. Valletaux himself was killed; his beaten troops fell back upon Leon, and Serras retired upon Benavente; whereupon Santocildes uniting his entire force moved forward on the 2nd of July against Bonnet. There was a sharp engagement between the two on the 15th; but by the 17th the divisions of Serras and Dumoustier had come up, with Bessières himself at their head; and Santocildes with good sense and prudence retired westward into the mountains. Bessières was unable to follow, for, before he could attempt pursuit, he received the alarming news that his headquarters at Valladolid had been attacked on the 15th by the guerilla-bands of Mina and Longa. Hastily returning to Valladolid with Dumoustier's divisions, the marshal there found letters signifying that the emperor had recalled him from his command. Bessières in consequence vanishes at this point from the Peninsula, his successor being General Dorsenne.

Meanwhile Bonnet and Serras had stationed themselves on the east bank of the Orvigo; but were presently compelled by Santocildes, who advanced against them with his whole force, to retire to Leon. The guerillas immediately flooded the whole of the province, isolating all outlying garrisons, even that of Salamanca; while their comrades farther to the east gave terrible trouble to General Roguet's division on the lines of communication. But now two misfortunes stemmed the tide of Spanish success. Dorsenne was reinforced by a new division under General Souham, and Santocildes was superseded by General Abadia, a leader upon whom Wellington had founded great hopes, which were too soon to be disappointed.

Turning over the care of the province of Burgos to Souham, Dorsenne marched on the 9th of August from Valladolid with two divisions of the Young Guard and both of his brigades of cavalry upon La Bañeza, while Bonnet simultaneously moved forward from Leon upon Astorga. Upon the advice of Santocildes Abadia retreated westward; but Dorsenne, following him up, beat him after severe fighting at the passes above Astorga, and forced him still farther back. Thereupon

Abadia decided to retire southward to Orense; and Dorsenne, unable to pursue through so barren a country, turned about from Villafranca on the 29th of August for Astorga, burning villages in all directions as he went. He had good reasons for so doing, as the guerilla-bands had been unusually busy during his absence. Porlier on the 14th had stormed Santander and captured three hundred prisoners; other bands were daily worrying all the French garrisons; Julian Sanchez had foiled every effort to revictual Ciudad Rodrigo; and lastly Wellington, as we shall see, had reappeared in his old quarters on the Agueda. The British commander, thanks to the skill of Santocildes and the boundless activity of such men as Mina, Longa, Porlier and Sanchez, had been able to march to the Guadiana and back with perfect safety to himself and to Portugal; and upon his return the northern provinces became once more the field chiefly of minor operations.

Let us now look to the second diversion whereby Wellington had broken up the combination between Soult and Marmont. Blake, after crossing the Guadiana at Juromenha on the 17th of June, had turned south through Alemtejo, recrossed the river about thirty miles from its mouth at Mértola six days later, and on the 30th was at Niebla. He was now within forty miles of Seville, which was so weakly garrisoned that it could hardly have resisted him; but he preferred to besiege one of Napoleon's nondescript foreign battalions in the castle of Niebla. Having outmarched his guns, he could do no more than invest this stronghold until the 2nd of July, when he learnt that Soult had detached the divisions of Godinot and Conroux against him. Thereupon he embarked Zayas's division at Ayamonte on the 8th and returned to Cadiz, whither Ballesteros, after evading the French for some weeks in the mountains, followed him at the end of August. It cannot be said that Blake distinguished himself in this enterprise, but at least he succeeded in keeping Soult distracted for a short time.

Elsewhere in the south the Spanish Army of Murcia had remained quiet since its disastrous defeat at Baza in November 1810, until Soult withdrew, for the campaign of Albuera, a portion of the troops opposed to it. Then in May General Freire began slowly to advance from Murcia eastward; and Leval, who had succeeded Sebastiani in command of the Fourth Corps, was too weak to stand before him. In the middle of July Blake obtained leave to carry to Murcia the two divisions which he had brought back from Albuera, and landed with them at Almeria on the 31st. On the 3rd of August they joined Freire at Baza; but he, though now in command of seventeen thousand men, would make no attempt upon the weak French garrison of Granada, and remained halted in a strong position about forty miles to east and north of the city. Nevertheless Leval's danger was so manifest that Soult on the 3rd of August marched with four regiments of cavalry and a part of Conroux's division for Granada, in order to manoeuvre against Freire's post, ordering Godinot's division at the same time to move by way of Jaen upon his right flank and rear.

On the 7th Soult reached Granada, and by the 9th came up before Freire's position at Gor; on which same day Godinot utterly defeated a detachment which the Spanish general had sent out to parry his turning movement. Freire therefore retreated under cover of night; but he was overtaken by the French cavalry next day, and his troops were broken up and hunted in two separate bodies into the hills. They rallied, however, and reunited under the command of Blake before the city of Murcia, where they proceeded to fortify a strong position. Soult meanwhile pressed the pursuit no farther than to the frontier of Murcia, but, returning to Granada, organised a number of flying columns under Godinot to quell the insurrection within the mountainous quadrilateral that lies between Granada, Baza, Motril, and Almeria. This work proved to be long, hazardous, and difficult, and it was still in progress, not unchequered by galling reverses to the French, when a new combatant came upon the scene in the person of Ballesteros.

This officer, realising that a diversion was needed in favour of Murcia, landed on the 4th of September with three thousand men at Algeçiras, and marching up to Ximena rekindled the whole of the insurrection in the Sierra de Ronda. Sundry little successes soon compelled Soult to despatch against him a strong column, which sustained a serious defeat near San Roque on the 25th of September. Much irritated, Soult summoned Godinot from the east, and calling up simultaneously two columns from Victor's force before Cadiz, endeavoured to pen in Ballesteros between these three bodies. The Spanish general thereupon quietly retired southward and took refuge beneath the guns of Gibraltar, from which secure position he laughed at the ten thousand men of Godinot.

Exasperated by his failure, Godinot marched against the second base of Ballesteros, Tarifa; but there was only one road—that running along the coast—by which he could take his cannon with him, and he was driven from that with some loss by the fire of the British cruisers. Meanwhile the French troops from Cadiz marched away from before Gibraltar in two separate bodies; and Ballesteros, following after one

31

nem commanded by General Semele, surprised it, dispersed a battalion of Spaniards enlisted by the French, and captured furthermore one hundred French prisoners and a gun. Soult, infuriated by this petty disaster, threw the blame of his own failure upon Godinot, and reproached him so savagely that the unfortunate general committed suicide. The Duke of Dalmatia, notwithstanding his temporary success against Freire, had in fact accomplished nothing by all his multitudinous operations since he had returned to Seville from Badajoz in June; while his troops were worn out and discouraged by long marches after an elusive enemy and by frequent petty defeats.

Let us now leave him for the present and turn northward to Catalonia and Aragon. There it will be remembered that in May Suchet, with the Seventh Corps and half of the Third, was about to undertake the siege of Tarragona, while Macdonald, with the remainder of the Third Corps, was set down to recover the fortress of Figueras. To follow first the fortunes of the former, Suchet's advanced guard came before Tarragona on the 3rd of May, but, owing to the slow march of the siege-train from Tortosa, was unable to break ground until the night of the 7th. On the 10th, General Campoverde was able to enter the city by sea with four thousand men, thereby raising the garrison to a strength of ten thousand regular troops. The first act of the besiegers was to construct a battery to drive the British men-of-war, under Captain Codrington, to an anchorage out of range of the shore, which was accomplished by the 13th; and the French engineers then turned their attention to a detached work, named Fort Olivo, which commanded the lower town.

This was successfully stormed on the night of the 29th with very heavy loss to the defenders; and on the 31st Campoverde sailed from the fortress to collect an army of succour, leaving the garrison still in good heart under the command of General Coutreras, and strengthened by two battalions which had just arrived by water from Valencia. By the middle of June he had gathered together about eleven thousand men; but meanwhile Suchet pushed forward his operations rapidly against the lower town, and on the 17th carried the last of the external defences of Tarragona. The situation of the city was now critical, but Campoverde confined himself to distant diversions without any attempt to molest the besieging force. On the 21st, therefore, Suchet stormed the lower town and thereby closed the harbour to the besieged, though the British squadron still lay in a roadstead not more than a mile away.

On the 24th Campoverde came so close to Tarragona that Suchet concentrated a portion of his army to meet him; but the feeble Spanish general never fired a shot, and busied himself with a plot to depose his colleague, General Coutreras, upon false suspicion of cowardice.

On the 26th new hope was kindled in the garrison by the arrival in the roadstead not only of small Spanish reinforcements from Murcia and Valencia, but of between eleven and twelve hundred British troops under Colonel Skerrett, (2/47th, a small detachment of 3/95th, ½ company of artillery, and some light companies from Gibraltar), which had been detached by Graham from Cadiz. Rough weather kept Skerrett on board ship until the evening, but on the 27th he went round the defences with General Charles Doyle, Captain Codrington, and other officers, when all unanimously agreed—as indeed Coutreras himself admitted—that the town was untenable. Graham's orders to Skerrett were clear and strict: He was not to land his troops unless he could be sure of embarking them before a capitulation.

Since Skerrett himself had only gained the shore with difficulty owing to the surf, it was very clear that he could not be certain of getting twelve hundred men into boats if the French should make a successful assault. He therefore declined to disembark his men at Tarragona, though he agreed to do so farther up the coast in order to strengthen Campoverde's army of succour. The position was extremely unfortunate, and it is to be regretted that the British detachment should have come upon the scene at all; for it was too weak to give any help to Coutreras, and yet strong enough to make its departure most depressing to the garrison.

A day later the end came. The French breaching batteries opened fire on the morning of the 28th with great effect, and at five o'clock in the evening the storming parties rushed to the assault. In half an hour the French were masters of the fortifications; but the Spaniards resisted desperately in the streets, and the exasperated assailants, breaking loose from all control, gave themselves up not only to massacre but to every description of outrage. Not until the next day could the officers with all their efforts restore order; and the streets were then encumbered with four thousand Spanish corpses, more than half of them civilians, and over one-tenth women and children. Of the Spanish regular troops nearly two thousand perished and eight thousand were captured. The army of Catalonia was, in fact, reduced to insignificance; and with Tarragona the chief centre of Spanish resistance within the province as well as the main channel of communication with the British fleet was lost. It was a great and genuine success for Suchet, and was achieved at a cost of something over four thousand French soldiers killed and wounded.

Losing no time after his triumph, Suchet marched north to reopen communications with Barcelona, and on the 30th seized Campoverde's depot, together with several ships, at Villanueva. Campoverde himself retired inland to Cervera, where on the 1st of July he decided, pursuant to the vote of a council of war, to abandon Catalonia entirely, although Figueras was still holding out, and there could be no immediate danger from Suchet. Happily Codrington refused to embark any Catalonian troops, though ready to convey the Valencians back to their own country. Campoverde therefore marched to Arenys de Mar, about twenty-three miles east and north of Barcelona, where the Valencian infantry, over two thousand strong, was shipped off by Codrington.

The cavalry, however, some nine hundred men, refused to part with their horses, and rode away to Tudela, where they crossed the Ebro and struck southward to Valencia, eventually rejoining their own general, Carlos O'Donnell, at the end of August, after an amazing march of six weeks over seven hundred miles of country. Campoverde then retired to Vich, where he handed over to General Lacy, who had been sent to supersede him, such miserable remnant of an army as desertion and discontent had left under his command. Too weak to attempt any operation, Lacy withdrew to Solsona, about fifty miles north-west of Barcelona, there to reorganise and recruit his dilapidated forces.

Meanwhile Suchet, who had reached Barcelona on the 9th, moved northward to Vich to restore communications with Macdonald, and finding that the blockade of Figueras was prospering, led ten thousand men to the great stronghold of Montserrat, which was weakly garrisoned, and stormed it with trifling loss on the 25th of July. The capture of this sacred place made a profound impression on the Catalonians, and all the more since the fall of Figueras appeared now to be inevitable. Nevertheless that garrison by heroic endurance of extreme privation held out for another month, until at last, after a vain attempt to break through the beleaguering lines, it was compelled by famine to surrender on the 19th of August. The siege had lasted for over four months, during which time fifteen hundred of the defenders and four thousand of the French had perished.

Overjoyed at the success of his arms in Catalonia, Napoleon now urged Suchet to hasten to the work which he had already prescribed for him in Valencia, and gave him positive commands that his head-quarters must be established in that province by the 15th of September. Let a battle be won and Murviedro be captured and, in the emperor's opinion, the city of Valencia would surrender. Suchet was not so confident, but obeyed orders; and it will presently be our task to follow the course of his campaign. Meanwhile, however, Catalonia was so far from being subjugated that Lacy, even before Figueras had fallen, made a raid into France with about a thousand men and, to the frantic rage of Napoleon, raised contributions in the region of Puigcerda. (See his wild orders to Suchet of 22nd August 1811. *Corres. de Napoléon*). Five weeks later, with the help of British men-of-war, Lacy drove the French from the Medas Islands at the mouth of the Ter, and built a fort upon one of them to serve as a base for predatory operations both by land and sea. Having heartened his troops by these successes, he set himself in October to harass the French in earnest on the line of communications between Barcelona and Lerida.

On the 4th he surprised a French post at Igualada, inflicting considerable loss, and followed up this spirited action first by the capture of a convoy, and next by seizing the posts of Cervera and Belpuig, in which, over and above killed and wounded, he took more than two hundred prisoners. Finally he closed the month by a second raid into France. As a consequence of these events the French were obliged to evacuate Montserrat; and the flickering flame of insurrection, thanks to the enterprise of this daring leader, flared up once again to brightness in Catalonia. Napoleon recalled Macdonald from his command in consequence of these mishaps. Truly Catalonia was entombing the reputations of many French marshals.

So ebbed and flowed the tide of war around the centre of all resistance to the French in Spain—the forty thousand red-coats under Wellington's command. It cannot be said that the Spanish generals made the most of their opportunities; and Wellington was bitterly disappointed with one and all of them. He had hoped that Blake would have destroyed the stores at Seville; but Blake had been afraid even to look at the city. Moreover, instead of taking post in the mountains of Ronda where, threatening both Seville and the besieging lines at Cadiz, he would have been a perpetual thorn in the side of Soult, he had hurried away to Murcia for no good purpose whatever. Elsewhere the miserable feebleness of Campoverde had sacrificed both Tarragona and Figueras; and only Santocildes in the north had shown both enterprise and judgment. Wellington to Dumouriez wrote:—

One would have thought that, when the whole of the enemy's disposable force was assembled in Estremadura, the French scattered all over the rest of Spain would have had their throats cut, and that every Spaniard being hostile to the French (as I really believe to be the case) there would have been a general rising. Nothing of the kind! That is the extraordinary feature in this war. This is the third time in less than two years that the entire disposable force of the enemy has been united against me, but no one takes advantage of it except the guerillas.

He wrote on the same day to Liverpool:—

The greater number of the French would have been destroyed if all the Spaniards were like the lower orders. However, we must have patience, and we may yet be able to root them out of the country. (*Wellington Desp.* To Dumouriez and Liverpool, 4th, 5th July 1811).

It is pleasant to catch the echo of Marlborough, and of his "patience which conquers all things," in a second great captain after the lapse of a century. Patience and trust in the unconquerable peasantry of Spain had already wrought more than Wellington himself realised; and the landing of the siege-train, so long kept afloat upon the Tagus, was a circumstance pregnant with meaning for the future. Let us therefore return to the camp at Portalegre, and follow the British army to the close of this fateful year.

CHAPTER 2

Action at Arroyo Molinos

The cantonments of Wellington's army were distributed as follows:
On the 18th of July the Third and Sixth Divisions were at Castello
Branco, the Seventh at Niza, the Light Division at Castello de Vide,
the First and Fifth at Portalegre, and the Fourth at Estremoz, within
easy reach of Hill; the entire line measuring from seventy to eighty
miles in extent from north to south. As to the operations next to be
undertaken, three courses were open to the British general: to renew
the siege of Badajoz, to attempt the relief of Cadiz, and to besiege
Ciudad Rodrigo. The first of these he rejected as impracticable in
summer owing to the unhealthiness of the climate. The second likewise he dismissed at once; for it was certain that Marmont would
follow him to Andalusia, in which case he would find himself confronted with the armies that had faced Graham at Barrosa, Beresford
at Albuera, and himself at Fuentes de Oñoro, all united into one.

Success was not to be hoped for in such conditions; and, moreover,
as has already been said, there was no object in forcing Soult to amend
his original blunder of locking up an indefinite part of his troops in the
lines before Cadiz. There remained therefore Ciudad Rodrigo, which
upon the whole seemed to be the most promising enterprise. Wellington reckoned Marmont's army very accurately to number about thirty-
six thousand men, and that of Bessières (of whose departure he was
not yet apprised) at ten thousand more, making forty-six thousand in
all. His own force he returned at about fifty-six thousand British and
Portuguese, with the prospect of receiving very shortly an additional
five thousand, giving a total of some sixty thousand. But, while pursuing
the siege, he would be obliged to leave from ten to fourteen thousand
men in Alemtejo to watch the Fifth Corps in Estremadura; and thus
the margin of superiority on the Agueda would be cut so fine that it

might vanish altogether. Still there was always hope; and accordingly on the 18th of July the momentous order was given for the siege-train to be disembarked on the Douro, carried by water to Lamego, and thence overland to Trancoso. (*Wellington Desp.* To Liverpool, to Colonel Framingham, and others, 18th, 19th July 1811).

This very arduous duty was entrusted to Major Dickson of the artillery, who at once started for Oporto, where he found two companies of British artillery, and having obtained further three hundred gunners from the Portuguese, proceeded to his work. One hundred and sixty boats were required to take the guns and stores to Lamego, and over a thousand country carts, besides nearly four hundred pairs of bullocks, to transport them over appalling roads to their destination. Indeed the track from Moimenta to Trancoso was so impossible that Dickson asked and obtained leave to establish the depot at Villa da Ponte, some twelve miles short of Trancoso, from which point the train could be moved by way of Pinhel to Almeida. Of Dickson's trials in the course of this duty full details may be read in his journal. (Printed by the R.A. Institute, *Dickson MSS.* chapter 3). There were no proper carriages for the conveying of the Ordnance for long distances; and he was obliged to fit the limbers with special poles, and to prepare sledges for the mortars.

Moreover, certain descriptions of shot were not too abundant, and it was necessary to hunt through many Portuguese fortresses to supplement the number. However, by the first week in September the bulk of the train had arrived at Villa da Ponte, and by the third week the whole of it was safely stored there; many of the carriages, indeed, much shaken by a sudden journey over rough roads after three years' stay on board ship, but easily to be repaired and made fit for a farther march. This, however, for reasons now to be explained, was a trial which was to be spared them for some months.

On the 1st of August Wellington shifted his headquarters to Castello Branco, and on the following days marched with two divisions and one brigade of cavalry northward for the Agueda. On the 11th the French outposts were driven in and the blockade of Ciudad Rodrigo was established on the south by the Light Division with headquarters at Martiago, and by the Third Division with headquarters at Carpio, the northern side being left to the care of Julian Sanchez and his guerilla-band. On the 12th Wellington moved his own headquarters to Fuenteguinaldo, and the remaining divisions were distributed on a broad front more or less in alignment with the blockading force.

Farthest to north the Sixth Division lay between Barba del Puerco and Nave de Haver; next to south was the Seventh Division between Villar Maior and Sabugal; and then in succession the First Division at Penamacor and the Fourth at Pedrogão, six to seven miles farther to the south. Lastly, the Fifth was stationed in advance at Perales and Navas Frias to guard against any north-westward movement of Marmont from Plasencia.

The cavalry was extended in front of the infantry and beyond its right flank, reaching its extreme southerly point at Idanha a Nova. The line of the infantry cantonments from Barba del Puerco to Pedrogão measured, roughly speaking, seventy miles, (Oman has given the distance from Barba del Puerco to Penamacor at 80, it is really 53 as the crow flies, but quite 70 by road); but Wellington had now a competent second in command at Penamacor, who could be trusted to handle efficiently all troops not under the commander-in-chief's own eye. For on the 9th of August Graham, having been summoned from Cadiz, took over the First Division from Spencer; and the latter, not relishing the advent of a senior officer, went home on pretext of sick leave, and will be seen by us no more.

Marmont, meanwhile, was struggling with the usual difficulty of French commanders in Spain, want of supplies. The districts made over to him for the support of his army were, as he complained, inadequate for the purpose; while Joseph, far from helping him, threw every obstacle in his way. Intimately connected with the question of supply was, of course, that of transport, necessary even in easier times for the formation of magazines, but now more than ever important since the French Army had, as Marmont frankly admitted, exchanged the offensive for the defensive, he wrote to Berthier on the 14th of May:

> Without regular means of transport, it is impossible to move in a country devastated by war, constantly overrun by guerrilla-bands and where requisitions are extremely difficult to enforce. . . . This army at the beginning of the last campaign had three hundred provision-waggons; it has now thirty-four. I beg urgently for twelve to fifteen hundred pack-mules for my supplies; no doubt they can be speedily bought at Bayonne. The English have twelve thousand pack-animals for their artillery and supplies; hence all their movements are made at ease, and they draw most of their beasts from Spain.

On the 5th of August he reiterated his request, now representing that Massena had left him no more than ten provision-waggons; and, as it chanced, both letters were intercepted and brought to Wellington. (Both letters are printed in *Wellington Desp.*, v.). His comment upon them was grim and pithy;

> We have certainly altered the nature of the war in Spain; it has become to a certain degree offensive on our part. . . . Marmont says that he can do nothing without magazines, which is quite a new era in the French military system. . . . They will soon, if they have not already, come upon the resources of France; and, as soon as that is the case, you may depend upon it the war will not last long. (*Wellington Desp.* To Liverpool, 27th August; to Wellesley, 30th August 1811).

Singularly enough the ideas even of Napoleon had changed in respect of this question. There was no more talk of twenty thousand men being able to live in a desert. Bitter experience had put an end to nonsense of that kind; and the great soldier, learning from his enemies, was actually trying to organise a service of "rolling magazines" to carry twenty days' provisions for sixty thousand men. ("*Magasins ambulants*," see *Corres. de Napoléon*). He sagely observed:—

> This method could be very advantageous employed in Holland, Portugal, and all countries where supplies are dear.

Had he thought of it a little earlier he might have saved the lives of hundreds of thousands of soldiers, and perhaps have driven the British out of the Peninsula. But such a system had little place in his conception of war.

Another terrible obstacle to Marmont's progress was the interception of drafts and convalescents, on their way to rejoin his army, by the generals upon the lines of communication. These small parties, placed for the time under officers who had no interest in them or authority over them, were constantly stopped by the commanders aforesaid to perform any troublesome work or fatigue which would otherwise have fallen upon their own troops; and, being nobody's children and under nobody's care, they soon sank into a state of moral and physical deterioration which ruined them as soldiers even when it did not destroy them as men. The emperor's orders were hardly efficacious to check this evil.

According to the arrangement of the Chief of the Imperial Staff, over seven thousand men and eleven hundred horses were to have left

Burgos in the first fortnight of August for the army of Marmont; but they did not reach him until the 15th of September, and then only by special intervention of Napoleon himself. (*Mémoires du Duc de Raguse*, iv.). Nevertheless the marshal had an advantage, of which Wellington for some time remained ignorant, in the arrival of two divisions, jointly about thirteen thousand strong, under Generals Caffarelli and Souham, which had been sent from France by Napoleon to reinforce the armies of the North and of Portugal. Wellington, unaware of their coming, had naturally made no allowance for this in his calculations for the approaching campaign, and the error was one which might prove to be serious.

For the first fortnight the two hostile armies remained quiescent. Various rumours as to Wellington's intentions were current in the French camp, but intelligence as to his preparations for a siege gave Marmont the clue to his true design. It was therefore certain that sooner or later the marshal must take measures for revictualling Ciudad Rodrigo; but there was no immediate hurry, for the supplies within the place were still abundant. Accordingly for the present he contented himself with shifting his headquarters to Plasencia, moving his Sixth Division and his cavalry to the Pass of Baños, bidding Foy drive away the troops of Castaños from the vicinity of Truxillo and prepare to cross the Tagus, and sending proposals for concerted operations to Dorsenne. Meanwhile, by the 21st, Wellington had ascertained that large French reinforcements had entered Spain; and in the course of the next week intercepted papers gave him a much truer idea of the strength that might be brought against him.

On the 26th Marmont advanced his headquarters and the whole of his troops slightly northward; and, combining this movement with his latest intelligence, Wellington divined that the marshal would not pass the mountains until Dorsenne could join him on the Tormes, when the two French armies could operate together against him. A report, that Napoleon on the 19th of July had himself reviewed some of the reinforcements for Spain, led Wellington even to conjecture that the emperor was about to take command in the Peninsula in person. (*Mémoires du Duc de Raguse*, iv. *Wellington Desp.*, to Liverpool, 21st, 28th Aug.; to Craufurd, 28th Aug. 1811).

And here a very short digression may be permitted in order to explain that Napoleon had no idea of entering Spain, but was busily planning a diversion on the British coast. Early in June he had begun the formation of a new camp at Boulogne, and a few days later he gave orders for the flotilla to be again prepared for sea. The numbers of the military force which he proposed to employ varied from thirty to eighty thousand men; and these were to be used at one time for a landing in Ireland, at another for the burning of Chatham dockyard, at a third for a descent upon the Channel Islands. At any rate the flotilla was to be moored ready for sea at any moment throughout the months of September, October, and November, and England was to be kept for all this period in trembling suspense. The British Ministry was indeed a little uneasy; but Wellington, with his usual common sense, pointed out that an old French regiment had lately been sent from Cherbourg into Spain, and that this would never have been done if Napoleon had seriously contemplated a disembarkation on the British Isles.

The camp at Boulogne was in fact simply a device for converting the training of raw conscripts into a diversion. As such it was ingenious enough, and Napoleon carried his feint so far as to embark himself at Boulogne on the 20th September and superintend a very feeble and harmless attack upon a British frigate off the harbour. The exploit ended on the 21st in the capture of a French *praam*, and consequently did not find a place in the pages of the *Moniteur*. (*Corres, de Napoléon*, James's *Naval History*, 1811. *Wellington Desp.*, to Liverpool, 21st Aug. 1811).

In view of the return of Marmont northward, Wellington on the 27th ordered the First and Fourth Divisions to draw nearer to Fuenteguinaldo; and on the 29th an intercepted letter from Foy confirmed the British commander's conjecture that a combined movement of Marmont and Dorsenne upon Ciudad Rodrigo was at hand. Information was received on the 3rd of September that Dorsenne, having driven back the Galician Army, was advancing by forced marches upon Salamanca from Zamora, and that his troops numbered some twenty-five thousand; from which Wellington inferred that the Allies would shortly have to do with at least fifty thousand men. His own force at the moment counted about forty six thousand, not quite thirty thousand of them being British.

The low strength of the redcoats was due to the fact that fourteen thousand men were on the sick-list, the sufferers belonging chiefly to regiments which had either just landed in the Peninsula, or had taken part in the expedition to the Scheldt, though fever had left its mark also upon all who had been encamped on the Guadiana.

With the certitude of inferiority of numbers, it was very clear that

Wellington could not fight a battle to prevent the revictualling of Ciudad Rodrigo; but it was at any rate something to have compelled the concentration of a large force for that purpose; and the British commander, fully alive to the importance of diminishing French pressure upon other districts and to Marmont's difficulties of transport and supply, determined to hold his ground at all risks for a time. He had selected two strong positions on the edge of the central mountain chain of the Peninsula, where he could turn and form a front if the French should attempt any offensive movement. At the best he might find that their numbers had been as greatly diminished as his own by sickness; at the worst he could, by forcing them to remain together, compel them to consume the greater part of the supplies which they had brought up to revictual Ciudad Rodrigo. (*Wellington Desp.* To Liverpool, 18th Sept. 1811).

Meanwhile Marmont had begun his march over the Sierra de Gata, leaving Foy's division only behind him with orders to make a demonstration towards the Pass of Perales. On the 22nd of September Montbrun's cavalry and one division of infantry reached Tamames, while on the same day Dorsenne's force reached San Muñoz, some miles farther to the north. On the 23rd the two armies united with a joint strength of some fifty-eight thousand men, of whom between four and five thousand were cavalry. On the 23rd also Wellington, leaving the Third and Light Divisions in their former station, brought up the Fourth to Fuenteguinaldo and echeloned the rest of the army, with the exception of the Fifth Division, (this was at El Payo at the summit of the Pass of Perales), between that place and Fuentes de Oñoro. Graham, who was in command of the left wing of the army, was uneasy at this dispersion of the troops, and would have preferred that his chief should concentrate at once about the chosen position at Fuenteguinaldo.

In the course of the day the French advanced guard came up and communicated with Ciudad Rodrigo; and on the 24th they entered the city and pushed a large force of cavalry to west of it. Still Wellington made no change in his dispositions; and on the 25th Marmont decided to make a strong reconnaissance, in order to ascertain the truth about the British preparations for a siege. Dorsenne was persuaded to spare some of his cavalry for the purpose; and it was agreed that this force should proceed towards Espeja while Montbrun with the greater part of his division should advance upon Fuenteguinaldo.

Accordingly at about eight in the morning General Wathier with his own and Lepic's brigades—about thirteen hundred sabres,—after leaving six squadrons in Carpio, advanced with the remaining eight across the Azava. The British fell back before them; and Wathier, halting half of his squadrons close to the river, pushed the rest through a wood after the retiring British. These were charged by two squadrons, one of the Fourteenth and the other of the Sixteenth Light Dragoons, and were driven back; but they rallied and were again advancing when they were staggered by a volley from the light companies of Hulse's brigade, which Graham had ordered up to the edge of the wood. Before they could recover themselves two squadrons of the Fourteenth and as many of the Sixteenth dashed into them and hunted them for two miles back to the Azava with a loss of nearly fifty killed, wounded, and taken. The British casualties did not exceed twelve, so that upon its own scale this was a brilliant little affair.

On the side of Fuenteguinaldo matters were more serious. Starting with four brigades, say twenty-five hundred sabres, Montbrun made straight for the ground occupied by the Third Division, which was split up into three fractions along a front of six to seven miles. Half of Wallace's brigade, (late Mackinnon's, who had gone home on sick leave), was at Pastores, the other half at El Bodon five miles to south-west; while one battalion, the Fifth Fusiliers, of Colville's brigade was astride the road from Ciudad Rodrigo some two miles north-west of El Bodon, and the remaining battalions two to three miles farther south-westward. Moreover there were two roads leading to Fuenteguinaldo, the one by Pastores, La Encina, and El Bodon, the other passing west of the last-named village over the ridge held by the Fifth; and hence it was impossible to arrange any final disposition of the British troops until Montbrun had shown which route he meant to take.

No sooner was it seen that he had chosen the western road than Wellington sent two Portuguese batteries, the Seventy-Seventh Foot and five squadrons of Alten's brigade to the support of the Fifth, at the same time calling up the 21st Portuguese and a brigade of the Fourth Division from Fuenteguinaldo to the same point. The situation was perilous; for, if Montbrun succeeded in breaking through this detachment upon the road, he would cut off the battalions at Pastores and El Bodon from the main body. Happily Marmont could not believe that Wellington would have kept the Third Division so dangerously scattered unless there were some more solid array concealed in their rear; and he therefore gave orders for his cavalry to advance alone without sending for infantry to second them.

Meanwhile Wellington in person had drawn up his little body of men so as to cover the position to the best advantage. The ground which he occupied was a rocky ridge, intersected by stony hollows, through one of which ran the road. In this central hollow were posted two squadrons of the 1st German Hussars, with the two batteries, backed by the Fifth, on their right, and another squadron of Hussars, together with two squadrons of the Eleventh Light Dragoons, in echelon to their left rear. Montbrun for his part divided his cavalry into three columns and pushed them up the steep ascent against the three sections of the defending force, the Portuguese batteries plying them with a murderous fire as they advanced. As his central column drew near the crest of the hill, the leading squadron of the German Hussars charged and, being well supported by the second squadron, forced the French back to the foot of the ascent. On the British left the third squadron and the Eleventh were equally successful; but on the right the French dragoons in spite of heavy losses broke into one battery and captured four guns.

Before they could rally, however, Major Ridge brought forward the Fifth in line; and these, after pouring in a heavy fire, charged with the bayonet and drove the dragoons headlong down the slope. The Portuguese gunners thereupon returned to their pieces and reopened fire; while Montbrun sent out fresh squadrons to renew the attack. Wellington's cavalry, however, by repeated charges of single squadrons kept them back for a time, the Seventy-Seventh, which had meanwhile come up, likewise taking a share in the defence. Thus the combat was maintained for some hours, until Thiébault's division of infantry, which had been summoned by Marmont from Ciudad Rodrigo, was seen approaching in the distance, when Montbrun, abandoning frontal attacks, sent a part of his force round the right flank of the British.

Soon after two o'clock in the afternoon Wellington formed the Fifth and Seventy-Seventh—about a thousand bayonets jointly—into a single square, with the Twenty-First, which had by this time come up, in another square in advance, and ordered a retreat. (Beamish and Schwertfeger say 3 o'clock; but Beamish adds that the force reached Fuenteguinaldo, which he describes as six miles distant, by 4, which is absurd. The real distance, according to Wyld's *Atlas*, is about four miles and a half). It was high time, for a few more minutes would have seen the British force surrounded. The cavalry, fearing to be enveloped, galloped away to take refuge with the Twenty-First; and the Fifth and Seventy-Seventh were left to bring up the rear alone.

Montbrun's horsemen, accompanied by a light battery, instantly swarmed after them on all sides; but, though their round shot fell thick among the red-coats, they could find no weak spot nor perceive any wavering. More than once they dashed close up to the bayonets, but fell away at the critical moment before the steady fire of the infantry. Meanwhile Picton, having with some trouble withdrawn his three battalions from the intricate ground about El Bodon, joined Colville's brigade; and the whole continued the retrograde movement in square, much harassed by the French artillery, but presenting always an unshakable front to the cavalry. At length the British reinforcements from Fuenteguinaldo began to come up, with the Third Dragoon Guards at their head; and Montbrun calling off his cavalry left his enemy to go in peace.

The loss of the French in this engagement was probably about two hundred men; that of Wellington did not exceed one hundred and sixty. Of this number seventy belonged to the cavalry, which had behaved superbly, having delivered from thirty to forty separate attacks in the course of the fight. The whole affair of course was a repetition on a smaller scale of the retreat of the Light Brigade at Fuentes de Oñoro; and in both actions the same features are conspicuous, namely the powerlessness of the French cavalry against the British squares, and the ease with which it could be thrust back by a mere handful of British or German horse. The latter point is especially remarkable; but it must be mentioned that the ground over which the French advanced to the attack was exceedingly bad, for it was broken by cliffs and precipices, (the expression used by Londonderry, who was present), so that it must have been difficult to bring the squadrons forward a second time when once they had been repulsed.

At the same time it should seem that Montbrun's tactics were exceedingly faulty, and that, if he had made his turning movement at the first instead of at the last, he might have accomplished much more— might indeed have done Wellington very serious mischief. Even as things were, the escape of the Third Division was due mainly to the fact that Dorsenne had summoned Thiébault's division before Marmont did so, and that consequently it had marched for some distance in the wrong direction before the marshal's messenger could reach it. As a matter of fact the detachment at Pastores was actually cut off; but Colonel Trench of the Seventy-Fourth with excellent judgment crossed to the right bank of the Agueda, made his way to Robleda, recrossed the river there, and brought both of his battalions safely to Fuenteguinaldo at midnight, having captured a French patrol on the way.

Thus by his own coolness, the admirable behaviour of the troops, and some good fortune Wellington had brought off the Third Division from a most perilous situation with little loss. But the danger was not yet over. At nightfall of the 25th he had in his chosen position at Fuenteguinaldo only two British divisions and one Portuguese brigade of infantry, with Alten's, De Grey's and Slade's divisions of cavalry, making from fifteen to sixteen thousand men in all. While the engagement was in progress he had directed Graham to draw back the First and Sixth Divisions and all the troops on the left to Nave de Haver; sending at the same time orders that the Seventh Division was to move to Albergueria and Casillas de Flores, and that the Light Division was to come in close to Fuenteguinaldo. But these instructions were by no means adequate to the occasion. Graham at Nave de Haver was still ten to twelve miles from the main body of the Allies; and meanwhile Marmont had summoned every man of his infantry to him by forced marches, so that noon of the 26th found him with at least forty thousand men in front of the British lines.

Moreover Craufurd for some reason had not obeyed Wellington's commands. He had set out indeed at nightfall, but had halted after traversing three or four miles, and did not move again until daylight, with the result that his division did not reach Fuenteguinaldo until late in the afternoon. His disobedience greatly increased the peril of Wellington. Graham had received exact directions concerning the line of his retreat in certain contingencies, so that the commander-in-chief, except for Craufurd's absence, might have retired during the night before the bulk of Marmont's forces had come up; but, for the sake of the Light Division, he was obliged to remain in position throughout the whole of the 26th, with an enemy of twice to thrice his strength . within striking distance. "I am glad to see you safe," observed Wellington dryly to Craufurd, when that officer at last appeared.

"Oh, I was in no danger, I assure you," answered Craufurd.

"No, but I was through your conduct," retorted the other. "It is very desirable that the general officers commanding divisions should understand that the divisions under their command respectively are only parts of an army, which must be governed by system and rule, and that every departure from the system ordered and the rule laid down, however convenient to the particular division, must be inconvenient to the army at large and therefore detrimental to the service."

So had Wellington written to Craufurd less than two months before this; but the principle was one which, with all his undoubted merit and ability, the headstrong little subordinate was unable to grasp. "He's damned crusty today," was his muttered comment, as Wellington left him to digest his two curt sentences. It occurred to him readily that the commander-in-chief might be ill-tempered, never that Robert Craufurd could be in fault. (Larpent's *Journal*. Wellington to Craufurd, 30th July).

Happily no harm came of the late arrival of the Light Division. The lessons of Bussaco and other actions had not been lost upon Marmont; and he had no intention of rushing blindly to the attack. Some portions of the position of Fuenteguinaldo had been fortified, though very incompletely, with field-works; the numbers and dispositions of the Allied troops were unknown; lastly, Wellington was a cautious commander and unlikely to offer battle unless he felt sure of success. Marmont accordingly after much reconnaissance decided not to hazard an action; and the British troops were regaled with the spectacle of the entire French Army, division after division, coming up and deploying from daylight until dark as though for a great battle on the morrow. As a matter of fact Marmont had no intention of attacking; but Wellington had likewise no idea of giving him anew the opportunity that he had lost.

Soon after dark the Allied troops began their retreat southward in two columns by Forcalhos and Aldea da Ponte upon Wellington's second chosen position at Alfaiates; the Light Division and the 1st Hussars being left to keep the watch-fires burning and to follow at midnight. At the same time the Fifth and Seventh Divisions were directed upon the same point from El Payo and Albergueria, and Graham's force was bidden to retire upon Bismulla. Singularly enough Marmont likewise turned about and retreated at precisely the same time; but towards midnight General Thiébault (according to his own account, *Thiébault: Soldier of Napoleon:* Volumes 1 and 2, published by Leonaur), noticed that the British fires were burning low and, sending men to verify his suspicions, discovered that the British camp was deserted. Marmont, being apprised of this, ordered his columns to counter-march; but the bulk of his army had already withdrawn to some distance, and only the cavalry of Wathier and Montbrun, with the infantry divisions of Thiébault and Souham, were on the spot to begin the pursuit at once. With so small a force Marmont was in no condition to give Wellington serious trouble before the concentration of the Allied army should be accomplished.

Following the routes taken by Wellington, Montbrun and Souham marched by Forcalhos, Wathier and Thiébault by Aldea da Ponte. The former column, finding the Fifth and Light Divisions in position by Aldea Velha, about three miles south-west of Forcalhos, was brought to a stand; but Thiébault, on discovering that Aldea da Ponte was held only by the light companies of Pakenham's brigade, (1/7th; 1/23rd; 1/48th), manoeuvred them out of the village with three battalions and occupied it. Unwilling to give up this advanced post, Wellington drove the French out again in turn with Pakenham's brigade, supported by a Portuguese regiment; but, Souham having joined Thiébault, the British were dispossessed of the village once more at nightfall, when Wellington left it in the hands of the French. The casualties of the Allies in this trifling affair numbered just one hundred men, thirty of them falling upon the cavalry brigades of Slade and De Grey, which had skirmished for a long time with the French horse. The losses of the French numbered one hundred and fifty.

On the following morning Wellington's army, now completed by the arrival of Graham at Rendo, was drawn up in the position which he had chosen for action, on a line from five to six miles long across a great bend of the Coa between Quadrasaes and Rendo. On the right the Fifth and Light Divisions, with Alten's, Slade's and De Grey's brigades of cavalry were massed between Quadrasaes and Souto, a village about three miles north and west of it. In the centre the Third Division was at Cardeal, with the Seventh Division in second line; the Fourth Division was at Boucafarinha; and Pack's Portuguese brigade at Villaboa.

On the left Anson's cavalry brigade and the First and Sixth Divisions were at Rendo, with a brigade in advance at Ruvina. Far out to the left, on the other side of the Coa, M'Mahon's Portuguese infantry were at Rapoula, and Madden's Portuguese cavalry at Minxella, eight miles to north, to watch the fords at that point and to communicate with the Spaniards of Carlos d'España at Castello Mendo, yet another seven miles farther north. Rather less wide on the right flank a brigade of the Fifth Division was thrown out to Valle d'Espinho. The position was exceedingly strong, so strong indeed that although the river (everywhere fordable at the moment) ran along the rear of it with only a single bridge at Sabugal, Wellington asked for nothing better than for Marmont to attack.

★★★★★★

Misled by the false date of 28th of September at the head of the orders printed in *Suppl. Desp.* xiii. 710 (which is correctly given in *Despatches*, v., as 27th), Oman has placed the troops on the 28th where they were, more or less, on the 27th, between Aldea Velha and the bridge of Rapoula. He none the less describes the position as having both flanks resting on the Coa, and as seven miles long. Aldea Velha, however, lies beyond the source of the Coa; and the distance from Aldea Velha to the bridge of Rapoula as the crow flies is ten miles.

★★★★★★

It was not likely, however, that Marmont would accommodate him, now that the Allied army was really concentrated on such formidable ground, when he had declined to attack him on very favourable terms at Fuenteguinaldo. After reconnaissance the marshal decided that his enemy was too powerfully ensconced to be assailed, ordered his columns to cantonments once more, and brought up the rear with the troops at Aldea da Ponte. His brief campaign had been to outward appearance successful. He had revictualled Ciudad Rodrigo, and had destroyed a large supply of gabions and fascines which had been prepared by Wellington for the siege of that fortress.

But he had missed his chance of striking a telling blow; he had spared Wellington when isolated at Fuenteguinaldo, and Graham when isolated at Nave de Haver; he had left the British siege-train, of whose existence he had gathered information, untouched and even unthreatened at Villa da Ponte; and lastly, in order to keep his army in the field, he had been obliged to draw upon the magazines in Ciudad Rodrigo and had consumed four out of the six months' rations which he had thrown into the place for the garrison. In his report to the emperor, (*Wellington Desp.*, v.), he of course suppressed the fact that he had begun his retreat on the night of the 26th, and represented that he had made his dispositions for attack on the 27th. He added the further fictions that he had taken two hundred prisoners, and that the loss of the Allies amounted to six or eight hundred men. Marmont was a good and gallant soldier, but too weak to escape from the atmosphere of falsehood in which Napoleon's Empire lived, moved, and had its being.

On the 1st of October Marmont and Dorsenne parted company; and the Army of Portugal returned to the posts which it had evacuated at the beginning of September. Headquarters were at Talavera; and three divisions of infantry besides Montbrun's cavalry lay in adjoining villages to westward, with the light cavalry and another division of infantry beyond them on the Alagon. Clausel's division was about Avila to gather supplies; and Foy's was despatched to Toledo. It will be remembered that this last division, after long endurance of the bad climate of Truxillo, had been sent up the Pass of Perales to make a diversion during the advance of Marmont upon Ciudad Rodrigo; but in spite of most trying marches it had reached El Payo only on the 29th, when Marmont and Dorsenne were both in retreat, and had then hastened to retire from a dangerous position. In consideration, therefore, of the sickness and hardship that had thinned its ranks, it was stationed in a healthy quarter where food was abundant; and the intermediate post of Truxillo for communication with the Fifth Corps was abandoned.

Dorsenne for his part left Thiébault's division and one brigade of Souham's with some light cavalry at Salamanca, and led the rest of his army to its former posts in the valley of the Douro. One division of the Guard was employed in supporting the advance of Bonnet to re-occupy Asturias, which had been imperatively ordered by Napoleon. Bonnet reached Oviedo and Gihon practically without opposition from the Army of Galicia, and resumed his hopeless task of holding down with eight thousand men a country which was never still except where it was under the shadow of the French bayonets.

Wellington also put his troops into winter quarters; the First, Fifth and Sixth Divisions about Guarda, Celorico and Freixedas; the Seventh at Penamacor; the Third and Light at Fuenteguinaldo, El Bodon, Martiago and Zamarra; the Fourth about Gallegos; the light cavalry along the line of the Coa from Freixedas to Castello Mendo; and De Grey's heavy brigade about Alverca. For the present he could do no more than watch Ciudad Rodrigo and recommence the provision of material for the siege. The only active work done during the winter months was a foray carried out by Julian Sanchez on the 15th of October, which resulted in the capture of the cattle belonging to that fortress, and by happy chance of the governor also. In fact matters were again at a deadlock, though Wellington could congratulate himself upon the year's work. He had driven the French from Portugal; and, though he had since taken great risks in the presence of their army both at Fuentes de Oñoro and at Fuenteguinaldo, he had, partly through his own skill, partly through great good fortune, come off the better rather than the worse.

It is now necessary to return to the doings of Hill and his detachment, who had been left with about sixteen thousand men to watch the Fifth Corps, which was of much the same strength, in Estremadura. Hill's headquarters were at Portalegre, and his troops were stationed about that place, Ville Viçosa and Santa Eulalia; with the remnants of the defeated Spaniards of the Gebora—three or four thousand strong under Castaños—to north and east of him at Valencia de Alcantara and Caçeres. The duty enjoined upon Hill was simply that of neutralising d'Erlon who, with headquarters at Zafra and a strong detachment at Merida, had received from Soult instructions to neutralise Hill. Both generals had been cautioned by their respective Commanders to retreat at once if threatened by superior numbers, Hill by Gavião upon Abrantes, and d'Erlon either north-eastward towards the Army of Portugal or southward towards the Army of the South, as might seem to him best. Meanwhile it was d'Erlon's business to maintain communications between those armies through Foy's division at Truxillo. During August and the first half of September both corps remained quiet, the only distraction being occasional raids of Castaños's cavalry upon d'Erlon's posts; but on the 15th of September Foy's division, as we have seen, was summoned from Truxillo to take part in the operations of Marmont about Ciudad Rodrigo, and at the close of the campaign was sent to Toledo.

D'Erlon therefore was ordered to fill up the gap thus created in the chain of the French posts to north-eastward, a duty which could not fail to tax his resources severely. He was obliged to send Girard's division to close the space between the Tagus and the Guadiana, and to extend Claparède's division, with two brigades of cavalry, from the latter river southward to the Sierra Morena. Such dispositions naturally led to a dangerous dispersion of force; but Wellington's information from Cadiz gave him to understand that Soult was meditating a return to Estremadura before the end of September, and there were many reasons—the revictualling of Badajoz among them—which made such a movement the reverse of improbable. The British commander was therefore unwilling at first to take advantage of this dispersion, and reiterated to Hill his original orders not to venture into the plains. It must be added that he was strengthened in this decision by the anxiety of Castaños to strike a blow at Girard, for he suspected that the Spaniards had their own motives for wishing to involve him in operations in Estremadura. (*Wellington Desp.* To Hill, 8th August, 4th, 10th, 16th October 1811).

Soult, however, was too busy with the affairs of Andalusia to spare any attention for the neighbouring province; and on the 15th of October, Hill, being satisfied of the safety of the operation, asked for leave to join Castaños in dealing a stroke at Girard, upon which Wellington at once gave his consent. The moment was propitious, for Girard, anxious to enlarge his sphere of supplies, had just marched northward from Merida with some six thousand men to drive back the Spanish detachments, and had advanced as far as Caçeres.

Accordingly on the 20th Hill wrote to ask Castaños for the help of a portion of his troops, promising for his part to bring with him some eight thousand horse, foot and artillery, so as to make up a total force of over ten thousand men. Castaños assented, whereupon Hill with all possible speed and secrecy assembled two British brigades of infantry, one of cavalry, and nine Portuguese battalions at Portalegre, (see list below), and began his march before daylight of the 22nd. Climbing the Serra de São Mamede by execrable roads, the column passed Alagrete and made its first halt at La Cordosera, having battled against a terrible storm of wind and rain ever since noon.

★★★★★★

Howard's Brigade, 1/50th, 1/71st, 1/92nd; *Wilson's Brigade* (late Abercromby's), 1/28th, 134th, 1/39th; *Long's Cavalry Brigade,* 9th and 13th L.D.; 2nd Hussars K.G.L.; 4th, 6th, 10th, 18th Portuguese (each 2 batts.), 6th Caçadores (1 batt.).

★★★★★★

Early on the 23rd the leading troops reached Alburquerque, where Hill received intelligence from Castaños that Girard, after moving as far westward as Aliseda, had fallen back to Arroyo del Puerco and Caçeres, and that the Spanish contingent under Morillo and Penne Villemur had reoccupied Aliseda. Accordingly on the 24th Hill started north-eastwards in two columns, which met at Aliseda on the 25th; and on the same day Penne Villemur drove the French advanced parties out of Arroyo del Puerco.

That night the column made another march in pouring rain to Malpartida, within six miles as the crow flies of Caçeres, only to learn on arriving that Girard had left the latter place on the previous afternoon. Unable to gather information of his direction, Hill halted his own men at Malpartida, and pushed the Spaniards forward to Caçeres. However, intelligence having come in that Girard had taken the road to southward by Torremocha, Hill set his troops again in motion at three in the morning of the 27th, directing them upon Aldea de Cano and Casas de Don Antonio, well to south of Torremocha, in the hope of intercepting his enemy. Once more he was disappointed.

On the way he was informed by the peasantry that Girard had again marched on south-eastward over the Sierra de Montanchez to the village of Arroyo Molinos, (so Arteche writes the name of the village, full title, according to the large Spanish map, is Arroyo Molinos de Montanchez—stream of the mill of Montanchez—not Arroyo dos Molinos—two-mill-stream—as borne on the colours of the 34th), leaving a rear-guard at Albalat on a by-road some six miles east and south of Aldea de Cano. There was consolation in this last detail, for it showed that Girard was ignorant of the movements of the Allies; and accordingly Hill resolved to make a final effort to overtake him.

The pursuit was therefore resumed, without changing the route, to Alcuescar, six miles to south and east of Casas de Don Antonio, and twenty-four as the crow flies from Malpartida. The troops reached their destination after dark, the Seventy-First occupying the village and throwing out a chain of sentries to prevent anyone from giving information to Girard, who lay quite unconscious of his danger some four miles away. The rest of the column bivouacked with all possible silence and quietness a little short of the town, excepting one brigade of Portuguese, which was halted at Casas de Don Antonio. At Alcuescar, over six thousand feet above the sea, all fires were forbidden, and a terrific storm of wind and rain, which blew down all tents and soaked every one to the skin, increased to the utmost the discomforts of the weary and much-tried soldiers.

At two o'clock on the morning of the 28th the sergeants went round their companies and roused them in whispers; the column again moved forward, and four hours of stumbling over an infamous road in the darkness brought them at last undiscovered and veiled by a dense fog to within a mile of Arroyo Molinos. The village itself lies under the south-western extremity of the Sierra de Montanchez, an impassable chain of mountains, of which one spur effectually blocks all egress to the east. Five country roads branch out from Arroyo Molinos north towards Montanchez, west towards Alcuescar, north-east upon Truxillo, and southwest upon Medellin and Merida respectively. Hill therefore divided his force into three columns. Of these Howard's brigade supported by Morillo's Spanish infantry, the whole under command of Colonel Stewart of the Fiftieth, was to advance straight upon the town, holding the Fiftieth and three guns in reserve; Wilson's brigade and three Portuguese battalions, with three guns, under General Howard were to move to the right so as to cut off all retreat by the two southerly roads; and lastly the cavalry under Sir William Erskine was held ready for any emergency.

Girard, as it happened, had arranged for an early start; and one of his brigades—that of Rémond—together with a regiment of cavalry had marched away before daylight, and was gone past call or view. The remainder of his troops were actually filing out of the village, the rear-guard and baggage being still within it, when the Seventy-First and Ninety-Second came charging down the street, sweeping everything before them at the bayonet's point. A few of the French cavalry, forming part of the rear-guard, appear to have attempted resistance, for they cut down some of the British infantry; but the surprise was so complete that they found no support. Dozens of prisoners were captured before they could escape; and Girard himself had only taken the alarm a few minutes earlier, and was hurrying his troops out of the village with all possible haste. Having brought them clear of the streets he faced them to west, so as to present a front towards his enemy, and formed his six remaining battalions in two squares with their right flank within a hundred yards of the town, and the left, covered by cavalry, midway between the two roads to Merida and Medellin.

His design was evidently to retire to Merida; but, before his formation was complete, the Seventy-First opened fire from behind garden-walls upon his right flank, while the Ninety-Second filed out, formed line at right angles to it, and prepared to charge. The latter regiment, however, was forbidden to fire, and suffered some slight loss, until the three guns attached to Howard's brigade came up and began to ply the helpless French column with grape. Then the enemy attempted to move off; but finding the road blocked by the Allied horse, Girard ordered his mounted troops to drive them off at all costs, and changing the direction of the infantry from south to east, headed straight for the road to Truxillo.

Bad roads and darkness had delayed the arrival of Long's brigade; but Penne Villemur and his Spanish squadrons gallantly assailed the two French regiments of cavalry, until the 2nd German Hussars, together with a squadron of the Ninth Light Dragoons, came up, and after a sharp conflict defeated the French completely, capturing over two hundred prisoners. Among them was the French brigadier, Bron, who after shooting two dragoons of the Ninth, finally gave up his sword to a trumpeter of the same regiment.

★★★★★★

Cannon's *Record of the Ninth Lancers*, This states that the whole regiment was engaged. Schwertfeger and Beamish on the contrary say that one squadron only of the Ninth was with the 2nd Hussars, and I believe them to be correct. Beamish states that Bron was ridden down by the Hussars and picked up by the 9th. Cannon's account affirms that Bron was trying to escape in his carriage, when he was captured, which seems incredible. Oman, following another story, says that Bron was taken in the village before he could mount his horse. The incident is of no great importance.

★★★★★★

Meanwhile Howard's column was marching with all its speed round the southern flank of the French, striving to reach before them a promontory of the Sierra, about which runs the road to Truxillo, so as to cut off their last hope of retreat. The French guns led the way at a trot, and the light companies of Wilson's brigade diverged from their true direction in a vain effort to overtake them, until Hill bade them leave the guns to the cavalry. The British general then galloped on alone with his *aide-de-camp* and orderly to the point of the promontory, where the light companies presently joined him just as the French column came up. Hill would not allow them to fire, but ordered them, though no more than two hundred against fifteen hundred, to charge with the bayonet. They charged accordingly, led by Lieutenant Blakeney of the Twenty-Eighth; but Girard, who was himself wounded, had already given the order to his men to disperse, and showed the way by throwing himself upon the rocky hillside above him.

Some two or three hundred men seem to have had time to follow him before Blakeney's troops closed with the main body which, seeing the British converging upon them from all sides, laid down their arms. Girard and his companions pursued their way over the hill, which just at this point ran out into a long spit, with the light companies in eager chase; descended again into the plain on the other side; and finding cavalry awaiting them there, climbed into the mountains once more. Morillo's Spaniards then took up the pursuit, which they pressed for over thirty miles, killing or capturing many of the fugitives, though failing to take Girard himself and his brigadier, Dombrowski. Meanwhile the Thirteenth Light Dragoons had overtaken and captured the guns; and the work of the British column was thus completed.

Of about twenty-six hundred French, who were at Arroyo Molinos, some thirteen hundred were taken, from seven to eight hundred were killed, and only from four to five hundred contrived to escape. Hill's casualties, British, Portuguese, and Spanish, barely exceeded one

56

hundred killed and wounded.

Directly the action was over Hill sent Long's cavalry and the Portuguese regiments, which had not been engaged, in pursuit of Rémond; but that general, having been warned by some flying dragoons of Girard's mishap, had marched steadily southward without a halt. Hill therefore moved off next morning to Merida, and after two days' rest there, returned by Wellington's order to his old quarters at Portalegre, which were reached on the 4th of November. As Wellington said, he had done his business handsomely; and if by unlucky chance half of Girard's force had not started before he came up, he would have made the blow still more telling. Napoleon was intensely annoyed with Girard, and deprived him of his command, not failing at the same time to express dissatisfaction with Soult for exposing so small a detachment to danger, (*Corres, de Napoléon*); but Girard was soon employed again, and did noble service for his master.

For the rest it must be observed that the loyalty of the Spanish peasants in giving no warning to the French was an essential feature in the enterprise; and that Hill's success gave extraordinary pleasure not only throughout Wellington's army, but wherever he was known in Spain. "The man seems to be beloved by all," wrote an officer of the German Legion, who could have had no motive for such words beyond that he shared in the general devotion to Hill; and when in response to Wellington's recommendation the Order of the Bath was conferred upon Hill and he became Sir Rowland, there was for once applause and satisfaction in all ranks from the private to the commander-in-chief.

★★★★★★

Of all the regiments engaged at Arroyo Molinos the 34th (1st batt. Border Regiment) alone bears the name on its colours. Why this should be so, I know not, unless it was because the 34th of the French Line was captured in the action, but I imagine the honour to be due to some job. If any regiment deserves to bear this name it is the 92nd, which suffered more heavily than the rest; but it would be impossible to make the change now without giving the honour also to all other regiments present which, for so small an affair in a really great war, would be absurd. The best account of Arroyo Molinos is in Blakeney's Autobiography; but there are also narratives in Sherer's *Recollections*; Hope's Military Memoirs; *The Adventures of Captain Patterson*; and *The Journal of a Soldier of the 71st*; Dickson MSS. iii. 495;

Hill's despatch is printed in *Wellington Desp.*, v.; Girard's *ibid.*
★★★★★★

Lastly it remains to narrate very briefly, in order to conclude the campaign of 1811, the operations of Suchet on the eastern coast. With some misgivings, for he could not forget the outcome of former invasions of Valencia, Suchet hastened his preparations, and moving from his advanced base at Tortosa crossed the boundaries of the province on the day appointed by Napoleon, (Sept. 15), with some twenty-two thousand men. Blake, who was in command of the forces opposed to him, could bring into the field about thirty thousand men, including the troops which had fought so bravely at Albuera; but the Spanish Army had little coherency or moral strength, and its commander was not a man who could supply these deficiencies. He made practically no opposition to the advance of Suchet, and before the arrival of the French forces at Murviedro on the 23rd fell back to an entrenched position behind the Guadalaviar, leaving his adversary confronted by the fortress, formidable through its great natural strength, of Sagunto.

After a vain attempt to carry this stronghold by escalade, the marshal was constrained to send for his siege-train; and, having first freed his communications by the capture of Oropesa, opened fire upon Sagunto upon the 17th of October. On the 18th he made a second assault, which was once more beaten off with serious loss, and he now realised that his misgivings as to the task set to him by the emperor were but just. It was everything to him to make short work of Sagunto, if it were humanly possible, and yet two attempts to capture the place by surprise had failed completely. At the same time, the successes, already related, of the guerrilla leaders in his rear filled him with apprehension for his communications.

Now, however, Fortune came to his aid. Blake deemed it his duty to march forward to the relief of Sagunto, and, having collected nearly forty thousand men, on the 25th attacked Suchet's force of less than half his numbers with his usual unskilfulness. He was, of course, totally defeated with the loss of five thousand killed, wounded and prisoners, and of twelve guns, the casualties of the French not exceeding eight hundred. As a consequence Sagunto capitulated on the following day; and thus was removed from Suchet's path an obstacle which, if the garrison had emulated their fellows of Zaragoza and Gerona, might have detained him yet for several weeks.

The marshal then advanced to the north bank of the Guadalaviar, over against Valencia, where only the river separated him from the city and from the entrenched camp of Blake upon the southern bank. The Spanish general, by calling up garrisons and small bodies from Murcia, had raised his army once more to over thirty thousand men, and having command of the bridges could at any time take the offensive. Suchet, what with losses in action, the occupation of captured places, and detachments for minor services, had now little more than fifteen thousand troops at his disposal. He was therefore fain to fortify himself in his new position and await reinforcements, which he did with the better hope inasmuch as the guerilla-bands in his rear sustained during the month of November more than one serious defeat.

CHAPTER 3

Napoleon and the Peninsula

It will hardly be believed that during the last six months of 1811, when scarce a tricolour flag dared show itself at sea, when the Grand Army had begun to concentrate for the march upon Moscow, and the state of affairs in the Peninsula alone might have sufficed to engross all the attention of one man, Napoleon wrote no fewer than twenty orders—many of them long and elaborate—concerning a projected descent upon the British Isles. Fatigued and worn down by hard and inexorable facts, he seems to have found solace and recreation in framing plans for an impossible enterprise against his inveterate enemy, even as a jealous woman finds relief in stabbing the image of a rival with a pin. And yet within the same twenty-four hours the dreamer regained his transcendent common sense, triumphed over an old illusion, and patiently worked out the organisation of the transport-corps, which has been already mentioned, for service in the Peninsula.

★★★★★★

For the transport-corps see *Corres, de Napoléon,*; and compare with the first the project of invasion written on the following day. See also his complaint that the *prefect* of Boulogne must take the preparations for the English expedition seriously and not as a joke.

★★★★★★

Thus we are brought back once more to Spain, where the emperor appeared intent upon complicating as much as possible the details of an already intricate problem before leaving it in great measure to solve itself. On the 18th of September 1811 he had written orders which showed that for the moment he built all his hopes upon Marmont. The Duke of Ragusa was to take d'Erlon's corps under his orders, obtain three thousand cavalry from Soult, and, with an army thus raised to fifty-seven thousand men, was to lay siege to Elvas. Wellington would be bound to hasten to the rescue of the fortress, but, being obliged to leave two divisions to hold Dorsenne's Army of the North in check, he could do so only with inferior numbers, and might therefore be beaten.

This, said the emperor, was the only way to regain the offensive, make the English tremble, and take a decisive step towards ending the war. Meanwhile Suchet would have taken Valencia by the time that Elvas had fallen, and could then send Marmont a division. The letter closed with a warning, however, that this scheme was only feasible on the supposition that Wellington possessed no siege-train; otherwise by beleaguering Ciudad Rodrigo he could force Marmont to forsake all other objects and march to its relief. The last condition, as it happened, vitiated the whole scheme, for Marmont had found evidence enough that Wellington harboured designs upon Ciudad Rodrigo; but the marshal's only answer was that he was wholly occupied with the business of feeding his army, and that, when this difficulty had been overcome, he would submit an offensive project of his own.

Before matters could go further, however, the emperor changed his plans entirely. So far his one successful general in Spain had been Suchet; and on the 18th of October, at the moment when Suchet was before Sagunto, he issued fresh orders to Marmont, which showed that he had transferred his faith to the commander who had just found his baton in Tarragona. Henceforth the principal object was to be Valencia; therefore Joseph's Army of the Centre must be extended to Cuenca so as to second Suchet; and the Army of Portugal must fill the gaps thus created in New Castile. A month later the same injunctions were repeated with further developments. By that time Sagunto had fallen, and the capture of Valencia was deemed so urgent that Marmont was instructed to detach six thousand men to reinforce Suchet. The English, said the emperor, had eighteen thousand men sick, and seemed determined to remain on the defensive; consequently there would be plenty of time for the advance upon Elvas at the end of January, when the fall of Valencia would release plenty of troops for the field.

The letter containing these orders was dated the 20th of November: by the 21st Wellington's sick list had swelled in the emperor's imagination to twenty thousand men, and his effective army had diminished to as many more. The English were therefore in his view helpless; and Marmont was accordingly ordered to detach at once twelve thousand men to Valencia, besides three to four thousand more to hold the line of communications, and to hold himself ready to support Suchet generally. When once Valencia had been taken, Marmont would receive forty thousand men from the Armies of the South and West, and then the final conquest of Portugal would be near at hand.

The actual results of this change of policy shall be fully described in their place. For the present it is sufficient to note two things: the first, that the scheme was built wholly upon the fiction that Wellington had only twenty thousand men in his army fit for duty, whereas he had over thirty-eight thousand British and Germans, besides twenty-four thousand Portuguese; the second, that the weakening of the army of the senior Marshal, Marmont, for behoof of a junior Marshal, Suchet, was a very doubtful remedy for healing jealousies, and the practical transfer of Joseph's small army of the Centre to Suchet's command a very singular method of upholding that king's authority. Apart from these two considerations there was undoubtedly not a little to be said in favour of making the capture of Valencia a prime object.

In the first place the majority of the Grandees of Spain possessed estates in that province, upon which they had lived when all other springs of income had failed; and the loss of their last resource was likely to hasten their submission. Further, the French would not only cut off the supplies of Valencia from the most formidable of the guerrilla leaders, but by appropriating the provisions and money in that district would be able to found, as it were, a new and advantageous base of operations. If Soult should move eastward and aid Suchet in the reduction of Alicante and Carthagena, the greater part of Andalusia might be turned to this use, and their united hosts might then march in full strength upon Estremadura and Portugal from the east. But even if Soult should find such an undertaking beyond his strength, the possession of the city of Valencia would enable the Army of Aragon (to give it the old title) to communicate by a shorter route than ever before with the Army of the Centre towards Madrid, and with the Army of Portugal on the Tagus. In fact, as Wellington at once perceived, it would greatly enhance the French powers of concentration, upon which depended their ultimate mastery of the Peninsula. (Wellington to Liverpool, 4th Dec. 1811).

These were unquestionably great advantages; but no mere change of plans could make good the vital defect of the French armies in Spain, the want of unity in command. Joseph, as we have seen, after endless complaints and threats of abdication, had proceeded to Paris in person for the baptism of his nephew, the King of Rome, hoping to obtain some increase both of pecuniary assistance and of administrative authority from his great brother. The emperor declined to grant the whole of his demands, doubtless realising that Joseph was too much in love with his royal title to abandon it readily; but it was, after all, a part of his system to make over outlying possessions to his family, as feudatories; and, with the prospect of a long absence in distant lands before him, he was prepared to go to some lengths in conciliation. He therefore informed Joseph that his monthly dole from Paris should be augmented, that the chief commanders of all the armies should report to him daily, that a royal commissioner should be attached to the Armies of the North and South, so as to secure for the king one-fourth of all receipts, and that, whenever His Majesty were actually present with any army, his orders should be obeyed.

But even so the Army of Portugal was left independent; and, whatever the emperor might have promised to his brother, his commands to his generals omitted all mention of the daily reports to be made to Madrid, and of the quarter of all contributions to be reserved for Joseph's use. The monthly payments from Paris were irregular and incomplete; and the Army of the Centre was used as a milch-cow for the feeding of the remaining forces. Moreover, Joseph had not left Paris two months before there were signs that a part of his realm was to be torn from him. The general commanding the Army of Catalonia was instructed on the 25th of August 1811 to address no correspondence to the king and to answer none of his letters; and there were ominous rumours concerning the annexation of that province to France.

Joseph wrote frantic protests. He had always declared that, if there were any violation of what he called his territory, he would resign his crown. This was in fact precisely what Napoleon wished him to do; but, when fairly faced with the alternative of submission or abdication, the poor creature could not bring himself to play the man and forget the king. True to his usual habit on such occasions Joseph sent his wife to mediate with the emperor, who, by reason of his respect for her as a virtuous woman (a rare thing in the Bonaparte family), yielded so far as to promise that Joseph's allowance should be regularly remitted, and the Army of the Centre left intact.

Still not a word was said as to Catalonia; and in December and January came new signs more than ever alarming to Joseph. The emperor's special campaigning-equipment, which ever since 1809 had been kept ready, first at Bayonne and later at Vitoria, for his descent upon the Peninsula in person at any moment, was finally removed to

France; and this was presently followed by the recall of the whole of the Imperial Guard and of all Polish troops from Spain. (Berthier to Joseph, Jan. 1812. *Arch. Nat.*). Napoleon had been careful to prepare his brother for this withdrawal of troops, promising that every man taken away should be replaced by another; and he did indeed presently send forty-two battalions of conscripts to fill the room of forty battalions of seasoned soldiers. But the Army of Spain was not, as he tried to represent, a gainer by the change. At the same time he reorganised the whole of the troops in the Peninsula, according to a plan which shall be shown on a later page, and redistributed the commands all over the country without a word to Joseph.

Moreover, at this same period he determined upon the final stroke, the incorporation of Catalonia with France. The public announcement of this alteration was omitted; but the province was divided into four departments; and a few weeks later an army of civil officials entered it to take up the work of administration. The story of their arrival forms one of the most singular episodes in the history of the Empire. The newcomers were men of high rank and station, who had rendered eminent service in other posts, and had been rewarded by titles of dignity. The French officers, from the general to the subaltern, refused to recognise their authority for a moment. They regarded them as intruders and encroachers upon their own domain, jostled them unceremoniously aside, and, in defiance of the emperor's orders, forcibly retained all powers of government in their own hands.

To put the matter briefly, the French armies in Spain were so much demoralised by indiscipline that they had become a number of independent bands under independent chiefs, who claimed autocratic power within the districts assigned to them, and would not yield it up to the emperor himself.

It was hardly likely that such men would pay any respect to Joseph; and indeed they treated him with open contempt, not scrupling even to appropriate to the service of their troops a part of the monthly allowance sent by Napoleon for the king's own use. Such an outrage would, it might be thought, have stirred even the mildest man to revolt; but Joseph accepted it, accepted even the official information that Catalonia was taken from him, rather than resign his shadow of a crown. He was unwilling, he said, to increase existing difficulties, and was prepared to stay at Madrid till the Russian War were ended; and a few days later, (March 13), he received his reward in the shape of a letter to the effect that Jourdan was appointed to be chief of his staff, since the emperor intended, if he should find himself obliged to go to Poland, to place Joseph in command of all the armies in Spain. The king at once informed Jourdan, who had returned to Madrid in December 1811, of his appointment; and thinking that the time was come for himself to send an ultimatum, he wrote that, if the annexation of Catalonia were openly proclaimed, and if he were not left in supreme authority, both civil and military, in Spain, he would abdicate his throne.

The letter was intercepted and printed in the Spanish newspapers; but Napoleon judged it to be a forgery and took no notice; for he had already on the 18th of March issued the final order that Joseph was to command all the troops in the Peninsula in chief, and that Suchet, Soult, and Marmont were to obey all orders that they might receive from him, "to ensure unity of action on the part of the armies." ("*Pour faire marcher les armées dans une même direction.*"The phrase is explained a few lines lower down by the words "*la nécessité de mettre de l'ensemble dans les armées.*" Napoleon to Berthier, 16th March 1812. *Corres.*). The wording of the directions to the generals was a little obscure, for it could be construed as permitting them to disobey any commands from Joseph which, in their judgment, would not contribute towards the result desired by the emperor; while the omission to mention by name the chiefs of the Armies of Valencia and of the North might be interpreted as exempting them from the duty imposed upon their colleagues of the other armies.

On the 3rd of April the emperor complicated matters still further by declaring first that he gave Marmont a free hand with the Army of Portugal; secondly, that he entrusted to Joseph the supreme command of the Armies of Portugal, Valencia, and the South, the remaining armies being still unmentioned; and thirdly, that he committed likewise to Joseph the political and military direction of all affairs in Spain. (*Corres. de Napoléon*). Such contradictory solutions of a difficult problem show that Napoleon felt his embarrassments in Spain to be beyond remedy. There was, however, still another means of escaping from them. Joseph was once more empowered either to negotiate with the Cortes at Cadiz for the recognition by them of his sovereignty in return for his acceptance of the constitution, which they had lately promulgated, and upon the basis of this arrangement to agree to the restoration of Catalonia and the withdrawal of all French troops from Spain; or he might summon a Cortes of his own which should adopt that same constitution with the same results.

In this latter case the ground was to be carefully prepared by the intrusive king; and it was judged that the chance of getting rid of the British as well as of the French would offer strong temptation to the Spaniards. So sanguine was the emperor of the success of one or other of these expedients that on the 17th of April he tendered to Castlereagh the following propositions as the basis of peace.

The integrity of Spain and of Portugal was to be guaranteed, and France was to renounce all extension of her boundaries towards the Pyrenees. In Portugal the House of Bragança would continue to reign; in Spain the dynasty of Joseph would be declared independent, and Spain would be governed by a national constitution of the Cortes. The kingdom of Naples would remain with Murat, and the kingdom of Sicily with the reigning house of Bourbon; and all forces, both naval and military, of France and Great Britain would be withdrawn alike from the Peninsula and from Sicily. All other subjects of discussion were to be settled upon the principle that each of the contracting powers should keep what the other was powerless to take from her. (*Corres. de Napoléon*). The bait was tempting; for such an arrangement would have left England in possession of practically all the French and Dutch colonies; but Castlereagh refused to look at it. Within less than a week he answered that England could entertain no overtures which involved the acknowledgment of Joseph in lieu of Ferdinand as King of Spain.

Therewith vanished the emperor's last hope of concluding matters in the Peninsula before he invaded Russia, of securing his rear in the south and west, as we may put it, before advancing north and east. What his ultimate designs as to Spain may have been, it is impossible to say; it is only certain that for the time being he left his affairs in that country to chance; and it should seem that he was guided not a little towards this fatal step by Joseph's childish craving for the phantom of a crown.

CHAPTER 4

Tarifa

Returning now to the scene of active operations, let us deal first with events in the south of Spain. Here Soult, looking to the uniform success of Suchet's campaign, had conceived the idea of joining him in the sieges of Carthagena and Alicante, and of establishing himself so firmly in Andalusia as to make it a regular base for offensive movements against Estremadura and Portugal. But to accomplish this it was necessary first to cut short the career of Ballesteros, who had already done much mischief. It was, however, difficult if not impossible to crush this chief so long as he could find refuge not only at Cadiz but at Tarifa and Gibraltar, could put to sea at any one of these ports when hard pressed, and land again at a fresh point to swoop down anew upon the French posts and communications about Cadiz.

The marshal therefore decided first to attack Tarifa, primarily because it gave the British complete mastery of the Straits of Gibraltar, and secondly because it was the one place of the three where he might hope for some success. He was the more inclined to this course inasmuch as he had sent a mission to Barbary, and had obtained from its ruler a promise that the supplies hitherto sent to the Allies would in future be directed to the French, if Tarifa were occupied by them as a port of entry. This promise, it may be added, was not fulfilled; for Mr. Stuart, by sending a counter-mission, armed with richer presents, to the same potentate, quickly persuaded him to confine his good offices, as heretofore, to the British.

Soult, nevertheless, resolved to pursue his design; and to that end ordered a small siege-train of twelve pieces with over one hundred waggons of ammunition and siege-equipment to be secretly collected at Puerto Real, just outside Cadiz, in the first days of November. The force appointed for the operations numbered something over twelve thousand men, drawn from the First and Fourth Corps, and was placed under the command of Marshal Victor. (See list following).

First Division. Barrois.

1st Corps	1st brigade : 43rd Line, 7th and 9th Poles, about		3,000	
	Cavalry brigade . { 16th Dragoons, 500 }{ 21st „ (det.) 85 }			. 585
	Divisional artillery (say)	.	.	. 50

Second Division. Leval.

4th Corps	1st brigade, Pécheux { 16th Light, 3 batts. }{ 94th Line, 1 batt. }			
	2nd brigade, Chasseraux { 51st „ 2 batts. }{ 95th „ 1 batt. }		about 6,000	
	3rd brigade, Cassagne { 54th „ 2 batts. }{ 27th Light, 1 batt. }			
	Divisional Artillery (say)	.	.	. 50
	Artillery and Engineers	.	.	. 765

Covering Force.

3 batts. of 8th and 63rd Line (say)	.	.	1,800
2 squadrons 2nd Dragoons „	.	.	150

12,400

The first requisite was to fend off any attempt by Ballesteros, who was in the neighbourhood of Ximena, to interrupt the siege; and Soult appears to have planned his operations with some hope not only of fending him off but of annihilating him. For on the 21st of November the division of Barrois, thirty-six hundred men, moved southward from Ronda upon Los Barrios and San Roque, while Pécheux's brigade of the Fourth Corps occupied the passes which lead from the westward into the plain of Gibraltar; and Leval, with a third force of about the same strength as that of Barrois, closed in upon the Spanish General from Malaga. With some difficulty Ballesteros again found safety under the guns of Gibraltar, where for the present his army remained, without shelter from the winter rains and without any food but that supplied by the governor.

Victor, having left Cadiz a few days later with three battalions and two squadrons, reached Vejer, midway between Cadiz and Tarifa, on the 2nd of December, and being there joined on the 8th by the siege-train, resumed his march on the next day. Little progress was made on the 9th owing to bad weather; and in the night the rain came down in torrents, continued for forty-eight hours, and laid the whole country under water. Leval's division had already joined Pécheux, but that of

Barrois at San Roque and Los Barrios was completely cut off by the floods both from Cadiz and Malaga; and it was only at great peril of drowning that an officer succeeded in carrying to Barrois the order to unite his division to the rest of the army.

Not until the morning of the 13th could he do so; and meanwhile the whole of the French force had fasted for two days in a desert of mud and water. With great difficulty supplies were brought up from Cadiz, the whole of the horses of the transport, besides those of the field-artillery of the First Corps, having been already taken to drag the siege-train.

On the 14th the march was resumed, and, by dint of harnessing forty or fifty animals to each gun, the train with infinite trouble was brought forward about fifteen miles in five days. Meanwhile on the 17th Ballesteros, in combination with some Spanish troops of the garrison of Tarifa, made an attack on the French outposts, but was beaten off with loss; and on the 19th Victor's soldiers debouched into the plain of Tarifa. On the 22nd the train, having braved the fire of a small British squadron at one point of the road, was safely brought in, and the work of the siege began.

Tarifa, then a little town of three thousand inhabitants, lies nearly at the point of a promontory which juts out almost at a right angle to the sea, and is connected by a causeway about five hundred yards long with a circular island of some seven hundred yards diameter. The town itself stood within an old rampart about six feet thick, surmounted by a crenulated battlement and flanked at intervals by towers; but there was no ditch within the rampart, and the extent of the entire *enceinte*, which was nearly square in form, did not measure more than four hundred yards from north to south and rather less from east to west. The southern front, being within one hundred yards of the sea, was of course practically inaccessible to an army which had no ships to support it; and the British men-of-war were able to afford efficient defence also to the western front, though this was already protected by two important works ashore. These were the castle and tower of the Guzmans at the south-western angle, and a battery mounting one heavy gun upon a sandhill, called Santa Catalina, on the foreshore about three hundred yards south-west of it.

These two strongholds commanded all the ground between the walls and the island, which last, being surrounded by sheer cliffs and having a battery constructed at the head of the causeway, was to all intents inaccessible. The northern and eastern sides were far more ole, being dominated at close range by heights from which wn could be seen to its foundations. On the northern front demolition of a suburb and the conversion of a convent, about a ndred yards from the wall, into an outwork, had done something to increase the strength of the defences; but on the eastern side there were not only ridges which offered good sites for hostile batteries, but additional danger from a hollow way, formed by the bed of a torrent, which ran actually to the foot of the rampart and passed through the town. This last was barred at its entrance by a tower, known as the Retiro, with a portcullis, before which was a line of palisades; but even so it furnished such good cover for an assaulting party as positively to invite an attack.

The engineer in charge of the place, Captain Smith, had noted all these peculiarities, and divining that the French would almost certainly attempt to make their breach by the portcullis, had retrenched the position with consummate skill. In the first place the guns of the Retiro tower swept the whole length of the torrent; and, to gain a flanking as well as a frontal fire, he fortified and loopholed the houses and barricaded the streets on each side of the torrent's bed so as to confine the enemy to it. At the same time he provided means of egress to the rear, so that the defenders, if hard pressed, could retreat to the strongest part of the fortifications—Guzman's castle and tower on the southern side—and thence make their way over the causeway to the island.

The full strength of the garrison was slightly over three thousand of all ranks, (see list following), nearly eighteen hundred of whom were British and the remainder Spaniards, the former being under command of Colonel Skerrett of the Forty-Seventh, and the whole under command of the Spanish General Copons. Of the British, about eleven hundred were in the tower, one hundred were in the convent, fifty at Santa Catalina, and some six hundred, under Major King of the Eighty-Second, on the island. Eleven guns in all were mounted on the walls, towers, and outworks of the fortress, and twelve on the island.

Spanish.		Officers.	Men.
Infantry	. .	67	1073
Artillery	. .	5	101
Sappers	. .	4	79
Cavalry	. .	1	16
		77	1269 (Arteche, xi. 521, table.)

British.

Light cos. 11th
   2/47th
Det. 82nd
   2/87th
1 co. 2/95th
Det. R.A.
Det. 2nd Hussars, K.G.L. } 67 officers, 1707 men.

The operations opened with two little sallies on the 21st and 22nd, in the latter of which the French lost over twenty killed and wounded, including four officers; and on the 23rd the French broke ground, as Smith had expected, on the eastern heights upon both sides of the torrent, at a distance of about three hundred yards from the wall. Before dawn they had completed their first and begun their second parallel, and on the five following nights they pushed their works forward vigorously under a heavy fire from the defenders. And now there ensued a curious complication which might easily have brought disaster not only to this but to any military enterprise. The idea of holding Tarifa had originated not with Wellington nor with General Cooke, his deputy at Cadiz, but solely with General Campbell, the Governor of Gibraltar. Skerrett's brigade was under the command of Cooke, but the artillery, engineers, and part of his infantry had been lent by Campbell.

Realising the weakness of the place when the French attacked it by the regular operations of a siege, and unable, perhaps, to appreciate the subtlety of Smith's plan of defence, Skerrett had hesitated to take responsibility by risking his troops in the venture, and had applied to Cooke for orders. On the 24th Cooke's answer came that the brigade was to be at once re-embarked for Cadiz; and on that night Skerrett held a council of war wherein opinions were divided between Cooke's party, represented by Skerrett, and Campbell's party, represented by Major King and Captain Smith. Gough of the Eighty-seventh, though his regiment belonged to Cadiz, appears to have carried the decision of the council against Skerrett; and it was resolved that resistance should be continued.

On the 26th the wind blew so hard that the British squadron was obliged to seek shelter in Algeçiras Bay; and a deluge of rain poured down for another forty-eight hours, filling the trenches with mud and water. However, with great difficulty and labour the French dragged their guns into the batteries on the night of the 28th, and at eleven o'clock on the following morning opened fire from ten heavy pieces upon the town and the island. The garrison answered with a cannonade from the towers and from four small vessels, which had returned to the roadstead in spite of persistent bad weather. In a few hours a practicable breach had been made in the spot where Smith had anticipated, just to south of the Retiro Tower; and now once more Skerrett's heart misgave him, and he decided to withdraw his brigade and abandon the place. He even went so far as to order the garrison's single heavy gun, which was mounted on Guzman's tower, to be spiked. Major King, however, reported this determination to General Campbell, who took effective measures to neutralise it by ordering the transports to return from Tarifa to Gibraltar without taking a man on board. Campbell had just faith in the ability of Smith, who had indeed been indefatigable in making good all damage wrought by the enemy's cannon.

Owing to the slope of the ground towards the torrent, the level of the street at the damaged point was thirteen feet below that of the rampart; but, although the enemy poured showers of grape into the breach, the defenders contrived to keep it clear of rubbish, and to cover the space within with iron gratings, torn from the windows of the houses, with every alternate bar broken and turned upwards. At daybreak the French renewed their fire under a sharp fusillade from the marksmen of the garrison; and at noon the breach was thirty feet wide. Leval, who was in charge of the siege, then sent in a summons, which was rejected. The cannonade began again; and by nightfall the breach had been enlarged to a width of sixty feet. Leval therefore ordered the assault to be delivered at dawn of the next day.

In truth he had no choice but to storm or raise the siege. Incessant rain forbade any further work upon the trenches, and cut off all communication with Victor's magazines at Vejer. The besiegers were in a miserable state; their trenches flooded; their camp a sea of mud. They had neither shelter, nor food, nor fuel to dry their clothes; many had succumbed to sickness, and all were utterly wretched. Soon after sunset of the 30th the rain streamed down with unusual violence; the bed of the torrent became a torrent indeed, and washed down such an accumulation of corpses, gabions, planks, and other material from the besiegers' camp that the palisades before the portcullis were swept away, and the portcullis itself was so much bent as to leave an opening into the town.

Many of the defensive works were also ruined; and only by the utmost exertions were the necessary repairs effected before daylight. Fortunately the enemy had suffered even more from the weather than had the Allies; and it was not until eight o'clock, when the rain was still falling in sheets, that the French columns were seen to be moving. They were composed of the grenadiers and *voltigeurs* of the besieging army, sixteen companies of each, massed into four battalions and numbering perhaps two thousand men.

The grenadiers formed the actual storming party, while the *voltigeurs*, supported by Cassagne's brigade, made a demonstration on the right of the allied line, and Pécheux's brigade a similar demonstration on the left. The grenadiers advanced along the right bank of the hollow formed by the bed of the torrent, where they should have been sheltered almost to the last moment from fire; but, mistaking their way, they followed this direction straight to the portcullis, instead of turning to their right towards the breach. Thus they came under a terrific fusillade from the Eighty-Seventh, who defended the breach and the eastern wall. The leader of the storming party fell desperately wounded, and handed his sword through the bars of the portcullis to Gough; and the men, not knowing what to do, extended themselves, knee-deep in mud, to left and right along the ramparts, and opened a feeble fire. In this way some of them came upon the breach, and a few ascended it; but all who exposed themselves were instantly shot down, while a raking blast of grape from the north-eastern tower so devastated the attacking party that they shrank back into the shelter of the hollow, and returned beaten to their camp.

Their loss amounted to two hundred and seven, of whom forty-eight were killed; and no fewer than seven officers and eighty-one men of the fallen belonged to two gallant companies of the 51st. That of the Allies did not exceed thirty-six, more than two-thirds of whom belonged to the Eighty-Seventh. Yet such a check would never have daunted French soldiers but for the appalling state of their camps and their works. The trenches were waist-deep in water; the platforms of the guns were washed away; the guns themselves were sinking into the soil; the ammunition both for cannon and muskets was ruined; and the muskets themselves were unserviceable.

The men were barefooted and their clothing in rags; they could get no sleep in their flooded quarters; they had been obliged to travel eight miles to discover fuel, which after all proved useless when found, owing to the rain; all supplies were now cut off by swollen torrents, and for four days they had received only quarter-rations of bread. For some time they had suffered such hardships with patience, but they had now reached the limit of human endurance. Hundreds had already succumbed to fever, and on the day after the assault the guards deserted their posts, leaving the trenches to take care of themselves, and scattered all over the country in the vain hope of finding some kind of shelter.

At length towards the evening of the 2nd of January 1812 the deluge abated, and the weather improved. The French gunners returned to their pieces, but one of them jumping on the embrasure of the breaching battery sank waist-deep into the mud, and could only be extricated by rough methods which left him half dead. On the night of the 2nd the besiegers fired a few shot from their cannon, and Victor gave orders for a new attack which should batter a breach in a different position. Leval protested against this attempt, alleging that the men were worn out, the tools buried in the mud, and most of the transport-animals dead; but Victor persisted, saying that a week's fine weather would deliver Tarifa into his hands. The arrival of provisions and a belated opportunity of drying their clothes cheered the men back to their work; but on the night of the 3rd the rain began again; all communications were once more cut off; and Victor, fully alive to his critical position, hesitated no longer to raise the siege.

All through the day of the 4th the storm continued to rage, and in the evening an English *felucca* from Tangier was driven ashore at Tarifa. The crew were saved; but the French soldiers, in spite of the fire from the walls, swarmed down to pick up the shattered timbers for fuel, and to take such food as they could find from the wreck. Throughout the night they laboured to bring off the guns; but, though over two hundred men worked their hardest, they could save only three of the light pieces, which were dragged, each by a team of forty horses, to Torre Peña. On their return the horses drew off a field-smithy and two waggon-loads of wounded; and it was then necessary to abandon the rest of the cannon together with the whole of the ammunition, and to collect the waggons and stores in piles to be burned.

Finally at three in the morning of the 5th the retreat began, covered by Barrois's division. The garrison made a sortie and saved many of the stores from the flames, but the pursuit was not pressed, and, though there was some firing, the losses of the French were insignificant. On the 6th with the help of one hundred horses, which had been sent with guns and ammunition to Tahibilla, eight miles from Tarifa, the wounded and two of the siege-pieces were taken back to Vejer, but the third gun and the newly-arrived loads of ammunition were engulfed with all their teams in the quagmires of the road.

Altogether the expedition cost the French over five hundred men, at least three hundred horses and mules, nine guns, and a great quantity of stores. The loss of the British in the entire siege did not reach the number of seventy killed, wounded, and missing.

Taken as a whole the defence of Tarifa was creditable to the British, though it seems a ridiculous exaggeration to call it, as Napier does, a splendid achievement. The repulse of the assault, as it happened, was simply child's play, for the storming party could hardly move in the sea of mud over which they had to advance. That the place was worth holding, if it could be maintained without undue risk, may be admitted; and all praise is due to Captain Smith for perceiving, as he did, the possibilities of a long and stout defence. But, after all, it is very evident that the weather was chiefly responsible for the failure of the French attack; and indeed it was within Smith's calculations that the garrison might at any time be driven into the island.

Suppose that it had been driven into the island, and that then there had supervened such a burst of stormy weather as prevailed throughout the siege, with a continuous downpour of rain and a wind which drove the ships to some safer harbour. There was no shelter whatever on the island; the troops would have perished of wet and cold; and, as the only place of embarkation was within five hundred yards of Santa Catalina, it is difficult to believe that the French would not have contrived somehow to move a howitzer or two to that hill, from whence they could have made things very unpleasant both for the garrison and for the shipping. Indeed an officer, strongly prejudiced in favour of holding Tarifa, pronounced the island to be untenable with the enemy in possession of the neighbouring heights.

The behaviour of Campbell must not be allowed to pass unnoticed. It was he who had originally occupied Tarifa in 1809, and he claimed it to be a dependency of Gibraltar. The defence was in fact his doing, and was only made possible by his usurpation of command over part of the troops in Cadiz. Those troops were under the orders of Cooke; and he in his turn was under the orders of Wellington, to whom Cooke of course reported all the circumstances, not omitting to point out that he had recalled Skerrett and his brigade from Tarifa, but that his directions had been frustrated by Skerrett's subordinates, acting under the influence and inspiration of Campbell. Wellington treated the matter, which contained abundant material for controversy, with his ordinary strong good sense. First and foremost he entirely upheld the propriety of Cooke's order of recall, he said:—

We have a right to expect that His Majesty's officers and troops will do their duty upon every occasion; but we have no right to expect that comparatively a small number would be able to hold the town of Tarifa, commanded as it is at short distances, and enfiladed in every direction, and unprovided with artillery and with walls scarcely cannon-proof.

But he declined absolutely to be drawn into a quarrel with Campbell. The incident was over and brilliantly over; and if Campbell chose to conceive of Tarifa as under his orders (in Wellington's contemptuous phrase) he was very welcome to do so, for the place was really of no importance at the stage which the war had reached. Of course this was not Campbell's view, and one of his officers went so far as to say that:—

If Soult had once become possessor of Tarifa, the entire coast of Andalusia would soon have come over to King Joseph, and the struggle in the south of Spain would have been over.

This is flat nonsense. Wellington with his usual acuteness pointed out that the French would never have been able to hold the place against the efforts of Ballesteros, backed by the co-operation of the British fleet and the resources of Gibraltar, unless they had kept an army at hand on purpose to protect it; and if Soult had been foolish enough to waste troops upon so comparatively unimportant an object, nothing could better have suited the Allies. It is not surprising therefore that Lord Liverpool, upon receiving Wellington's reports concerning the whole matter, sharply censured Campbell for meddling with troops which were not under his control, and risking their safety for no commensurate end. The truth is that Campbell was always burning to conduct little campaigns of his own, with greater zeal than intelligence; and in this instance he did not hesitate to sacrifice to his petty operations the discipline of the army and the unity of command in the Peninsula. Liverpool's censure, therefore, was not only just but imperatively needed. (See note following).

★★★★★★

Note:—The authorities for the siege of Tarifa are Belmas, iv.; Jones's *Sieges of the Peninsula*, ii.; Arteche, xi.; Raitt's *Life of Lord Gough*, i.; Napier (particularly appendix vi. to vol. iv.); Leval's journal of the siege (*Archives du Ministère de la Guerre*).

I have dwelt on the story at some length because Napier, from blind partiality towards Campbell and Soult, has given the affair of Tarifa a wholly factitious importance. He doubles the losses

of the French, solely upon Campbell's conjectures; entirely ig-
nores the influence of the weather, which was the most important factor of all, upon the French operations; accepts without
question, and actually prints the most absurd and self-contradictory nonsense from Campbell's officers; affects to believe
that Wellington did not know what he was saying when he upheld Cooke's authority and slighted the importance of Campbell; and of course sneers at the censure passed upon Campbell
by the Tory Minister, Liverpool. I do not know the reason for
Napier's prejudice in Campbell's favour, but it undoubtedly ex-
isted, as is shown by his inaccuracies in the account of Lord
Blayney's affair as well as in the present case.

★★★★★★

While these events were passing Suchet had at last received his reinforcements and pushed forward to the siege of Valencia. On the 4th
of November Reille's French and Severoli's Italian divisions, jointly
some fourteen thousand men, received Napoleon's orders to move
southward from Aragon and Navarre, and on the 24th of December
they were within two days' march of Suchet's camp. On the 26th,
therefore, the marshal crossed the Guadalaviar in the face of Blake's
army, and manoeuvred to pen the entire force of the enemy under
the walls of Valencia. He was successful; capturing twenty-four guns
and some hundreds of prisoners, with trifling loss to himself, and accomplishing the investment of the city before nightfall. On the night
of the 1st of January 1812 the French troops broke ground, and by
the 4th their batteries were armed. Blake then hastily abandoned his
entrenched camp without the walls, and gathered his force within the
old walls of the city
    All was confusion and dismay among the defenders. Owing to a
bitter quarrel between the general and the civil population provisions
were scarce; and the soldiers, with the exception of those under the
command of Zayas, were deserting almost in companies. Suchet added
to the prevailing disorder by pouring a rain of heavy shells upon the
city; and on the 9th Blake was fain to capitulate. Something over sixteen thousand men laid down their arms, (Suchet gives the number
at 18,219, but I prefer the statement of a return which I found at the
Archives de la Guerre. Even this is possibly exaggerated); and when
Suchet entered the city in triumph on the 14th he was received with
loud cheers by a portion, and that not the least distinguished or the

most obscure, of the population.

Thus fell Valencia, which at the outset of the war had so bravely defied Moncey, in shame, scandal, and disgrace; and with it fell Blake, having proved by this last of a long series of defeats that he was useless for any purpose whatever. Wellington latterly had foreseen the disaster, and had conjectured with grim accuracy that, though a Spanish general and his army might starve in Valencia, the French would find there abundance both of money and provisions. (*Wellington Desp.* To Liverpool, 4th, 18th Dec. 1811). The reduction of Peniscola after a short siege completed the subjugation of the province; and the annihilation of a French detachment of eight hundred men near Reuss by General Lacy on the 19th of January was counterbalanced by his total defeat at Altafulla on the 24th at the hands of General Maurice Matthieu. All seemed therefore to be well with the French on the east coast of Spain. It must now be told how none the less the campaign of Valencia was their undoing.

CHAPTER 5

The Attack on Ciudad Rodrigo

Wellington at the end of October was reposing in his cantonments on the Agueda, distraught by great anxieties, though animated by yet greater hopes. In the first place, his army was still terribly sickly. Large reinforcements had reached him in July, both of cavalry and of infantry, made up in great measure of young soldiers and of battalions which had passed through the campaign of Walcheren; and these had fallen down by scores and hundreds under the stress of the Peninsular summer. The distemper, which was due in great measure to the intemperance of the men in the consumption both of fruit and liquor, was not generally fatal, but none the less it filled the hospitals and reduced the ranks of many regiments to one-half their strength. At one moment there were no fewer than seventeen thousand men on the sick-list, and in the Fourth Division there were as many men prostrate as fit for duty. Moreover, the Horse Guards had insisted as a general principle upon the return of battalions which had become attenuated in the field, and the substitution for them of their sister battalions from home; whereby the Peninsular Army gained in numbers, but lost old and seasoned soldiers.

★★★★★★

The Duke of York to Wellington, 23rd July 1811. "Let the rule be this: when the incorporation of the effectives of the two battalions of any regiment shall not exceed 1200 rank and file, merge the two together, and send the officers and non-commissioned officers of the second battalions home." *Wellington MSS.*

★★★★★★

In obedience to this rule Wellington had taken leave with a heavy heart of the Twenty-Ninth and of two other battalions which, though the three of them counted little more than a thousand men jointly, could not easily be replaced as regards the quality of the rank and file. Happily, as the winter drew near, the health of the force improved, though in November there were still fourteen thousand men in hospital; and when the New Year came the strength of the army amounted to thirty-eight thousand British and Germans of all ranks present with the colours, besides twenty-two thousand Portuguese. (*Wellington Desp.* To Liverpool, 1811).

Another difficulty—one that was constantly recurring—was the dearth of capable generals. The divisional organisation was now so far developed that each division had become, to use Wellington's own words, a complete army, composed of British and foreign troops, artillery and sundry departments, requiring "some discretion and sense," to say nothing of experience, for its proper management. But as fast as the divisional commanders had mastered their business, they had broken down in health. There was not one who had stayed with the army continuously since 1809, as had Wellington himself; and the brigadiers had been changed as often as their superiors for much the same reasons. Graham, whose frame seems alone to have been comparable for toughness to that of his chief, was beginning to feel the weight of his sixty-three years.

Hill had been driven home for a time by wounds, though after his recovery he did not return again to England until the close of the war. And now Generals Dunlop and Sontag, "the former a real loss," had broken down hopelessly; Alexander Campbell was about to seek more lucrative employment elsewhere; Houston, who had gone home on leave, was not expected to come back; and Cole had departed for the time to his place in the House of Commons. There were at least two other officers, respectable in command of a battalion but unfit for any higher charge, of whom Wellington was anxious to be rid, one of them evidently an undesirable individual.

The outlook therefore was not very cheerful, more particularly since Bentinck desired to keep two very good officers, Generals William Clinton and Macfarlane, for his own petty requirements. Colonel Torrens, however, at the Horse Guards, worked indefatigably to satisfy Wellington's demands, with the result that by December there were almost more generals than could be disposed of. The most notable of the newcomers were Henry Clinton; Le Marchant, a brilliant officer whose career was too early cut short; John Byng and Richard Hulse, both of the brigade of Guards; and James Kempt, whom we last saw on the field of Maida. Among the truants who returned was Tilson, who had now taken the name of Chowne; and Leith, who resumed his former place at the head of the Fifth Division. (*Wellington Desp.* To Torrens, 1811).

In the matter of administration the chief difficulty now as always lay in the dearth of specie, with which was intimately bound up the question of transport and supply. Wellington had written in August that he had never been in such want of money. At that time the pay of the men was two months, and the allowance of the officers six months, in arrear; and there was no prospect of any amelioration, but rather of increased embarrassment, owing to two principal causes. First, the flow of specie into the Peninsula was checked at its fountain-head by the quarrel between Spain and her colonies; secondly, owing to the prohibition by President Madison of the trade of the United States with England, American ships required payment in specie for the corn that they brought to Lisbon, instead of taking home its value in English manufactured goods. It was even to be feared that the American Non-Intercourse Act (as it was called) might produce still more serious consequences; for the harvest of 1811 had failed in England, and, as she could no longer count upon her old sources of supply in the Baltic, it was not easy to divine how she could furnish herself, to say nothing of her army in the Peninsula, with corn, even could she have afforded to pay for it with precious metal.

Moreover, supposing that this difficulty were overcome—as in matter of fact it was—and that the army were supplied with a sufficiency of flour, there remained still the problem how to carry it to the front without specie. The transport-service depended wholly upon hired Spanish muleteers; and the pay of these people in July was already six months in arrear. It was out of the question to purchase many mules, for their price had risen to £45 apiece, (150 dollars. *Wellington Desp.* To Beresford, 2nd Aug. 1811. The dollar at that time cannot be reckoned as costing the British less than six shillings in specie); and even had it been otherwise, it was useless to take them without the muleteers, whose attachment to their animals formed the sole warrant for their faithful service. There was, further, one failing in these muleteers which neither money nor usage could overcome. They would not knowingly work for the Portuguese upon any terms.

So long as Portuguese battalions were mixed up with the British, the haughty Spaniards could not tell whether or not they were serving their despised neighbours; but, if it were a question of victualling an independent Portuguese detachment, they would carry their beasts to the French rather than use them for such a purpose. Moreover, since the government at Lisbon was incurably slothful and negligent in providing for the transport and supply of its troops, there was always the danger lest the muleteers, wearied out by want of pay, should make their prejudice against the Portuguese a pretext for deserting the British altogether.

All these complications must from the first have been a grinding anxiety to the commander-in-chief; but now that he was meditating offensive operations and even a siege in form, the question of money became doubly perplexing. To make matters worse, his chief commissary, the very efficient and industrious Kennedy, seized this particular moment to resign his office, being incited thereto by the importunity of his wife, whose sister had already been the means of withdrawing from Wellington a valuable member of his staff, and no doubt had worked upon the feelings of Mrs. Kennedy. Happily Kennedy's successor, Mr. Bissett, who had been selected by the Commissary-in-Chief in England, was an officer of ability, and had enjoyed the further advantage of studying the commissariats of other countries in the field. It is to him that we owe an exact account of the organisation of the transport and supply in 1812, the year which may be taken as that in which it was finally perfected.

According to his book, the unit of infantry for the purposes of the commissariat was the division, consisting of two brigades of foot and one battery of artillery; the unit of the cavalry was the regiment; and the unit of horse-artillery the troop; while the reserve of artillery, exclusive of the batteries attached to divisions, formed another unit, and head-quarters of the army yet another. The item of forage of course accounted for the apparent anomaly that a regiment of cavalry, four hundred strong, was placed on the same footing with a division of infantry numbering six thousand. Even in the infantry the feeding of the field-officers' horses and of the baggage-mules, which were attached to each regiment, was a very heavy task, requiring, roughly speaking, one mule to every six men. But in the cavalry the allowance was one mule to every two men and horses; so that a regiment of four hundred dragoons, having nearly five hundred horses and baggage-mules, required for the filling of all mouths and for the provision of fuel—which was always scarce in the Peninsula—nearly three hundred commissariat mules to itself. Altogether for all units the British Army, at a strength of barely fifty-three thousand of all ranks,

needed between nine and ten thousand commissariat mules ove.
above those employed in regimental transport. (Bissett, *The Dutie.*
the Commissariat).

Looking to the fact that he contemplated a vigorous offensive in
1812, Wellington was obliged to supplement his train of mules by vehicles of some description. The native Portuguese car, with its primi-
tive system of wheels revolving together with their axles, he banned
altogether, as we know; so slow, cumbrous, and unmanageable were
they in the narrow Portuguese roads. He therefore set Bissett to design a suitable cart, and ordered others to be made after this pattern
at Oporto and Almeida during the winter of 1811, the wheels having
iron axle-trees and brass boxes, most of which had been captured from
the French. These carts were to be drawn by purchased bullocks under
the charge of native drivers hired for the purpose; and the full number
of them, to be ultimately constructed in England and elsewhere, was
fixed at eight hundred. They were to be organised into two grand
divisions of four hundred, every grand division being distributed into
eight divisions of fifty each, and every one of these lesser divisions into
two brigades, each of twenty-five carts and fifty four bullocks, two
bullocks being allowed to each cart and four to spare.

Each division was placed under the command of a clerk or other
subordinate officer in the commissariat. Trivial though such a matter
may seem to the unthinking, the appearance of these carts, which
put the finishing touch to the organisation of the transport, marks an
important stage in the progress of the war. The waggons of the wag-
gontrain, which had springs, were employed wholly for the service
of the sick and wounded, or, to use the modern term, as ambulances.
(*Wellington Desp.* To Commissary-in-Chief Gordon, 12th, 25th June,
21st Aug.; to C. Stuart, 4th July; to Liverpool, 1st Aug.; to Beresford,
2nd Aug.; to Torrens, 4th Aug.; to the Cavalry Brigadiers, 31st Aug.; to
Bissett, 20th Nov., 3 documents, 1811).

So much for Wellington's difficulties and preparations; let us now
look at his plans. All Europe was greatly excited by the prospect of
Napoleon's invasion of Russia; and there was expectation in various
quarters that for so great an enterprise he would withdraw his troops
from Spain. This idea seems to have been cherished alike by the English Court and by the Horse Guards, both of which, in Wellington's
belief, were anxious to move the army from the Peninsula to some
other scene of operations; and he appears to have feared that the fall
of Valencia might be made a pretext for the change. His own view of

was singularly sagacious. He admitted the possibility of a
...eeze in Europe" as he called it, but he deprecated prema-
...n, and foresaw no good from any combined rising against
...nless the sovereigns were prepared to fight on till they con-
...or perished.

...they pursued their old practice of sacrificing a part of their territory to save the rest, they could never hope to overthrow Napoleon's
system (so Wellington happily defined it) of making war as a financial
resource. Already the pay of the French troops in Spain was many
months in arrear; and the emperor had laid down the principle that no
men, except those actually with the colours, should receive the debts
due to them, so that, by saving the money owing to the dead, he was
able to put a million men into the field for the wages of half a million.
Meanwhile, whatever might happen, the British army must not be
withdrawn from the Peninsula. Napoleon (so Wellington judged with
remarkable correctness) would not greatly reduce his army in that
quarter, though he would not reinforce it; and forty thousand British
troops could occupy the attention of infinitely more French troops
there than in any other country. Moreover, even if Napoleon were to
evacuate Spain, an advance of the Allies upon the Pyrenean frontier of
France would compel the employment of two hundred thousand men
for its defence. (*Wellington Desp.* To Liverpool, 29th Oct., 4th Dec.; to
Sydenham, 7th Dec. 1811).

As to the details of the coming campaign, all must depend upon
the movements of the enemy. In view of the danger which would
threaten Carthagena if Valencia should be captured, Wellington sent a
detachment of troops from Cadiz to hold the citadel of that fortress,
(2/67th and a battalion of foreign detachments, together 1000 strong.
Wellington Desp. To Cooke and Henry Wellesley, 12th Dec. 1811); and
since Bentinck was intent upon operations in Italy rather than on
the east coast of Spain, this was the most that could be done upon
that side. For the rest he had completed his preparations for the siege
of Ciudad Rodrigo, in the hope that an opportunity might present
itself for an attack upon that fortress; but whether the place should
fall or not, he thought it imperative to move southward at the end
of February or the beginning of March, and to take advantage of the
healthy season, with its abundance of forage after the winter rains, to
attempt the capture of Badajoz. (*Wellington Desp.* To Liverpool, 18th
Dec. 1811).

The third week of December had come before Wellington received intelligence which set him instantly upon the alert. Foy's division of Marmont's army had passed the Tagus into La Mancha, but had since returned; and Brenier's division had suddenly broken up from Plasencia and crossed the Tietar towards Naval Moral. The explanation of the first of these two movements was that Marmont, under directions from Joseph, had ordered Foy's division to move from Toledo to Cuenca in order to replace a part of the Army of the Centre, which had been detached to Valencia; but, growing nervous over the attitude of the British on the Agueda, had recalled it. (Marmont (*Mémoires*, iv.) says that Foy marched on 22nd Nov.; Girod de l'Ain, *Vie du Général Foy*, says that Foy did not receive the order to march until the beginning of December; and this seems far more likely to be correct).

By the 10th of December Marmont was reassured, and on the following day he received definite orders from the emperor to send twelve thousand men towards Valencia, besides three or four thousand more to guard the lines of communication. Thereupon the marshal once more directed Foy to occupy La Mancha; ordered Montbrun's cavalry and Sarrut's division to march upon Cuenca; and, having propounded an ambitious plan to Joseph, declared his intention of following Montbrun in person with two more divisions. To that end he altered the disposition of his army in some respects, shifting Brenier's men from Plasencia into the valley of the Tagus. Foy in his journal reviewed the proceedings with dismay. In his view the entire operation was ill conceived. Marmont ought to have marched at once with seventeen thousand men, arrived before Valencia like lightning, crushed the Spanish Army of Aragon, and flown back to the lower Tagus, he wrote, with uncommon insight:—

> Perhaps, the English observing our evacuation of Plasencia will make active demonstrations upon our front, and then the marshal will never reach Valencia at all. (*Wellington Desp.* To Liverpool, 2 letters, and to Graham, 25th Dec. 1811. Girod de l'Ain; *Mémoires du duc de Raguse*, iv.; *Mémoires du Roi Joseph*, viii.)

Wellington was puzzled by all these marches and counter-marches. If Suchet had been beaten by the Spaniards, there would have been a reason why Marmont should close in towards him; but Wellington could not believe in the possibility of such a thing. In the following days the situation gradually cleared itself up. Intelligence came in that the cavalry of the Guard had re-entered France, that the infantry of the Guard was starting northward from Valladolid, that there was a general movement of the French troops about Bejar and Avila to east-ward, and, most important of all, that Clausel's division had marched from the upper Tormes to Avila. Wellington concluded that a great effort was making to deliver Suchet from the guerillas who had tormented him so much in the north, and to ensure the capture of Valencia; and, though his information was necessarily imperfect, he was not altogether wrong. The Imperial Guard and five regiments of Poles were really withdrawing from Spain in order to proceed to Russia; but the news of the French movement from Avila was premature.

Moreover, Marmont had received on the 29th the emperor's final orders, which involved a considerable dislocation of his force. The territory now assigned to the Army of Portugal for subsistence and to the Duke of Ragusa for government consisted of the provinces of Avila, Salamanca, Plasencia, Ciudad Rodrigo, Leon, Palencia and Asturias; and his army was to be increased by the addition of Souham's division in the region of Salamanca, and of Bonnet's in Asturias. Lastly, the marshal was to betake himself in person at once to Valladolid, as his head-quarters military and administrative. He accordingly made over to Montbrun the command of the troops detached to Valencia, and prepared to obey; though until the 5th of January 1812 he remained still at Talavera. (*Mémoires du duc de Raguse*, iv. *Wellington Desp* To Liverpool, 1st Jan. 1812).

Meanwhile on the 1st of January Wellington had issued his orders for the attack upon Ciudad Rodrigo. He had as yet no further intelligence of his enemy's movements than that above stated; but he knew at least that Marmont with the bulk of the Army of Portugal was still in the valley of the Tagus; and he reckoned that, even if he should fail to capture the fortress, he would at any rate compel a part of the corps both of Marmont and of Dorsenne to return with precipitation towards the Agueda. The operations, however, promised, whatever the event, to be costly, for the entire country was covered with snow, which not only made transport the more difficult, but threatened heavy losses among the men from exposure. The opening days of the month were occupied in the construction of a trestle bridge over the Agueda at Marialva, and in anxious arrangements for bringing forward the materials for the siege. Wellington had hoped to break ground on the 6th, but, as he said, there was no counting on Spanish and Portuguese carters and muleteers, and there were many vexatious delays.

However, on the 4th matters were sufficiently advanced for the troops to be set in motion; and on that day the four divisions selected for the work of the siege left their cantonments, the First Division marching to Gallegos and Espeja; the Third occupying Martiago and Zamarra; while the Fourth and Light crossed the Agueda, the former to San Felices, and the latter to Pastores, La Encina, and El Bodon. On the 8th the first convoy of stores left the depot at Gallegos and passed the trestle-bridge towards Ciudad Rodrigo; and at noon of the same day the Light Division forded the Agueda once more at La Caridad, a few miles down the water from their cantonments, and invested the fortress. Simultaneously the Fifth and Sixth Divisions crossed the Coa to the vicinity of Almeida; while the Seventh, leaving Penamacor on the 11th, occupied Fuenteguinaldo on the 13th. To complete his dispositions Wellington on the 9th sent orders to Hill to fall back from Estremadura to his former station between Portalegre and Castello Branco, in order to check any diversion that might be attempted by the French in the valley of the Alagon towards Lower Beira. (*Wellington Desp.* Instructions and Memoranda of 1st Jan. To Liverpool, 7th Jan.; to Hill, 9th Jan. 1812. Simmons; Tomkinson; Green's *Vicissitudes of a Soldier's Life*).

Ciudad Rodrigo stands on the right or northern bank of the Agueda, crowning the summit of a low oval hill which rises to a height of perhaps one hundred and fifty feet above the water. The city, which is a network of narrow streets, is enclosed within a mediaeval wall thirty-two feet high, and covers, roughly speaking, a quadrilateral, measuring about three furlongs east and west by two furlongs north and south. This wall is in turn enclosed by fortifications which were then modern, consisting of a *fausse-braie*, or low rampart, with a revetted ditch, but without a covered way. The whole is constructed so far down the slope of the hill as to afford scanty cover to the interior wall, and the glacis is so steep as to give but slight protection to the rampart. On the southern side towards the river the declivity is almost precipitous; but towards the north the ground descends gradually to a slender rivulet, beyond which rises a long narrow ridge, hardly more than two hundred yards from the outer defences.

Northward this ridge, which is called the Little Teson, declines again to a second rivulet, from whence the ground swells into a second and more commanding height called the Greater Teson. This was the weakest side of the place, the Greater Teson rising at six hundred yards distance thirteen feet above the level of the ramparts; and accordingly the French had erected upon it a small redoubt. This outwork presented a salient angle towards the country, and mounted two cannon and a howitzer. Its rear, which was on the slope of the hill, was closed by a low loopholed wall, with a gate in it, and by *chevaux de frise* on the outside; and the three remaining sides had a good parapet, a ditch eight feet wide and twenty feet deep, with much water in its lower parts, and very strong palisading at the foot of the counterscarp.

The redoubt was further supported by a battery of two pieces on the flat roof of the convent of San Francisco four hundred yards to east and south of it, and by the fortified convent of Santa Cruz about seven hundred yards to south and west. Outside the city were two principal suburbs; one of them on the other side of the river and connected with the fortifications by a bridge, which is completely commanded by the guns of the southern defences; the other, that of San Francisco, which lies three hundred yards beyond the north-eastern angle of the outer works. Both had been so far strengthened as to be safe against any attack with small numbers. The place was crammed with artillery and munitions of war, for Marmont had thrown into it the siege-train of the Army of Portugal; but, owing to the extreme difficulty of victualling it in the presence of Wellington's army, it was not overstocked with provisions. The garrison counted just over eighteen hundred combatants of all ranks, (infantry, 34th Light, 13 3rd Line, 1552; artillery, 2 cos., 168; engineers, 15; Staff, etc., 40 sick, 163—Total, 1928; deduct dead and deserted, 120. Grand Total, 1818); and the governor, Barrié, was, if Marmont be believed, a detestable officer, endowed neither with vigilance nor with resolution.

The ground being rocky on every side except the northern, it was obvious that the Great Teson, which possessed the further advantage of commanding the northern front, must be the point of attack. Therefore, after great parade of examining the fortress from every aspect, Wellington formed a brigade on the northern slope of the hill under cover of darkness; and at eight o'clock ten companies of the Light Division, (4 cos. 52nd; 2 cos. 43rd; 2 cos. 95th; 1 co. each from the 1st and 3rd Caçadores, this is Colborne's list, but Craufurd in his report mentions 1 officer and 12 men of the 3rd Caçadores), under Colonel Colborne advanced to the assault of the redoubt. Four companies, (apparently 2 cos. of the 52nd and 2 of the 43rd), led the way to occupy the crest of the glacis and open fire; and these were followed by the escalading party with the ladders.

The movement was undetected until at a distance of fifty yards Colborne gave the word "double quick," when the trampling and jingling of the assailants betrayed their approach; but the defenders had time only to discharge one cannon-shot before the leading companies opened fire and drove them from their guns.

The ladder-bearers then came up and placed the ladders in position; the escalading party, (1 co. 43rd; 1 co. 52nd), quickly descended into the ditch, where they suffered some loss from shells and hand grenades; but some swarming up the parapet, while others entered through the gate in the gorge, which had been accidentally burst open by a French shell, they were in a few minutes masters of the redoubt. Of the defenders four only escaped into the town, three were killed, and forty-eight captured. (See Barrié's letter in Belmas, iv. Belmas himself states the number of the garrison at 50, in contradiction to his own printed authority). The loss of the British did not exceed six killed and three officers and seventeen men wounded, so admirable were Colborne's arrangements. Thus a troublesome little obstruction, upon which the enemy had reckoned for a respite of at least five days, was swept away in twenty minutes. (The best account of this little enterprise is in Moore Smith's *Life of Lord Seaton;* with which compare Moorsom's *Hist. of the 52nd.* The redoubt is described in Wrottesley's *Life of Burgoyne,* i.)

No sooner did the garrison ascertain the fall of the redoubt than they opened a terrific fire upon it; but Colborne had been careful to collect his men and lead them down to the rivulet at the foot of the glacis, to cover the working parties until the moon should rise. Meanwhile one division of workmen reopened for a distance of one hundred and fifty yards the first parallel made by the French in the siege of 1810, the left flank of the trench resting on the redoubt; while another party dug the communication over the Great Teson to a depot which had been formed on the reverse side of the hill. Thus the siege had been well begun when on the 9th the First Division came to relieve the Light; for Wellington had ordered that each of the four divisions in rotation should do the duty in the trenches for twenty-four hours, so that the men should have three days in quarters for every day of exposure to the bitter cold of the weather. (The rotation was Light Division, First, Third, Fourth).

On the 9th the first parallel was continued, and three batteries for twenty-seven guns were commenced; and the work was pushed steadily forward on the succeeding days, though, owing to the intensity of the cold and the destructive fire of the enemy, progress was not rapid. The French gunners, having found the range exactly, swept away the

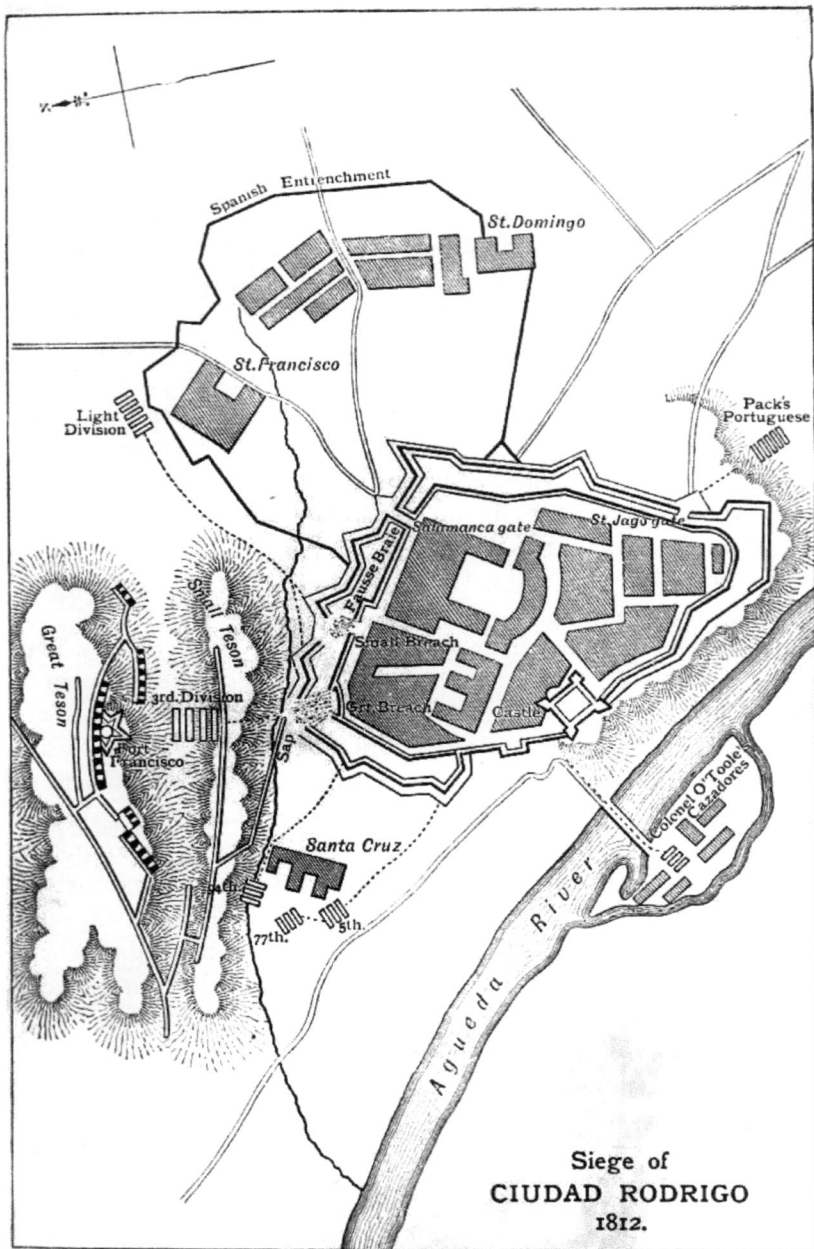

Siege of
CIUDAD RODRIGO
1812.

besiegers' parapets with salvoes of shell, causing so many casualties that the engineers were fain to abandon exterior excavations altogether, and to sink their batteries into the earth, so as to obtain the necessary soil for protection. Even more serious was the discovery that part of the first battery had been so faultily designed that five, if not more, of the guns were below the crest of the hill and out of sight of the objects to be aimed at; with the result that much time was lost in lengthening another battery and transferring the pieces to a situation where the gunners could see their mark. (Wrottesley's *Life of Burgoyne*, i. Jones's *Sieges*, i., tells only half the truth about this incident).

On the 13th matters came to a crisis. Much of the ammunition necessary for the siege was still at Villa da Ponte, some fifty miles away over the mountains; and Wellington had every reason to believe that, before it could be brought up, Marmont would have moved to the relief of the place. By this time he was vaguely aware that there was still a French Division on the Tormes and another at Avila, though he could not guess that the first was Souham's, newly arrived upon the scene, and the second Clausel's, which had been relieved by Souham's at Salamanca. (*Wellington Desp.*, to Graham, 5th Jan. 1812. *Mémoires du duc de Raguse*, iv.)

Wellington's original intention had been to erect batteries for thirty-three guns on the Great Teson, work forward under their protection to the Little Teson, raise fresh batteries there to breach the outer and inner walls, sap up to the glacis, and blow in the counterscarp according to good *poliorketic* rule. He now consulted his engineers as to the practicability of making a breach with the cannon on the Great Teson only; and, being answered favourably, he resolved that, if need were, he would storm the place with the counterscarp untouched.

Marmont on his side had shown no great disposition to haste. On the 1st of January Thiébault had written to him from Salamanca that Wellington was certainly intending to take the offensive, probably to attack Ciudad Rodrigo; and on the 3rd he repeated the warning, giving additional details which lent much force to his opinion. Dorsenne, in forwarding these letters on the 5th, declared that, having received the like alarming reports constantly during the last six months, he attached little importance to them; but he added that he felt no confidence in Barrié, and that he would be glad to see the marshal return. On that same day, the 5th, Marmont quitted Talavera for Valladolid, having set his division of heavy cavalry, his artillery, and the 3rd and 5th Divisions of infantry also on march for the Douro.

The rest of his army was scattered in all directions; the 6th Division in the valley of the Tagus; the 2nd at Avila; the 7th at Salamanca; the 8th in Asturias; and the 1st and 4th, together with his light horse, on the road to Valencia. Marmont broke his journey at Avila, and hence did not reach Valladolid until the 11th. Barrié had sent out three messages on the nights of the 9th and 10th to convey news of his peril to Salamanca; but these had been intercepted by the bands of Carlos d'España and Julian Sanchez; and hence, extraordinary as it may seem, Dorsenne was still ignorant that anything unusual was going forward at Ciudad Rodrigo when Marmont joined him at Valladolid. Wellington ascertained later that information concerning the siege reached Salamanca on the 13th; but it seems certain that neither Marmont nor Dorsenne knew anything of the matter until the 15th. (*Mémoires du duc de Raguse*, iv. *Wellington Desp.*, to Liverpool, 15th Jan. 1812. Dorsenne in a letter of 13th Jan. to Berthier talks only of revictualling of Ciudad Rodrigo, and says not a word of relief before a second letter to the same of 17th Jan., *Arch, de la Guerre*).

It is therefore manifest that Marmont's return to the Douro, which so troubled the peace of the British Commander as to make him alter his plans, was entirely unconnected with Wellington's operations, and due merely to orders written by Napoleon nearly five weeks earlier. Such is the irony of war.

Wellington now resolved to begin at once the second parallel and, as a first means to that end, to expel the French garrison from the convent of Santa Cruz. The building was accordingly escaladed and taken by three hundred men of the Sixtieth and of the King's German Legion on the night of the 13th after a sharp fight, which cost the assailants thirty-seven killed and wounded. Twenty-seven guns were placed in the battery in the course of the night; and the sap was then carried forward to the Little Teson until the forenoon of the 14th, when at eleven o'clock the French made a sortie with five hundred men, reoccupied the convent of Santa Cruz, destroyed the new trenches, and were only checked, as they were actually entering the batteries, by the advance of the relieving division under General Graham. At half-past four in the afternoon the guns opened fire, two of them upon the convent of San Francisco, and the remainder upon the most salient angle of the northern face of the fortress, where the masonry, having been already breached by the French in 1810 and since repaired, was considered likely to be still unstable.

The enemy responded vigorously, remarking with surprise that the besiegers turned all their guns upon the selected point, without attempting to silence the cannon on the ramparts. Since the garrison of the convent still clung to their position, a party of the Fortieth was ordered at dusk to drive them from it. This was gallantly done; and the Fortieth then established themselves in the suburb. In the course of the night or of the following day Wellington received more accurate intelligence of the actual situation of Marmont's army, which relieved him of much anxiety, but, as it appears, in no way altered his new plans for the conduct of the leaguer.

At dawn of the 15th the besiegers renewed their fire and continued it through that day, damaging both the outer and the inner walls so severely that it was thought time to mark out a new battery in a more advanced situation, so as to begin a second breach by a tower a little to eastward of the first. The place was cunningly chosen; for the inner wall just at that spot was wholly uncovered by the external wall; and the tower was the one point from which the garrison could pour a flanking fire of artillery upon the main breach. In the course of the night five additional guns were brought into the existing batteries; but the firing was stopped at half-past nine on the morning of the 16th by a dense fog which continued for over twenty-four hours. Advantage, however, was taken of the lull to extend the second parallel, and to place marksmen within it and in rifle-pits so as to keep up a constant fire on the breach and on the embrasures.

Singularly enough Wellington chose this evening to send in a summons of surrender, which was of course answered with defiance. At noon of the 17th the fog lifted, whereupon both sides again began a furious duel, which wrought much havoc among the besiegers and their defences; but the riflemen, in spite of heavy losses, subdued the storm of grape with which the enemy had endeavoured to overwhelm them. In the night the new battery, slightly in advance of the rest upon the Great Teson, was completed, and fire was opened at daylight of the 18th from thirty-two guns, with such effect that the main breach was considered practicable by the evening; while at about the same time the tower came down "like an avalanche," opening a second gap of little less extent than the other.

Nevertheless the accuracy of the enemy's artillery was such that the advanced sap could not be pushed forward, though the construction of a new battery on the second parallel was carried on without intermission. Late in the evening this work was completed, and a field-piece and a howitzer, being placed in position, poured a rain of projectiles upon the main breach throughout the night, so as to check any efforts of the enemy to raise an interior retrenchment. At daybreak the British resumed the cannonade with thirty heavy guns upon both breaches with great effect; and in the afternoon Wellington, after careful reconnaissance, ordered the artillery to be turned upon the fortifications at large, and sat down in one of the advanced approaches to write his orders for the assault.

The Fourth Division was on duty in the trenches on this day, but the Third and the Light were brought in towards nightfall to form the storming parties. (There is much conflict of statement as to this small matter; but it is to be remarked that it was the turn of the 4th Division to be in the trenches; and, though Burgoyne and others say that the 3rd Division was on duty, Grattan of the 3rd Division expressly says that the 4th was actually in the trenches when the 3rd formed for the assault).

The principal attack, however, was not to open until a series of preliminary and auxiliary movements had been executed. First of all the 2nd Caçadores with the light company of the Eighty-Third under Colonel O'Toole were to cross the Agueda, escalade an outwork immediately before it, and capture two guns which commanded the entrance to the ditch at the point where the outer fortifications joined the inner near the south-west angle of the place. This was to prepare the way for Campbell's brigade, (Under command of Colonel Campbell of the Scots Brigade during the absence of General Colville), to the four battalions of which were assigned the following tasks.

The Fifth Foot, provided with axes and short scaling-ladders, was to beat down the gate at the entrance to the ditch above referred to, scale the outer wall and follow it leftward to the main breach, so as to clear away all the enemy's posts thereon.

At the same time the Scots Brigade was to enter the outer ditch by means of ladders, and turn likewise to the left towards the main breach, so as to fulfil the same function in the ditch as was allotted to the Fifth on the wall of the *fausse braie*. Both regiments were to assemble beforehand at the convent of Santa Cruz, where the Seventy-Seventh also was to remain in reserve; while the Eighty-Third was posted in the second parallel to cover the advance of the storming party by a continual fire upon the walls. It was expressly ordered that the Fifth and O'Toole's detachment should set out at ten minutes to seven o'clock, and that Campbell's brigade should not attempt to ascend the breach until that of Mackinnon had passed through it.

At the same hour a party of one hundred and eighty sappers was to move out, unarmed, but carrying bags of hay and heather, which they were to throw into the ditch so as to enable the stormers to jump down with safety into it. Immediately after them were to follow the forlorn hope under Lieutenant Mackie of the Eighty-Eighth, five hundred volunteers of Mackinnon's brigade under Major Manners of the Seventy-Fourth, with the remainder of the brigade in support. On the left of Mackinnon the Light Division was formed behind the convent of San Francisco. Three companies of the Rifles were told off to enter the ditch between the two breaches, and, turning to their right, to scour it as far as the main breach. The remainder of Vandeleur's brigade, preceded by the 3rd Caçadores carrying bags of hay, was to attack the lesser breach, headed by a forlorn hope under Lieutenant Gurwood of the Fifty-Second, with three hundred volunteers, under Major George Napier of the same regiment, in support.

Vandeleur was instructed, upon mounting the gap in the outer wall, to send five companies along the top of that wall so as to support Mackinnon's assault; and, as soon as communication with the Third Division had been established along both walls, an endeavour was to be made to break open the Salamanca gate close to the north-eastern angle. Lastly Pack's brigade of Portuguese was to deliver a false attack upon the San Pelayo gate in the centre of the east front. The hour fixed for the advance of the main storming columns was seven o'clock; and the time was to be regulated, not by signal, but by the preliminary onset of the Fifth Foot; for the essence of the plan was that Mackinnon's brigade was to be covered upon both flanks as it swarmed up to the main breach.

A slight accident sufficed to upset Wellington's elaborate arrangements completely, though everything began with good promise of success. The night was fine though bitterly cold, with a bright moon which was occasionally obscured by heavy clouds. The Fifth, and not the Fifth only, but by some mistake the Seventy-Seventh also, stole out at the appointed hour from the convent of Santa Cruz, and moving swiftly and silently to the entrance of the ditch reached it absolutely unobserved. Above them the French manning the ramparts kept up an aimless and unanswered fire, quite unconscious of the danger that was threatening, the noise happily serving to drown the stroke of the British axes as the men plied them against the gate and palisade which barred the access to the ditch. A gap was soon cut in the timber; and all were pressing forward to pass through it when a young ensign, fresh from the wilds of Kerry, raised a yell of triumph which was promptly repeated by the soldiers.

In an instant there descended on them a rain of hand-grenades and light shells, while bullets flew thickly upon the column from all quarters; though happily O'Toole had done his task well and already silenced the two guns in the adjoining outwork. Three or four breathless minutes elapsed while the ladders were fixed, when the men of the Fifth crowded so closely after their beloved commander, Major Ridge, that one ladder broke and a mass of climbers fell down upon the bayonets below. The men struggled up again, however, and swept away a hostile picquet from the summit of the outer wall; and the column descending into the inner ditch rushed along it until checked by the heap of rubbish which marked the site of the main breach.

Here to their astonishment they found no sign of the storming party; but almost immediately the Scots Brigade appeared, having also reached the outer ditch unobserved and scaled the gap in the outer wall. Campbell, perceiving at once that hesitation and delay would be fatal, directed the whole of his men to form rapidly and threw them forthwith upon the main breach. They surged eagerly forward, but on reaching the summit were staggered for a moment by the firing of a train which kindled a number of shells that had been strewn upon the ruins, and by a sharp fire of musketry from a breastwork thrown up by the enemy in rear of the breach. Recovering themselves, they parted right and left to turn this unforeseen obstacle, and found their progress obstructed on all sides. In front of them was a sheer drop of sixteen feet into the town, and then a space filled with carriages, *chevaux de frise* and similar encumbrances, with the breastwork aforesaid rising above it; while to right and left the inner wall had been retrenched by two ditches, ten feet broad and ten feet deep, cut across it, and by two transverse ramparts thrown up between the ditches.

Blinded by the alternation of flashing lights and of darkness rendered denser by smoke, the column floundered on. Campbell and a small body of thirty or forty men dashed at the retrenchment on the right, and, finding the planks laid by the French for crossing the ditches still more or less in position, passed over, swept the defenders away, and ensconced themselves in a commanding post close by. From this point of vantage Campbell repelled a hostile party which was on its way to the rampart, and sent out patrols as far as the Agueda gate and to other points in the town, but was unable, in spite of all endeavours, to call any more men to him.

The rest of the stormers had, in fact, been irresistibly attracted toward the fire of the enemy in their front and to their left, where two guns, sweeping the head of the breach with a cross-fire of grape, caused frightful havoc. Mackinnon's brigade had by this time come up, and their rush bore the defenders back, when the sudden explosion, by design or accident, of a French magazine at the junction of the breastwork and the rampart, sent Mackinnon himself together with many officers and men flying into the air, and brought the assault momentarily to a standstill. The French hastened to recover their lost ground, but their opponents quickly rallied.

Many lay down and poured upon the breastwork in rear of the breach a very effective fusillade; while Major Thompson of the Seventy-Fourth, followed by three men of the Eighty-Eighth, dashed into the entrenchment on the left to seize the nearest and most deadly of the two guns that were playing upon the assailants. The French gunners, five in number, stood most nobly, loading and firing with the greatest coolness to the last, but were overpowered and slain every one of them at their pieces after a desperate resistance. Thus relieved from the scourge of grapeshot the Third Division carried the rampart and retrenchments, and passed on to confused fighting in the streets.

Meanwhile the Light Division had also made its way to the lesser breach somewhat late, for Major Napier was still receiving orders from Wellington at the convent of San Francisco when the attack of the Third Division began. Whether purposely or by chance few of the *Caçadores* carried bags, as had been ordered, (Costello and Kincaid say that the Portuguese would not come on. George Napier says that there was some mistake, and does not blame the *Caçadores*); but the storming party, having traversed the intervening ground at great speed, leaped without waiting for them straight into the ditch. In spite of the directions given by Wellington, the leaders mistook a ravelin for the bastion which had been battered, and only after some small delay discovered the true situation of the breach. During this brief interval the losses of the column were heavy.

George Napier was struck down by a grapeshot, and Craufurd by a bullet through the lungs; but the men dashed on, some of them to the right, where not a few were caught by the explosion which overthrew Mackinnon, but the principal portion into the breach, which, not being retrenched, was easily carried. The British then rushed on to the great square by the cathedral, which seems to have been reached almost at the same moment by a mob of soldiers from all the battalions of the Third Division; the enemy having given way in the streets near the main breach on hearing the cheers of the Light Division as they entered the town.

Thereupon all resistance appears to have ceased. Gurwood, pursuing the fugitives to the castle, received there in person the sword of Barrié. Pack's Portuguese, turning their feint into a real attack, likewise broke into the streets, and joined their comrades in the great square; and the French garrison, driven back from all quarters into the square or into corners of the ramparts, laid down their arms. The assault had been successful at every point, and Ciudad Rodrigo was won.

There followed a disgraceful scene of riot and pillage. Setting our wars in India aside, it may be said that a British force had never stormed a town of any importance since Cromwell had sacked Drogheda and Wexford in 1649. No orders or instructions had been issued for general guidance in the event of a successful attack, and no one appears to have known or to have considered what was to be expected or apprehended upon such an occasion. Officers noticed that the men's faces assumed an aspect of ferocity such as they had never seen before; but they seem neither to have known nor cared what this sudden expression of savagery might portend. Numbers of the men dispersed in search of plunder directly they entered the town; but a mixed multitude, as we have seen, drifted down to the cathedral square, where suddenly without any warning or reason they all began to fire at the windows of the houses, at the heavens, at each other, as though unable to remain quiet.

Picton's voice was heard above the din "with the power of twenty trumpets, proclaiming damnation to everybody"; while the coolest and most active of the officers, seizing the barrels of broken muskets for want of a better weapon, belaboured every man whom they saw loading or firing. Such was the disorder that, in the opinion of one who was present, the French prisoners, unarmed though they were, might by a single bold rush have recovered the town. Meanwhile the immediate effect of quelling the disturbance in the square was to scatter the stormers in small parties all over the town.

Colonel Macleod of the Forty-Third alone kept his battalion together for a time and endeavoured with its help to maintain order; but, despite of all his efforts, his men were gradually sucked into the whirlpool of indiscipline. A section of the mob discovered the French commissariat-store, over which some officer, with better intention than intelligence, had posted a single sentry. The unfortunate man—

a German—was bayoneted, and the plunderers, crowding in, made straight for the store of rum and broke in the heads of the barrels. A wild struggle ensued for possession of the liquor; and the first to reach it were tilted off their legs head-foremost into the butts and smothered. The rest soon drank themselves into a state of frenzy, and amid their scuffling and fighting they overturned a light and set fire to the building.

Many were burned where they lay, stupefied with spirits; and it was only by the utmost efforts of Barnard, who seems to have kept at any rate some men in hand, that the conflagration did not spread and consume the entire city. Parties of men invaded the chapels, carried off the candles to light them to their work, and proceeded, under the guidance of some rascally Spaniards, to blow off the locks of the houses with their muskets, and seize or destroy everything that they could find.

Men were seen, hopelessly intoxicated, with half a dozen silk gowns wound about them, or garnished with twenty pair of shoes hung round their waists. Nevertheless the disorder was not of long duration. By dawn there was already some reappearance of discipline, and by noon the last of the troops had been cleared out of the city. Many of them were so much encumbered by their booty that they could hardly move; and Wellington himself, seeing a column march out bedizened with every description of garment male and female, was fain to ask, "Who the devil are those fellows?" He was answered that they were the Light Division.

The capture of Ciudad Rodrigo after twelve days of open trenches was a great feat of arms; and the traveller, who wanders round the walls, little changed after the lapse of a century, cannot help marvelling that it was ever accomplished. Some training had indeed been given during the winter to selected battalions of the Third Division in the art of the sapper; but, generally speaking, the men were still unhandy and the officers still lukewarm where the work of the spade was concerned. Burgoyne complained that British troops never accomplished their tasks in the trenches within the time laid down in the French textbooks; and the engineer-officers themselves, though they toiled and hazarded their lives with blind devotion, were by no means faultless in their plans and their arrangements.

The organisation for bringing up the stores was bad; and the system of assigning the duty in the trenches to four divisions in rotation for twenty-four hours apiece was not found satisfactory. In the first place the divisions were of unequal strength; in the second, the men, having marched twelve or fifteen miles from their cantonments, were not fresh; and in the third, having in many cases to ford the Agueda on their way, they arrived with their clothes half frozen, could not be warmed except by work, and could not labour continually and energetically for twelve hours.

Still, in spite of all shortcomings and of a terrible fire from the ramparts, the besiegers made rapid progress, the more so since they conducted their operations upon a new principle. Wellington wrote:—

> The whole object of our fire was to lay open the walls. We had not one mortar, nor a howitzer except to prevent the enemy from clearing the breaches, and for that purpose we had only two; and we fired upon the flanks and defences only when we wished to get the better of them with a view to protect those who were about to storm. (*Wellington Desp.* To Duke of Richmond, 29th Jan. 1812).

It was this abstention from all effort to silence the enemy's guns which caused the losses during the siege to amount to five hundred and fifty-three, of whom one hundred and thirty-six were Portuguese.

The assault was more costly than it should have been, for reasons which have already been stated, namely the delay of the main columns in the advance, and the betrayal of the movements of Campbell's brigade by an excited Irish subaltern. Nevertheless the casualties did not exceed four hundred and ninety-nine of all ranks, of whom one hundred and five were killed. Some of the slain beyond question fell by each other's hands in the tumult after the town was gained; while the accidental explosion of the magazine alone is said to have slain or injured one hundred and fifty men. Among the wounded were Generals Vandeleur of the Light Division, John Colborne of the Fifty-Second (who was disabled for eighteen months by a very painful wound in the shoulder), and George Napier, who was shot down at the breach and lost an arm.

But the foremost of the fallen was Craufurd, who after lying in great agony for forty-eight hours died of his wounds on the 24th. Enough has already been said of him to show what manner of man he was, his great defects and his yet greater merits. His body was laid at the foot of the breach where he fell; but his name will never be forgotten while the British Army lasts, as that of the man who, after Moore, had the greatest share in the training of the Light Division.

The losses of the French are not easily ascertained. ("It is a remarkable feature," wrote Gomm at this time, "in the history of this siege, & one that will distinguish it perhaps from that of all towns carried by assault, that the loss of the besiegers doubles that of the besieged.") Wellington reported that he had taken close upon eighteen hundred prisoners of all ranks; but even if this figure be assumed to include the wounded, and the number of the killed be set down at no more than one hundred, the total exceeds the numbers of the garrison as stated in the French returns. I am bound to say, however, that I regard these returns with some suspicion. The besieged appear to have fought well, but to have been ill commanded; for all British accounts agree in condemning Barrié for lack of energy and vigilance. It seems certain that the assault was not expected by him; and it is said that an officer of the Fifth, who was carried off in the rush of the French as they retired from the breach, found him unwilling to believe even then that an attack was actually in progress.

His own account sets forth that his dispositions for meeting a storm had been made in the early morning; but this, in view of the British narratives, is incredible. In any case he made no attempt to retrench the lesser breach, which was obstructed only by a twenty-four-pounder gun placed lengthwise across the opening. Upon the whole I conceive that Marmont was right in condemning Barrié as a detestable officer, though it may be doubted whether, with so weak a force, any commander could have prolonged the siege for more than two or three days.

So short a delay would have made no difference to the result. Marmont, upon learning of the siege on the 15th of January, had at once ordered a hasty concentration of his troops at Medina del Campo and Salamanca. Besides the two divisions that had accompanied the marshal to Valladolid, Bonnet had been summoned from Asturias, Foy and Montbrun with all their soldiers had been recalled by forced marches from their journey towards Valencia, and Dorsenne had set six thousand of the Young Guard, as well as cavalry and artillery, in motion towards the same points. Thus on the 26th and 27th Marmont reckoned that he would have thirty-two thousand men, and on the 1st or 2nd of February forty thousand men, in front of the British on the Agueda.

Even if his expectations had been realised, he would have arrived too late. The fortress, which in the hands of five thousand raw Spanish levies had resisted Ney for twenty-five days, when transferred to two thousand French soldiers, succumbed to Wellington in twelve. "Never," wrote Marmont, surprised into unwilling eulogy, "was such an operation pushed forward with the like activity"; and for the moment he was fairly stunned by the blow. His advanced base for invasion of Portugal was gone; the gate which led into the country from the north-east was closed; and the key for reopening it—the siege-train for the Army of Portugal—had been captured in the lock, so to speak, within the walls of Ciudad Rodrigo.

CHAPTER 6

The Fall of Badajoz

The capture of Ciudad Rodrigo coincided in time, curiously enough, with Wellington's receipt of the news both of Victor's failure before Tarifa and of Suchet's triumph at Valencia; while at the same moment he became aware through an intercepted letter of Marmont's concentration on the Tormes. He therefore lost no time in effacing his trenches and repairing the fortifications, tasks which, together with the execution of several British deserters taken in the place, fully occupied the first days that followed after the assault. Yet, while taking every precaution in case Marmont should turn his position by the pass of Baños, Wellington divined that the marshal would probably make no movement when he found that he was too late to relieve Ciudad Rodrigo.

The British general was right. On the 21st Marmont reached Fuente Sauco, about eleven miles north-east of Salamanca, where he met the news that the fortress had fallen. (So Marmont says in his *Mémoires* (iv.). Napier, I know not on what authority, gives the day as the 26th). Under the shock of the misfortune he abandoned all idea of an advance, though he did not yet countermand his orders for concentration, lest Wellington should essay an offensive movement upon the Tormes.

But by the 28th Wellington had made up his mind that there was nothing to prevent him from proceeding with the siege of Badajoz. He therefore gave directions on that day for bringing up stores from Setubal to Elvas, and sent instructions to Hill to arrange an expedition for the purpose of destroying the bridge over the Tagus at Almaraz. The Army of Portugal would, as he calculated, need this bridge in order to advance to the relief of Badajoz, and, if deprived of it, might very likely be compelled by the swelling of the river to resort to the bridge of Toledo. (*Wellington Desp.* To Liverpool, 21st Jan.; to Hill, 22nd, 28th Jan.; to H. Wellesley, 29th Jan. 1812).

On the same day, however, the weather broke up; and the frost, which had so greatly facilitated the operations of the siege, gave place to heavy rain, which impeded not a little the repairs of the fortress. On the 31st the troops moved back to their former cantonments; and two days later the Agueda rose so high that the suburbs were two feet deep under water, the trestle bridge at Marialva was swept away, the stone bridge was rendered useless, and the garrison of Ciudad Rodrigo was left in isolation from the Allied army.

Such a situation naturally caused alarming rumours that Marmont was advancing; and every effort was made to render the defences proof against a sudden attack. The great English historian of the war has written that, if the marshal had but moved up to Ciudad Rodrigo at this moment, the place could not have resisted him; but this is extremely doubtful, for it seems that the river was not impassable for more than twenty-four hours, and it is certain that the French knew not whither to turn for supplies. (See Jones's *Sieges*, i. Napier says that the great flood came on the 28th Jan., and that the fortress was isolated for several days; but I prefer the solid facts in Jones's *Diary* to these loose statements, which are made chiefly to introduce the remark that "the greatest warriors are the very slaves of fortune.")

Be this as it may, Marmont had no sooner learned of the return of the British into their cantonments than he broke up his own army likewise. His headquarters were fixed at Valladolid; three divisions under Foy were sent to the valley of the Tagus and its vicinity; Bonnet's division, which was on its way from Asturias, was halted in Leon; a strong advanced guard with plenty of light cavalry was stationed at Salamanca under Montbrun; and the rest of the force was cantoned on the Douro and in the province of Avila. The mere catalogue of these movements, however, gives a very imperfect idea of their results upon the efficiency of the French Army. Bonnet had been dragged down from Asturias in midwinter; Montbrun and Foy had been recalled, the one from Alicante and the other from Villarobledo by forced marches, and in Foy's case certainly with a very slender supply of victuals; and as a consequence the detachments of all three commanders had suffered severely from sickness and fatigue. Moreover, new life was infused into the Spanish guerilla-bands in every quarter, and General Abadia was able to show greater activity in Galicia.

In the south Soult until the 15th of January remained exceedingly nervous about the intentions of Hill. He exhorted Marmont to make a demonstration towards Merida and Truxillo; indeed, being totally ignorant of what was going forward in the north, he seems even so late as on the 27th to have counted upon some such manoeuvre. Not until the 31st did he hear simultaneously of the siege and of the capture of Ciudad Rodrigo, when he at once conjectured that Wellington would shortly appear before Badajoz. Intelligence, received a week later, of the arrival of guns and ammunition at Elvas increased his anxiety for that fortress; and on the 9th of February he wrote an urgent appeal to Marmont to make preparations to succour it. Soult had reorganised the First, Fourth, and Fifth Corps into six divisions of infantry and three of cavalry, with a total strength of about fifty thousand men.

On the right the Fifth Division and one brigade of cavalry under d'Erlon were on the Guadiana about Medellin, the Sixth Division and one brigade of cavalry being also at d'Erlon's disposition in the same quarter; the Fourth Division and a division of cavalry under Leval occupied the provinces of Granada and Malaga; the Third Division and the rest of the besieging army round Cadiz was entrusted to Villatte; the First Division under Conroux watched Ballesteros about San Roque and Gibraltar; and the Second Division, under Latour Maubourg but subject, together with a brigade of cavalry, to the orders of Villatte, was in the interior of Andalusia.

In Murcia the wreck of Freire's and Mahy's armies were beginning to reassemble about Lorca, so that it was impossible to diminish Leval's force; Ballesteros was too dangerous to be left unsurveyed; Andalusia was barely safe with but five thousand men to watch it; and lastly, orders had arrived from Paris to send two complete French regiments of infantry, as many of cavalry, and all the Polish troops, altogether some seven thousand men, to Burgos, and thence to France. In the circumstances Soult informed both Marmont and Berthier, quite truly, that he was powerless to do anything for Badajoz, and pressed the latter for a reinforcement of twenty thousand men, urging that, since Ciudad Rodrigo had fallen, it would be more profitable to strengthen the Army of the South than the Army of Portugal. (*Arch, de la Guerre.* Soult to Berthier, 11th, 24th, 27th, 31st Jan., 1st, 7th, 21st, 22nd Feb.; to Marmont, 9th Feb. 1812. *Mémoires du duc de Raguse*, iv.; Soult to Marmont, 4th Jan., 7th Feb. 1812).

The situation of the two marshals, therefore, was not enviable. They had no wish to work together, though Marmont frankly recognised that without help from his troops it was utterly impossible for Soult to relieve Badajoz, if that fortress were besieged. Napoleon now interposed from Paris to make matters worse. First, on the 23rd of January he criticised, not perhaps without reason, Marmont's orders to Montbrun for the expedition to Valencia, and directed that detachment to be recalled at once, at the same time ordering Marmont to make over one of his divisions to Dorsenne and to take five thousand drafts in exchange. On the same day he censured Dorsenne for not sending a division to Burgos for the repression of Mina's guerilla-bands. Next, having heard that Ciudad Rodrigo was besieged, he instructed Dorsenne on the 27th (eight days after the fall of the fortress) to delay for the present the return of the Guard to France.

Shortly afterwards, having learned of the loss of Ciudad Rodrigo, he wrote on the 11th of February a succession of angry letters. Dorsenne he censured as the general to be held responsible for the disaster. Soult he reproved for asking help from Marmont against so weak an adversary as Hill. Marmont he blamed for not having advanced to Salamanca, so as to threaten Ciudad Rodrigo. Further, he gave Marmont positive orders to fortify Salamanca, assemble seven divisions there, collect his siege-train (which had, as we have seen, been captured), and hold the British in check by threatening Almeid, his words were such:

> You must think the English mad, if you suppose them capable of marching on Badajoz while you are at Salamanca, that is to say in a position to reach Lisbon before them.

Lastly, Napoleon directed the marshal to send Bonnet's division back to Asturias at once. The whole of these instructions were repeated in a second letter of the 18th of February, with an intimation that the Duke of Ragusa, by keeping a division in the valley of the Tagus, and generally concerning himself with operations in that quarter and in the valley of the Guadiana, was meddling with matters which were none of his business. The emperor (such was the purport of the missive) had given orders to Soult to place twenty thousand men under d'Erlon's command at Merida so as to keep Hill permanently in check and paralyse him completely; and that was sufficient. The truth is that Napoleon's thoughts at this time were occupied solely with the invasion of Russia, for on this same 18th of February he instructed Dorsenne to set the whole of the Imperial Guard on march for Bayonne within twenty-four hours. (*Arch, de la Guerre.* Berthier to Dorsenne, 23rd Jan., 11th, 18th Feb.; to Soult, 11th, 18th Feb.; to Marmont and

Joseph, 18th Feb. 1812. Ducasse, viii. Berthier to Marmont, 20th F 1812. *Mémoires du duc de Raguse*, iv. Berthier to Marmont, 23rd Jan., 18th Feb. 1812).

The absolute futility of these multifarious orders, issued in every case to meet a state of things that had ceased for several days to exist and based upon imagination rather than fact, is sufficiently apparent. Marmont was unable to concentrate anywhere because he had no supplies, and his troops even when dispersed had considerable difficulty in feeding themselves. To all intent a desert lay between him and Wellington, and this desert he was unable to cross. The British commander himself, with the ports of Lisbon and Oporto behind him and the sea always open to British shipping, could only just contrive to maintain his army unstarved in the field, after devoting vast trouble and expenditure to the organisation of transport. Soult was in the like difficulty with Marmont both for victuals and for money. His army was already overtaken by dearth and actually threatened with famine; and it was absolutely impossible for him to assemble twenty thousand men without withdrawing all garrisons from the interior of Andalusia. (*Arch, de la Guerre*. Soult to Berthier, 21st Feb. 1812). Meanwhile the departure of the troops needed for the Russian campaign, and the consequent redistribution of the forces in Spain into five armies, led to infinite trouble and confusion.

During this time Wellington had already entrusted to Dickson the task of collecting a siege-train at Elvas. His first idea had been to move the ordnance employed at Ciudad Rodrigo overland to its new destination; but the draft-bullocks were so weak that the project was abandoned, and it was decided to send sixteen heavy howitzers only by road, and to make good the deficiency by landing at Setubal sixteen twenty-four-pounders recently sent from England, together with twenty eighteen-pounders lent by the admiral from the fleet. Dickson set out accordingly for Setubal on the 28th of January, and the cannon started on their journey to Elvas two days later.

On the 2nd of February Wellington shifted his headquarters from Gallegos to Freineda, and promised himself a day with the hounds on the 3rd, (*Wellington Desp.* To Graham, 2nd Feb. 1812), but bad weather put a stop not only to all hunting but to all serious work for some days; and it became evident that the operations at Badajoz must necessarily be delayed. Hill also reported that the only road to Almaraz took such a direction as to make the capture of the enemy's bridge of boats almost impossible of accomplishment; whereupon that project likewise was for the present postponed. But these were only the first of a series of difficulties which cropped up to impede the enterprise against Badajoz.

There is no point upon which army and navy are so likely to misunderstand each other as a question of artillery; the purpose, broadly speaking, of naval guns being to strike a single object—namely, a ship—and of military guns to overthrow as many small objects—namely, men—as possible. When therefore Wellington applied to the fleet for guns, the admiral thought it sufficient to make over to Dickson twenty Russian eighteen-pounders which by chance were in the marine arsenal at Lisbon, assuring him that they were of the description named by the general, and would take the English shot very well. As a matter of fact the English shot was by nearly half an inch too small for these guns, and Dickson very respectfully protested against being saddled with such ordnance.

Sir Thomas Hardy, the captain of the fleet, however, showed no great alacrity in substituting other pieces for them; and Dickson finally decided to take what he could get, sifting out with enormous labour an adequate quantity of Portuguese and Russian shot which fitted the Russian cannon tolerably well. Wellington made no complaint to the admiral, but in his private correspondence he remarked sarcastically that the naval officers seemed to regard precision in the fire of artillery as no more necessary in a siege than in an action at sea. Ultimately the admiral consented to provide ten English cannon from a Danish frigate; but by that time Dickson had overcome the difficulties connected with the Russian guns, and at first declined to complicate matters by taking any others, though he appears in the end to have sent forward both the English and the Russian pieces. The incident is interesting chiefly as showing that the navy still thought that their worst was good enough for the army. (*Dickson MSS. Wellington Desp.* To Graham, 18th Feb. 1812).

Then followed the usual troubles with the Portuguese Government over the furnishing of transport for the siege-train from Alcacer do Sal, on the Setubal estuary, to Elvas. Wellington's relations with that government were not of the most cordial, nor his correspondence with it of the most friendly. By this time he had obtained authority to displace Principal Souza from the Council of Regency; but this would have been no remedy for the old and crying evil that the Ministers would not compel the magistrates to enforce the existing laws for supplying an army with carriage. The whole of the Portuguese authorities were afraid of incurring unpopularity, and therefore, while severe in exacting all that was required from the poor who could not resist, they were careful to exempt the rich and the well-to-do.

Wellington had already laid the utmost possible burden upon his own service of transport; but he was obliged to charge it in addition with the heavy task of bringing up munitions of war, simply because the Portuguese Government would not help him. There was no lack of carriages at hand, particularly in one town—Evora—which so far had not suffered from the war; but nothing could induce the Regency to make the people place them at Wellington's disposal. The result was that the operations were delayed until the breaking of the rains at the vernal equinox, which was exactly what the British general had desired to avoid. (*Wellington Desp.* To C. Stuart, 29th Feb.; to Liverpool, 27th March 1812).

Next, it was necessary to concert arrangements with the Spaniards for handing over Ciudad Rodrigo to the Spanish Government. Castaños had arrived at the place before the end of January, and Wellington, in order to make matters as easy as possible, had undertaken to execute the work of restoration at the expense of the British Government and with the labour of British soldiers, as also to supply the stronghold with provisions for five months. Though Wellington had particularly desired that no troops, except the actual garrison, should enter the fortress, the Spanish general at once fixed his headquarters there and began to draw extravagant rations for himself and his staff. Then, presumably in order to excuse his presence, he suggested that the handful of five thousand men, called "the 5th Army," together with the force of Ballesteros, should take an active part in the coming operations. Wellington at once set his foot firmly upon this proposal. He pointed out that the Spanish Government could not feed its troops in Castile, and that he most certainly neither could nor would; and he recommended that both Ballesteros and the 5th Army should be employed independently of each other in the south, threatening Seville in order to distract Soult's attention from Badajoz.

Castaños appears to have accepted this plan with docility; and Wellington then formulated his designs to meet all possible movements of the enemy. Four different courses were open to Marmont upon learning of the siege of Badajoz. First, he might leave two divisions to hold down Leon and Old Castile, and lead the rest of his army into Estremadura. In that case Abadia with the Army of Galicia, Carlos d'España with a part of the garrison of Ciudad Rodrigo, and all the guerrilla leaders in the northern provinces should endeavour to do as much mischief as they could. Secondly, Marmont might leave three divisions and his cavalry to support Soult against the British on the Guadiana, and invade Galicia with the five remaining divisions.

In this event Abadia would oppose him in front, while the Portuguese generals Bacellar and Do Amarante in Traz-os-Montes could harass his flanks and rear. Thirdly, Marmont might attack the frontier of Portugal north of the Douro; and then it would be the duty of the Portuguese to check the French as far as possible in front, while Abadia fell upon their flank and rear.

Lastly, Marmont might pass the Agueda below Ciudad Rodrigo, and possibly cross the Coa also, so as to cut off Almeida and Ciudad Rodrigo from the interior of Portugal. In that case Bacellar was to collect all the militia of the northern provinces behind the Coa, keeping touch with such part of Carlos d'España's force as was not in garrison, and endeavour to protect the British magazines on the Douro and the Mondego; while Carlos d'España should break down the bridges on the Yeltes and the Huebra, and, if necessary, those over the Azava at Castillejos and over the Agueda at Barba del Puerco. Full and minute instructions were furnished to Bacellar for his guidance in every one of these three last contingencies. (*Wellington Desp.* To Castaños, 16th, 24th Feb.; to H. Wellesley, 19th, 25th Feb.; to Bacellar, 27th Feb. 1812).

As regards the British Government there remained the old difficulty of specie, which Wellington had proposed to alleviate by the issue of a certain sum in English Exchequer-bills, hoping thus possibly to draw out of its hiding-places some of the coin that was undoubtedly hoarded in Lisbon and in Spain. Whether this plan would have been attended with any success Wellington himself was doubtful; but in any case it did not commend itself to the British Cabinet, and was accordingly abandoned.

★★★★★★

Napier of course says that Liverpool's objections to the plan were "futile," but does not condescend to particulars. I question whether Napier or anyone outside the Cabinet was competent to weigh them; and I think it extremely doubtful that he had the slightest idea what they were, for Lord Liverpool's letter is not among the Wellington Papers, nor have I been able to find it elsewhere.

★★★★★★

Another effort to persuade the principal merchants in the Peninsula to accept the Bank of England's notes as cash appears likewise to have failed; and Wellington was fain to manage as best he could without specie.

For the rest, he complained with righteous indignation of the bad quality of the entrenching and cutting tools, and indeed of all implements supplied by the store-keeper general, which had been found grievously wanting before Ciudad Rodrigo. He also pleaded for the formation of a corps of Sappers and Miners, beginning himself to train one upon the spot, with the result that in April a school was established at Chatham for the instruction of such a corps under the command of a very able officer of Engineers, Captain Pasley. (*Wellington Desp.* To Liverpool, 11th, 12th Feb.; to Peacocke, 14th Feb.; to Cooke, 29th Feb. 1812. Connolly, *Hist. of the Royal Sappers and Miners*, i.)

On the 16th of February the first of Wellington's troops began to move southward, many of the regiments marching by devious routes in order to pick up new clothing which had been brought up by water to various depots on the Douro, Mondego, and Tagus. (It is difficult to speak with certainty of the movements of the army at this time, but Tomkinson, under date of the 16th, says that some of the infantry had marched for the Tagus, that the 1st division had gone to Abrantes to get its clothing; and that Anson's Light Cavalry Brigade started for Thomar on the 18th).

All this could be done without anxiety, for by the 2nd Wellington had ascertained with fair accuracy the quarters into which five out of Marmont's eight divisions had been dispersed; and by the 19th he knew exactly the stations of the entire eight. He had arranged, as we have seen, to distract Soult and Dorsenne; and, having put two British regiments into Carthagena, he felt little apprehension of any formidable movement by Suchet. The guerrilla-bands indeed kept the last-named general employed even at the very gates of Valencia.

By the 26th the whole of the army, except the Fifth Division, was in motion; but Wellington himself remained stationary at Freineda, desiring to delude the enemy by not shifting his headquarters until the last moment. Nevertheless Marmont on the 22nd had heard of the movement of the British towards the Guadiana; and he ordered Foy to push forward an advanced guard to Jaraicejo and to close up to rear of it the 1st, 4th, and 6th divisions, which were under his command, in readiness for the march. At the same time he left Bonnet in charge of two divisions on the Tormes, established Souham's division n the Douro and Esla, and prepared to set out with the 2nd Division in person to join Foy. By these dispositions he flattered himself, apparently till the end of his life, that he forced Wellington to suspend his enterprise; but nothing could be further from the fact.

The British general had foreseen exactly what Marmont was most likely to do, except that he had expected him to leave only two divisions instead of three behind him, and had no intention of being diverted from his own course. The only effect of Marmont's preparations upon Wellington was to delay his departure from Freineda for five days, since he knew that the removal of his headquarters would be the signal for the French to advance. In justice to the marshal, however, it should be added that on the 23rd he wrote a long letter to Berthier, predicting certain disaster unless the emperor's system of carrying on the war were altered, and begging to be relieved of his command. (*Wellington Desp.* To Bacellar, 27th Feb.; to Liverpool, 4th March 1812).

Soult was by this time before Cadiz, hoping to infuse some vigour into the siege by opening a bombardment with mortars, which he had ordered to be cast at Seville, with a range of close upon six thousand yards. On the 21st of February he had been expecting momentarily to hear that Badajoz had been invested by Hill under the protection of an imaginary corps of twenty thousand men which was reported to have landed lately at Lisbon under General Hamilton. Soult had therefore detained the troops which he had been ordered to send back to France, and had written to Marmont to ask definitely whether he could count upon the help of three of his divisions. But on the 22nd—the very day on which Marmont took the alarm—Soult decided, upon intelligence from d'Erlon at Villafranca, that Wellington had renounced his designs upon Badajoz for the present; and under this false impression he directed six French and as many Polish battalions, besides two regiments of cavalry and some odd detachments, to march at once for Burgos pursuant to Napoleon's instructions.

D'Erlon had evidently been completely deceived by Hill's retirement to his old cantonments after his raid to the eastward, and had no inkling of the wrath to come. A few days later Soult heard that a weak column under General Maransin had been attacked by Ballesteros at Cartama near Malaga on the 16th, and, but for the timely arrival of General Rey with reinforcements, would have been very roughly handled, Maransin himself being hurt and about one hundred and fifty of his men killed, wounded, or taken.

★★★★★★

Ballesteros reported this affair as a victory (*Wellington Desp.*, to Liverpool, 4th March 1812); and Arteche represents it as a rout in which the French were hunted into Malaga, quoting a Spanish account which reports that Maransin was brought into the town with seven or eight wounded officers, and that the ground was strewn with dead (xii.). Martinien's list, however, shows that not a single officer was killed and no more than five besides Maransin wounded, one of whom belonged to Rey's column, about which Arteche says nothing.

★★★★★★

Such events, however, were too common to occasion Soult any special anxiety; and he was satisfied when his flying columns compelled Ballesteros to retire to Tarifa, hoping before long to bring that troublesome partisan to action and so make an end of him.

Not until the 5th of March was he again perturbed by reports both from d'Erlon and from Philippon, the *commandant* at Badajoz, that the British preparations had been resumed at Elvas; and then he wrote to Berthier that, unless all his troops in the interior of Spain were sent down to him, and authority granted to him to give direct orders to twenty-five thousand of the Army of Portugal, he could not be responsible for the consequences. (*Arch, de la Guerre.* Soult to Berthier, 21st, 22nd, 24th, 27th Feb., 5th March 1812).

Meanwhile, the last of the British troops, the Fifth Division always excepted, had marched southward on the 26th of February; and Wellington himself, being now exactly informed as to Marmont's dispositions, quitted Freineda quietly on the 6th of March, leaving the 1st German Hussars under Major-General Victor Alten on the Yeltes to screen the withdrawal of the departing regiments, and to spread the report that the commander-in-chief contemplated hunting in that country. On the 10th, upon reaching Portalegre, Wellington received the news that he had been promoted to an earldom for the capture of Ciudad Rodrigo, and on the following day he arrived at Elvas.

There he found that, for reasons already stated, the stores necessary for the siege were not yet accumulated, and that several battalions, which had marched to the rear to get their clothing, had not yet returned. None the less he determined to invest Badajoz on the 16th. Marmont so far had made no sign of bringing down additional troops from the north, and it was doubtful whether he was yet aware of Wellington's departure from the Agueda. Soult was still at Cadiz, as we know, and his force in the field in Estremadura did not exceed two divisions of infantry and a brigade of cavalry, numbering perhaps eleven to twelve thousand men. Hence there was no reason to apprehend that the enemy would for some time be in a position to intervene in the operations.

Accordingly on the 15th a pontoon-bridge and a flying-bridge were after some delay thrown over the Guadiana, the former at a narrow point in the river about ten miles below Badajoz, the latter about a mile and a half above it; and in the evening a brigade of Hamilton's Portuguese division crossed the water to protect these bridges. (Napier mentions only the pontoon-bridge and says that it was four miles from Badajoz; I prefer the evidence of Burgoyne, Wrottesley, i.). On the 16th at daylight the First, Sixth, and Seventh Divisions under the command of Graham marched for Valverde on their way to Zafra, in order to watch the movements of d'Erlon and Soult; while the Third and Fourth Divisions bivouacked for the night on the heights to the south of Badajoz.

On the morrow the Light Division joined the Third and Fourth, making up a total of about eleven thousand men; and, under the direction of Beresford, who had rejoined the army, these completed the investment of the fortress on the southern bank of the Guadiana. At the same time Hill advanced from his cantonments with his own and Hamilton's divisions and Long's cavalry upon Merida and Almendralejo, to watch Marmont's force on the Tagus.

On the very day of the investment, however, Wellington received intelligence that Marmont was withdrawing three out of the four divisions from that quarter to the north, and leaving only that of Foy at Talavera. (Wellington does not mention Marmont's change of dispositions until his letter to Liverpool of 20th March; but Burgoyne knew of it on the 17th, Wrottesley, i., so Wellington must have known it too.) Wellington naturally inferred that some diversion towards Galicia or the north of Portugal would probably follow; but, having taken all necessary measures to meet such a movement, troubled himself little more about it. He knew not yet though intercepted despatches were shortly to reveal it to him that Marmont on the 3rd of March had received the emperor's orders to concentrate his army at Salamanca and with sad misgivings had obeyed them, leaving Foy to follow from Estremadura as soon as he should be relieved by a detachment from Joseph's Army of the Centre.

It was very well for the emperor to say that an advance upon Ciudad Rodrigo would cause Wellington to raise the siege of Badajoz

BREACHES

French Retrenchment

Sword blades

St. Maria

Trinidad

Holes

Cunette

Cunette

Light
Division

4th. Division

Siege of
BADAJOS
1812.

5th. Division

Mines

San Vincent

Portuguese

Siera de Viento

Pardaleras

Guadiana R.

Bridgehead

Christoval

Great Square

St. Vincent

Cash

Quarry

Lt. Division

Trinidad

Rivillas

4th. Division

Inundation

San Roque

Wilson's
attack

French
communication

Picurina

3rd. Division

French
Guns

San Roque

instantly; but the marshal had neither magazines, transport, nor siege-train; and the British general, being perfectly aware of these facts, would not suffer himself to be disturbed by a mere concentration. (See the correspondence printed in *Wellington Desp.*, v.). Soult was hardly more at his ease than was Marmont. He had begun the bombardment of Cadiz on the 13th with some vague hope of alarming the Allies for its safety; but he had heard of Wellington's arrival at Portalegre and could not doubt that it portended an attack upon Badajoz.

It was impossible for him to march to the city's relief without leaving all Andalusia open to Ballesteros; and even then he could take with him but twenty thousand men, too small a number to loosen the grip of the British upon the fortress and compel them to fight. Moreover he had just heard of the withdrawal of Marmont's three divisions from the Tagus, and foresaw that this movement might be fatal. (*Arch, de la Guerre*. Soult to Berthier, 15th March 1812).

A reconnaissance upon the 17th showed that Badajoz had been considerably strengthened since its last investment by the British. To speak first of the outworks: Fort San Cristobal had been greatly improved, and a strong redoubt had been built on the site of Wellington's breaching battery; while a covered communication between the fort and the bridge-head had been nearly completed. In the fort of Pardaleras the gorge had been enclosed, and the fort itself had been connected with the body of the place by intermediate works. In the main fortress a *cunette* had been dug in the ditch; on the eastern side the stream of Rivillas had been dammed up so as to form an impassable inundation; on the north front the breach battered by Wellington had been rebuilt in the shape of a tower and mounted with several guns; and on the western front, which was the weakest, and by the south-western angle, three ravelins had been thrown up, one of which was completely and a second partly revetted, while the third consisted of earth only. The whole of these last were covered by an elaborate system of mines, which by great good fortune were revealed to Wellington by a sergeant-major of the French sappers, who deserted in a rage and brought his maps with him.

The garrison numbered just over five thousand men of all descriptions, leaving, after deduction of sick men and non-combatants, about forty-five hundred efficient of all ranks, which was hardly enough for the extent of the fortifications. One hundred and forty pieces were mounted on the works, but there was insufficiency both of powder and of shell in the magazines, Hill having twice prevented the en-

116

trance of a convoy of ammunition from Seville. Of victuals there was six to seven weeks' store, gathered chiefly through the energy of the able, watchful, and valiant commander, Philippon.

Any attack upon the castle, as now strengthened, was hopeless; and the engineers, having neither trained sappers, trained miners nor mortars, shrank from the difficulties of attempting the western front. It remained therefore only to take advantage of a defect in the right or southern face of the Trinidad bastion at the south eastern angle of the fortress, which made it possible to breach the main scarp of the bastion from the heights of San Miguel over against it; and since these heights were themselves crowned by the Picurina redoubt, it was necessary first of all to master that work. Accordingly the park was massed in rear of the heights; and, when night fell, the working party began in wild wind and rain to open a trench of communication thirteen hundred yards long from the park to the first parallel, which was marked out about two hundred and fifty yards from the redoubt. The garrison, not expecting such a proceeding, did not detect what was going forward until daylight, when a heavy fire of musketry was opened from the redoubt and of cannon from the fortress.

At dusk of the 18th two batteries were traced out opposite the two faces of the salient angle of Picurina; though when morning broke the enemy's sharpshooters, having made themselves additional cover, annoyed the working parties greatly. At one in the afternoon eleven hundred French infantry and forty cavalry under General Veiland formed under shelter of the covered way which connected the *lunette* of San Roque with Picurina, and, favoured by a fog, made a rush upon the right of the British parallel, while another party from Picurina itself attacked it on the left. The British soldiers, working up to their hips in water, were caught unarmed and defenceless, and were driven from the trenches in disorder, nor was it for some time that they could be rallied; but at length, charging the enemy, they hunted them in their turn back to the town. The French cavalry, meanwhile, galloped round to the park and had time to cut down a few unarmed men before beating a retreat. (If we are to believe Grattan, he alone had caused his men to throw down their tools and pick up their arms, which enabled him to repulse the French at one point. *Adventures in the Connaught Rangers* in *The Complete Connaught Rangers* by William Grattan).

The enemy also carried off over five hundred tools, but suffered somewhat severely, having one hundred and eighty—including thirteen officers—killed and wounded. The casualties of the Allies were about one hundred and fifty, and among the wounded was the chief engineer, Colonel Fletcher, whom, however, Wellington still retained in charge of the siege, visiting his tent every morning to consult him as to the work of the next twenty-four hours. (The figures shown are given by Jones; and the casualty list, which shows 3 officers killed and 5 wounded, bears it out. On the contrary, Jones gives the number of tools captured at 200, while Belmas states the number at 545). After this experience a squadron of horse with a battery of field-guns was kept constantly mounted in rear of the heights of San Miguel.

On the following days the parallel was prolonged to the northward, beyond the *lunette* of San Roque, and four more batteries were begun; but the incessant rain greatly hindered the progress of the work. On the 22nd the garrison, having thrown up cover for three field-guns on the north side of the river; opened so destructive a flanking fire upon the trench that Wellington summoned General Leith, who was with the Fifth Division in Campo Maior, to invest the place on the northern side. In the afternoon there fell a terrific shower; all the trenches were flooded, the pontoon-bridge was carried away, and eleven pontoons were sunk at their anchors.

Cut off by this accident from his supplies and from the battalions which were on march to join him, Wellington became extremely anxious. "We are not within twenty thousand men so strong on the left of the Guadiana as we ought to be," he wrote to Graham, (*Wellington Desp.* To Graham, 24th March 1812); and he urged that officer and Hill to thrust d'Erlon's troops back from their positions in the district east and south of Medellin, called La Serena, in order at least to delay the junction of Foy's division with d'Erlon, if, as Wellington feared, such a movement were in contemplation. From this circumstance it seems reasonable to believe that, had Marmont kept his four divisions, as he originally designed, on the Tagus, Wellington might at this crisis have raised the siege.

On the afternoon of the 24th the weather cleared up, and in the course of the night the six batteries were completed and armed with twenty-eight heavy pieces, thirteen of them against Picurina, seven against the *lunette* of San Roque, and eleven to enfilade the south faces of the Trinidad bastion and the San Pedro bastion next to northward of it. At eleven o'clock on the 25th these batteries opened fire and were vigorously answered by the cannon of the fortress; but the guns of Picurina were none the less dismounted, and the parapet so much ruined that the defenders made every preparation against an assault;

repairing such damage as they could, distributing along the parapet loaded shells and powder-barrels to be thrown at assailants, and attaching fuses to three mines which had been dug on the crest of the glacis.

Apprised of these precautions, General Kempt, who commanded in the trenches, determined to deliver his attack as early as possible. He therefore assembled a reserve of one hundred men under Captain Powis of the Eighty-Third in the battery over against the salient angle of the redoubt, a detachment of two hundred men under Major Rudd of the Seventy-Seventh at the extreme left of the parallel, and a similar detachment of two hundred of the Eighty-Eighth under Major Shawe of the Seventy-fourth at about the same distance to the right of the reserve.

Of these the left column was to move round the southern flank of the work and attack the gorge, while the right column, leaving half of its numbers to intercept any reinforcements sent from the main fortress, was to turn the fort by the north and join the left column before the gorge. These parties, all from the Third Division, were preceded by about one hundred men of the Light Division with axes, crowbars and ladders; for the redoubt was known to be strong, and indeed proved to be even more formidable than had been supposed.

★★★★★★

Moorsom states that they were of the 52nd under their own officers, and it is certain that two officers of that regiment were wounded in the assault. Jones describes them as Sappers and Miners, and states their number at forty-eight.

★★★★★★

The gorge, though without a counterscarp, was closed by a triple line of stout, slanting palisades, so traced that the defenders could sweep it with a flanking fire. On the remaining faces the scarp rose perpendicularly above the bottom of the ditch for fourteen feet, at which height slanting stakes had been driven in above the revetment, the slope of sixteen feet beyond it being such as men could ascend with no great difficulty. Only at the salient angle had the parapet been damaged and the palisades overthrown, and this was the one point where the defences had been materially weakened.

About nine o'clock, at the signal of a gun from an adjoining battery, the columns of Rudd and Shawe moved out, and the former reached the gorge undiscovered; but, on attempting to destroy the palisades, the men were shot down so rapidly by musketry that after suffering very heavy loss they gave up the effort.

★★★★★★

"About 9 o'clock", so says Jones, who is confirmed (or copied) by Belmas; Napier gives the hour at "about nine"; Burgoyne at half-past eight; Grattan relates circumstantially that the great cathedral bell of the city tolled the hour of eight, and that the signal followed immediately upon the last stroke, which I take to be a picturesque untruth.

★★★★★★

Shawe's party, likewise failing at the same point, drew round to the left flank of the work, where Captain Oakes, finding the ladders too short for the ascent of the scarp, threw three of them across the ditch to form a bridge, and after a sharp struggle forced an entrance. These attacks had diverted the chief attention of the garrison to their flanks and rear, and Kempt now launched his reserve straight upon the salient angle. Planting their ladders on the stakes, Powis's soldiers waited until some twenty or thirty had mounted, and then pressing in together drove the French, not without sharp fighting, from the parapet. This decided the fate of Picurina.

A reinforcement sent from the fortress was met and routed by the detachment of the right column, which had been left behind for the purpose; the axe-men of the Light Division, finding the gorge no longer swept by musketry, were able to break in the gate and enter the work from the rear; and after a struggle of three-quarters of an hour the British were masters of the *lunette*.

★★★★★★

Napier quotes an anonymous officer to the effect that the assailants would never have carried the Picurina had not the axe-men of the Light Division, "compassing the fort like prowling wolves," found the gate and broken it down. This I believe to be nonsense; for all authorities, including Wellington and Belmas, agree that it was Powis's attack which decided the affair; and it is difficult to understand how the axe-men could have approached the gate in the gorge unless the defenders, who had at the outset foiled every assault on that side, had been diverted by an attack in another quarter. Meanwhile not a single other authority mentions this breaking down of the gate, and Napier does so obviously for the sake of flattering the Light Division which needs no flattery.

★★★★★★

Out of the French garrison of two hundred and thirty, only one officer and thirty-one men escaped; the commandant, two more officers and eighty men being captured, and the remainder killed, or drowned in the attempt to pass over the inundation. The British casualties amounted to four officers and fifty men killed, fifteen officers and two hundred and fifty men wounded, making three hundred and nineteen in all out of fewer than six hundred engaged.

Few officers indeed were left standing at the close of the assault, which was a desperate affair and very creditable to the Third Division. The fact is that, heavy though were the British losses, the French behaved badly. The mines were not sprung, nor were the shells and powder-barrels exploded; and, in brief, the attack ought not to have been successful. So strongly did Philippon feel this that he held up the misconduct of the garrison of Picurina to reprobation in a general order.

A lodgement was at once made in the captured redoubt, and, although this was swept away next day by a heavy fire from the fortress, it was quickly replaced by another. Both sides exchanged a violent cannonade until dark, when the two batteries which had been raised against Picurina were demolished, and three more were traced out: one (numbered Seven) of twelve guns immediately to the left of the captured *lunette*, to breach the south face of the Trinidad bastion; one (numbered Nine) of eight guns just outside the gorge, to breach the left flank of the Santa Maria bastion, next to westward of the Trinidad; and one (numbered Ten) of three guns on the first parallel, to enfilade the ditch in front of the principal breach. Philippon, now realising for the first time the true direction of the British attack, exerted himself to improve the defences between the Trinidad and Santa Maria bastions; and his sharpshooters, well sheltered behind sand-bags and gabions, prevented all work on the exterior of the new batteries after daylight.

During the three following days the second parallel was with some difficulty extended to the right, with the view of driving the enemy from the *lunette* of San Roque which protected the dam of the inundation; and a new battery (numbered Eight) of six guns was begun in the gorge of the redoubt, to play against the flank of the Santa Maria bastion. On the 30th the breaching battery, number Nine, opened fire, but the gunners suffered much from the musketry of the French sharp-shooters until a trench was thrown up in advance for riflemen to keep down this fire; and the explosion of a magazine by a shell from the fortress killed and injured many men. Moreover, the shot from the breaching battery seemed to make little impression upon the masonry;

l, to add to Wellington's embarrassments, there had arrived on this and on the previous day somewhat disquieting news from without.

Soult had left Cadiz for Seville on the 23rd, and had issued orders for the assembly of such soldiers as he could spare for a march to the relief of Badajoz; but he was obliged to leave two divisions behind him to beleaguer Cadiz and watch Ballesteros, and could bring no more troops to d'Erlon than would make up a total of twenty-one thousand men. He had expected to leave Seville on the 30th; and Wellington, being apprised of this, recalled Graham to Villa Franca and Zafra and Hill to Merida, at the same time ordering the Fifth Division to move to Graham's support, and replacing it before San Cristobal with a Portuguese brigade. He was anxious to keep Hill at Merida as long as possible, in case Soult should approach Badajoz by the north bank of the Guadiana; but, if the marshal should advance by the shortest route, Graham had orders to collect his force in the wood to south of the position of Albuera.

It is very clear that Wellington felt little anxiety as to the result of this menace from the south, and the less so since Morillo and Penne-Villemur were on their way to make a diversion in the county of Niebla; but in the north affairs wore an unpleasant aspect. Marmont had contrived by great exertions to scrape together fifteen days' supplies; and, after detaching a strong division to Asturias, had marched from the Tormes on the 29th with some twenty thousand men for the Agueda. He had of course no siege-train; but he had managed to collect a few heavy cannon, and there was a report that twenty more pieces had entered Spain from Bayonne a month earlier.

All this would have been of small importance if the Spaniards had taken due care for the safety of Ciudad Rodrigo; but they had signally omitted to do so. It had been arranged that the garrison should be three thousand strong, and Wellington had not only thrown into the fortress provisions for twenty-nine days, but had given an order upon the British magazines for two months' supply in addition, besides furnishing money for completion of the repairs of the fortress.

Yet in less than a month Carlos d'España was whining that he could not proceed with the restoration of the works for want of British masons, and that he had only victuals for twenty-three days; the fact being that, from sheer indolence, he had stationed four thousand men in the fortress instead of three thousand, and had omitted to bring into the place the supplementary supplies freely given to him by Wellington. The outlook therefore was serious; and the British general may be pardoned if he displayed considerable indignation with the Spaniards. It was just such incorrigible negligence and helplessness as these of d'España that drove British officers to distraction. (*Wellington Desp.* To d'España, 20th March; to Liverpool, 27th March; to Graham and Hill, 1st April 1812).

However, Wellington only pushed forward the siege of Badajoz with the greater vigour. Thirty-eight guns poured an unceasing stream of shot upon the bastions of La Trinidad and Santa Maria; but not until the morning of the 5th of April could the engineers report that the breaches would be practicable by sunset. At noon Wellington inspected them in person, and, having heard of Soult's arrival at Llerena on the 4th, gave orders for the assault to be delivered in the evening. But the engineers, after further examination, pleaded for the battering of a third breach between the two bastions, and accordingly at four o'clock the assault was countermanded.

On this evening Leith's division was brought round to the Cerro del Viento, about a mile and a quarter to south-west of the fortress; and Hill, after breaking down the bridge at Merida, fell back upon Talavera la Real, within twelve miles of Badajoz. It was further arranged that, in the event of Soult's nearer approach, two divisions should be left in the trenches, while the remainder of the army should offer him battle at Albuera.

In the course of the night fourteen heavy howitzers were moved into a new battery on the extreme right of the first parallel; and on the morning of the 6th fire was reopened from fourteen cannon upon the curtain between the bastion of La Trinidad and that of Santa Maria, with the result that by four o'clock a practicable breach had been made. Wellington therefore ordered all the batteries to be turned upon the defences, and issued his commands for the place to be stormed at half-past seven that evening, an hour which, owing to the impossibility of completing the preparations, was afterwards postponed until ten.

Once again, therefore, all the established rules of the besieger's art were to be ignored, from sheer want of proper means to apply them. By right the counterscarp should have been blown into the ditch, so that over its ruins and those of the battered scarp opposite to it a formed body of men could have rushed into the breach. Instead of this, the assailants would have to jump or climb down into the ditch, and there form for the decisive assault; and a commander so able and energetic as Philippon was not likely to permit them to do so with impunity. In the course of the siege he had already raised earthen counter-guards and retrenchments to cover the curtain between the bastions of Trinidad and Santa Maria at one point, and between those of San Pedro and San Antonio at another; and whether for the construction of this work, or independently of it, he had excavated a ditch at the foot of the counterscarp which raised its height to sixteen or seventeen feet.

Water had been admitted to this excavation, which was invisible to the besiegers, and the space in the ditch, upon which Wellington had calculated for the formation of his storming columns, was thus entirely filled. The French working parties had laboured with extraordinary devotion to clear away the ruins below the breached wall until the fire of the besiegers fairly forbade the effort; and as early as on the night of the 30th of March the commanding engineer had begun to retrench the ruined defences, and had erected a large battery on a level with the castle in a situation to overlook the great breach. Where the parapet had collapsed with the fall of the scarp, it was replaced by wool-bags and sand-bags; and, when the assault was seen to be imminent, *chevaux de frise*, made of swordblades, were placed in front of them.

The slope of the breach, further, was covered with planks studded with spikes a foot long, and below these again was a chain of buried shells; while powder-barrels had been made ready to be rolled down into the ditch and to be exploded, together with the shells, in the thick of the assailants. The garrison at noon of the 5th of April numbered a little over four thousand men, of whom seven hundred picked soldiers were allotted to the defence of the breaches, with a battalion of from four to five hundred more in support; three or more loaded muskets for each man being laid ready on the parapet. Philippon, though suffering from a wound received on the 3rd, was still and always the soul of the defence.

The orders for the assault were as follows: On the right the Third Division, furnished with long ladders, was to move out of the right of the first parallel shortly before ten o'clock, cross the Rivillas a little above its junction with the Guadiana, and carry the castle by escalade.

In the centre the Fourth and Light Divisions were to make for the curtain between the bastions of La Trinidad and Santa Maria, hugging the edge of the inundation as closely as possible, and leaving each a reserve of a thousand men in some quarries close by. The advanced party of each division was to carry twelve ladders, and the forlorn hope was provided with sacks of hay to break the fall of the soldiers into the ditch. The idea was that part of the men should be spread along the crest of the glacis to keep down the fire of the garrison, while the remainder rushed on to storm; the Fourth Division turning to the right to take the breaches in La Trinidad and in the curtain to west of it, while the Light Division should turn to its left towards that of Santa Maria.

On the left, Leith's division was to make a false attack on Pardaleras, but attempt in earnest to carry by escalade the bastion of San Vicente, by the north-western angle of the fortress.

Lastly, as supplementary attacks, the guards of the trenches, under Major Wilson of the Forty-Eighth, were to storm the *lunette* of San Roque; while General Power and the Portuguese were to make a diversion by a feint assault upon the bridge-head on the other side of the Guadiana.

The night closed in darkly, (It was not Easter Sunday, as Grattan falsely states, but the second Monday after Easter); and a thick mist rising from the waters hung low between besiegers and besieged. All was still and silent, for the batteries upon both sides were dumb. (Napier's story about the sentinels crying from time to time that "all was well in Badajoz" was evidently derived from a private soldier. Every hour they shouted, "*Sentinelles! garde à vous,*" which the British soldier construed to be "All well in Bada*hoo.*")

At eight o'clock the battalions appointed for the assault marched up to their places of assembly, and piling arms waited impatiently for the decisive hour. By half-past nine all was ready, and the British were formed in deep columns, the men parading without stocks or knapsacks, their shirt collars unbuttoned, their trousers tucked up to the knee. Many had not yet received their new clothing, and their rusty tattered jackets added to the wild appearance of brown faces half hidden in a ruff of unkempt beard. All were to outward semblance quiet and resolute; but there was hardly one who did not promise himself some revenge for previous failures before Badajoz, some reward for the past weeks of danger and hardship in flooded trenches; and there were many who, in Napier's phrase, had grown incredibly savage.

About twenty minutes to ten the silence was broken by a sharp crackle of musketry before the *lunette* of San Roque, where the British guard in the sap opened fire upon the two faces, while the escalading party stole round to the rear. So fully were the defenders occupied by the fire in front that the storming party scaled the rampart almost unresisted, and, coming in upon the backs of the French, mastered the work immediately. Measures were taken at once to destroy the dam which made the inundation, but this task was not completed in time to affect the main attack.

Almost simultaneously Picton's brigade came into action. The general had said before starting:—

> Some persons are of opinion that the attack on the castle will not succeed, but I will forfeit my life if it does not.

Under the guidance of an acting engineer, Lieutenant McCarthy of the Fiftieth, the column stole forward in perfect silence, Colonel Williams of the Sixtieth leading with three companies of his own regiment and the light companies of the division; after which followed in succession Kempt's three battalions, Campbell's brigade, and the two Portuguese regiments of Champalimaud. Hearing the fire at San Roque, Picton began to suspect that he had been led astray. He drew his sword, and was only with difficulty prevented from cutting down the unfortunate McCarthy; but was appeased when he found that he had reached the first parallel, where Major Burgoyne of the Engineers was awaiting him.

The advanced party under Williams then passed on quietly to the Rivillas, and some at least of them had crossed the water by a mill-dam and lain down on the further bank, when a French sentinel in the covered way discharged his musket. Not realising that they were so close to the enemy, and thinking that they had been discovered, the leading men of the Sixtieth began firing; and the alarm was promptly given. A blast of grape and musketry was instantly turned upon the division and was presently concentrated upon the mill-dam, which was so narrow that the men could only cross it in single file. Confusion arose at once, for nine battalions were huddled together at this narrow causeway, with shot and shell tearing through them.

Picton was struck down for a time by a painful wound before he reached the passage; Kempt, who took over the command from him, was severely wounded in the act of passing, (So says *Wellington's despatch.* McCarthy would make this happen later, but his narrative is extremely confused); several soldiers had slipped off the dam, which was knee-deep in water, and were drowning; while the bearers of ladders and axes were overwhelmed by the press of the crowd behind them.

McCarthy, however, struggling forward, with the help of a few men broke down a paling which blocked the way, and hurried on with the ladders to the front between the bastions of San Pedro and San Antonio. (Belmas's account (iv.), and it explains why the first escalade failed). This was a mistake, for Wellington had expressly ordered the escalade to take place at the actual wall of the castle; and the consequences were soon apparent. Caught under the cross-fire from the two bastions, and overwhelmed by a deluge of shells, logs, heavy stones, cold shot, and other missiles from the top of the wall, the men were swept away as fast as they came to the ladders. Five of these with great difficulty were eventually manned, but four out of the five were soon broken at the top and slid away into the angle of the abutment; and the few brave soldiers who mounted the fifth were killed as soon as they reached the summit. For nearly three-quarters of an hour, it should seem, the Third Division struggled vainly to scale the wall, when at last they fell back baffled and took shelter behind a mound off the south-eastern angle of the castle.

Meanwhile the Fourth and Light Divisions had also opened their attack upon the breaches, their storming parties advancing from the quarries close to the foot of the glacis very soon after ten o'clock. Just before they moved off, the enemy threw out two or three fire-balls in their direction; and shortly afterwards a single musket-shot was fired, evidently as a signal, from the ramparts. In unbroken silence the British stole up the glacis to the edge of the ditch, planted their ladders and descended, the enemy observing their every motion but quietly biding their time.

Then suddenly, when the ditch was crowded, the French kindled the train of shells which had been laid in the breach; and with an appalling explosion most of the storming party of the Light Division were blown into the air. The ditch had been filled with overturned carts, barrows, damaged gabions and other obstacles; and these catching fire blazed up to light the defenders to their work. Philippon had reckoned that so terrible a slaughter would have daunted the comrades of the fallen; but on the contrary the main bodies of both divisions flew the more eagerly to the assault, neither knowing nor caring what dangers lay before them.

The excavation dug at the foot of the counterscarp made the descent into the ditch twice as high as the engineers had supposed, and being full of water caused the death of many by drowning. Moreover, by some unfortunate error, both divisions made for the same point instead of for two distinct openings, and, meeting opposite the unfinished ravelin outside the appointed bastion, mistook it for the breach. Swarming up the rude earthwork they came into full view of the enemy on the ramparts, and were swept away in scores and hundreds by a concentric fire of grape and musketry. The sharpshooters left on the glacis to keep down the fusillade of the defenders had been driven off by a raking fire from the bastions, and the French could mow down their assailants at their ease. Crowded together, blinded and bewildered, the stormers exhausted themselves in a series of gallant but futile rushes at the right and left breaches amid a very hell of bursting grenades and powder-barrels, and neglected, in the confusion, the centre breach which was the easiest of all.

Many brave men reached the summit, but were there stopped by sword-blades set deep in trunks of trees, and fell pierced by a score of bullets. One rifleman tried to creep beneath this obstacle, and was found next day with his head battered to pieces and his arms and shoulders riddled with bayonet thrusts, having given way not an inch but struggled forward to the last. And amid the wild yells and curses of the British rose the loud laughter of the French as they stood gallantly to their work and shouted the taunt, "Why don't you come into Badajoz?"

After vain endurance of a terrific fire for an hour the survivors of the two divisions fell back, and climbed up the ladders to the glacis; but here they met the Portuguese Reserve of the Fourth Division; and the whole rushed down once more into the ditch to snatch victory, if they could, from the mouth of the pit. All that impetuous valour could do was done. Officers exerted themselves again and again to lead parties up the breaches; and one of them, Lieutenant Shaw, stood up for some time alone after all who followed him had been struck down. Messenger after messenger came to Wellington in the quarries, bringing ever worse news; until at last as a climax arrived the report that no progress had been made, nor could be made, since nearly all the officers and vast numbers of the men were fallen. Thereupon the recall was sounded, and in sullen rage the survivors trooped back to the quarries. As the last stragglers came in, the clock in the cathedral tower peacefully tolled out the hour of twelve.

Major Stanhope, who was with Wellington at the time, has recorded that the miserable anxiety as to the issue of the assault made those two hours the most terrible that he ever passed. One faint hope only was left. There had been some sound of musketry and of cheering far away to the north-west, where Leith and the Fifth Division had been appointed to escalade. Amid all the tidings of failure Wellington remained cool and unmoved. When the last hopeless report came in from the divisions at the breaches, his jaw dropped, and his face, under the torchlight, seemed deadly pale; but it was with perfect calm and firmness that he laid his hand on the arm of Dr. M'Grigor, who stood by him, and said, "Go over immediately to Picton and tell him he must try if he cannot succeed in the castle." Then seeing that he had unwittingly addressed the wrong man, he apologised and left the order unrepeated. (Col. James Stanhope's MS. Journal and M'Grigor's *Autobiography* both give an account of this period of waiting. Stanhope says that there was no change in Wellington's countenance; but I prefer the evidence of the doctor, whose medical eye would be the more searching).

Meanwhile, however, Picton, having recovered from the first shock of his wound, had reached the foot of the castle wall some time after the failure of the first attack, and had tried a second venture for himself. His second brigade having come up and formed, Colonel Ridge and Ensign Canch of the Fifth moved two ladders for some distance to the right until they reached the place in the wall where the British had battered a breach in the previous siege. (Maxwell's *Peninsular Sketches*, i. When visiting Badajoz I selected by conjecture this point as the likeliest for the escalade, and, with this confirmation, do not hesitate to assert the fact). The damage had been repaired, but the wall at this point was considerably lower—twenty feet as against thirty feet high—than at the spot selected for the first escalade; and Ridge and Canch with the grenadiers of the Fifth at their heels, gained the summit almost if not quite unresisted.

The enemy was in fact surprised; and the Fifth, after dispersing a small hostile party, groped its way in the dark along the ramparts, and found a passage into the centre of the castle. Following this they came upon a column of French, which after the exchange of a few volleys gave way; whereupon the regiment, leaving Ridge mortally wounded behind it, drove the retreating enemy from post to post until they finally chased them from the castle. Here the pursuit was checked, for the French barricaded the outer gate by which they themselves had escaped, and though they had left the wicket open, they fired heavily on any who attempted to pass it. Picton therefore withdrew his men within the inner gate and waited. (It seems impossible to determine if Picton were present or not; some authorities saying that he was, others that he was not). Presently the march of troops was heard, and a voice demanded admission in English. Philippon had detached four companies of the 88th to recapture the castle, and these, joining their comrades who had just been expelled from the stronghold, had arrived under a crafty leader to make the attempt.

Picton, detecting the trick, opened the gate and received them with a volley and a charge, which effectually drove them back; but the outer entrance again had been barricaded, and there no egress was possible from the castle. Philippon in fact had made his preparations for holding this citadel in case the town should be captured; and, with such resources as Picton had at hand, it was impracticable for him to break the barriers down. He therefore resolved to secure his position and await the coming of daylight, sending information to Wellington of his success.

This joyful intelligence appears to have reached the commander-in-chief a few minutes after the scene with Dr. M'Grigor which has been already narrated; and so welcome was it that the staff gave way to a general cry of exultation. Wellington, however, without moving a muscle of his face, merely gave orders for the Fourth and Light Divisions to be prepared to renew their attack in the morning. Harry Smith, who was brigade-major of Barnard's brigade, on receiving this command said:

The devil! Why we have had enough; we are all knocked to pieces.

Happily, as shall be seen, the two mangled divisions were to be subjected to no such trial.

While all this was passing Leith had been the victim of a galling misfortune. Originally his attack had been designed only as a feint, and only by much entreaty had he persuaded Wellington to give him a few ladders. The officer, whose duty it was to guide these ladders from the Engineers' park to the Fifth Division, lost his way; and it was past eleven o'clock before Leith could start for his appointed station. A little before midnight he reached the bastion of San Vincente, where the three battalions of Walker's brigade were selected to lead the way. While yet on the glacis they were discovered by the enemy, and greeted with a heavy fire; but they pushed on undismayed.

First they had to beat down the palisade over the covered way, then to descend twelve feet from the summit of the counterscarp into the ditch, then to cross the ditch itself with its *cunette*, six feet wide and five feet deep, and finally to scale the wall of the scarp, of which the first twenty feet were perpendicular, and the next twelve feet so steeply inclined as to be barely possible of ascent. Notwithstanding a frontal fire of musketry and a flanking fire of artillery, Walker's soldiers triumphed over all obstacles and, in spite of many mishaps, succeeded, with the help of three or four ladders only, in driving the French from the summit and making good their own footing in the fortress.

Instantly reforming his brigade, Walker advanced southward along the ramparts, sending half of the Fourth regiment into the town to dislodge the enemy from some houses near the point of escalade. By hard fighting he mastered three bastions in succession; but in the third he fell desperately wounded; and the flame of a port-fire, added to the cry of "Mine," struck sudden panic into the brigade. They broke and turned; and a party of French, charging them with the bayonet, drove them headlong back to San Vincente. Here, however, Leith had stationed his second brigade in reserve; and the Thirty-Eighth with one volley blasted the pursuing enemy into annihilation. The entire division then marched in two columns towards the breaches, its bugles sounding the advance in all directions.

The detachment of the Fourth had found itself too weak to take the ramparts in reverse unaided, and had been driven back with some loss; but, when Leith's bugles were answered by Picton's, the French resistance seems to have collapsed, except on the outworks, with singular suddenness. The troops at the breaches, wrote the leading engineer on the French side, broke their arms and abandoned themselves to their fate on hearing of the fall of the castle; and the remnant of the Fourth and Light Divisions entered the fortress unopposed. At one o'clock Philippon with such few men as he could collect crossed the bridge into San Cristobal, whence he sent word to Soult by his cavalry of the fate of Badajoz. Five hours later at the summons of Lord Fitzroy Somerset he surrendered.

Then the assailants gave themselves up to an orgy of rape, drunkenness, and pillage. It seems certain that there were at least some officers of high rank who had promised their men the sack of the town; and a soldier of the Third Division has recorded that, after the prisoners had been secured, he and his comrades were allowed to enter the streets for the purpose of plunder. (Donaldson. *Eventful Life of a Soldier*). According to some accounts efforts were made in certain regiments to preserve order; but, be that as it may, it is undeniable that for a time the British Army in Badajoz was dissolved into a dangerous mob of intoxicated robbers. The soldiers sacked every house from cellar to garret; they fired indiscriminately upon the locks of doors, upon the inhabitants and upon each other; they threatened such officers as tried to restrain them; and they are said even to have discharged vinous salutes with ball cartridge about the person of Wellington himself.

As at Ciudad Rodrigo men were actually drowned in spirits, and many were killed or wounded while fighting for liquor or booty. Philippon himself with his two daughters only escaped outrage because they were escorted by two officers with drawn swords. Two Spanish ladies fled to the British camp to throw themselves on the chivalry of the officers, and happened by chance upon those of the Rifle Brigade. The younger of them, a girl of not more than fourteen, was so beautiful that every member of the mess appears to have fallen in love with her; but she was won by Harry Smith, who married her upon the spot and was destined to carry her with him to every part of the British Empire. She died in 1872, twelve years after her husband, leaving no children, but perpetuating her name in a South African township, which since the year 1900 has found a place upon many regimental colours. (*Juana's Story* by Juana Smith is one of three books contained in *Ladies of Waterloo* published by Leonaur).

On the 7th Wellington issued an order that it was high time for the plunder to cease. On the 8th he sent in the provost marshal with strong picquets to put a stop to the disorder, and Power's Portuguese brigade to form the garrison of the town; but the picquets were impotent, and the Portuguese proved themselves worse plunderers than those whom they were expected to repress. On the 9th therefore Power's brigade was kept under arms all day, and a gallows was erected in the principal square, when the sight of a few men hanging by their necks was efficacious in driving the last of the stragglers back to the camp. It is useless to waste words in condemning the behaviour of the troops, already ten times condemned, or to point out that it was triply condemnable seeing that Badajoz was a city of friends. Shots were certainly fired at the Fourth Foot by Spaniards as they entered the town, and he would be a hard judge who would blame them for it.

Moreover, it is idle to blink the fact that the British much preferred the French to the Spaniards, and that the French looked upon the British as friends compared to either Spaniards or Portuguese. Nor would it be far from the truth to add that the Spaniards loathed all three nations with an impartial hatred. French soldiers actually guided the British to the quarters where money or liquor was to be found; and it is probable that the bad characters of all four nations joined together heartily in barbarous maltreatment of the unhappy citizens. The only excuse for the men is that savage fighting had turned them all into wild beasts, and that few of them had seen either wine or wages for many weary weeks. Wellington's wrath was indescribable.

Stanhope wrote:—

He fulminates orders and will hardly thank the troops, so angry is he.

But thunder as he might he could not stop the riot for three full days. The twenty-one days of siege cost the Allies nearly five thousand killed and wounded, close upon four thousand of them being British and the rest Portuguese; and of this number almost exactly three-quarters fell in the assault. Six generals were wounded, Picton, Walker, Colville, Kempt, and Bowes of the British Army, Harvey of the Portuguese; and four battalion commanders were killed, Ridge of the Fifth, Gray of the Thirtieth, McLeod of the Forty-Third, and O'Hare of the Rifles—all of them excellent officers, McLeod in particular, who was but twenty-seven years of age, being of remarkable promise.

The Forty-Third and Fifty-Second were the regiments that had the most numerous casualties, the former losing three hundred and forty-seven, and the latter three hundred and twenty-three of all ranks killed and wounded; while the Rifle Brigade came next to them with a loss of two hundred and fifty-eight. But these were all three of them strong battalions, and the regiment which really suffered most severely was the Fourth, of Leith's division; for this battalion out of a total of at most five hundred and thirty of all ranks present lost two hundred and thirty killed and wounded. The five battalions of the Fourth Division also, as well as the Thirtieth and Forty-Fourth of the Fifth Division, were punished quite as heavily, in proportion to their numbers, as was the Light Division.

Speaking generally, it may be said that the men endured more than anyone could have expected of them, and that their behaviour at the assault was beyond all praise. The Fourth and Light Divisions, though cooped up in a confined space under an appalling fire, tried again and again to achieve the impossible, undismayed by the terrible havoc wrought among them, and by the maddening circumstance that they were unable to touch their enemies. While the assailants before the breaches were swept away by hundreds, French writers claim and there seems to be no reason to question their accuracy—that not twenty of the defenders were killed or hurt. Troops that will persist in fighting under conditions so disheartening must be animated by no common spirit.

It remains to consider whether this terrible slaughter could to any extent have been avoided or diminished. Wellington pleaded that the want of skilled workmen forbade him to follow the common rules of poliorcetics and to blow in the counterscarp, while the advance of Soult and the movements of Marmont rendered imperative an early capture of Badajoz at any cost. Both pleas must be admitted; and yet the fact remains that the assault upon the breaches, on which Wellington undoubtedly reckoned for success, was a failure so disastrous as to deserve characterisation as a blunder. The question then arises, Was the right quarter chosen in the first instance for the attack? Colonel Lamare, the senior French engineer in the place, afterwards averred—and the same view was commonly expressed by the garrison—that Wellington might have stormed Badajoz out of hand on the first night of the investment with less difficulty than he experienced after twenty-one days of siege.

But this amounts only to an opinion that, if the commander of the British had known as much of the condition of the fortress and garrison as did the commander of the French, he would have found his task greatly facilitated; and such a proposition, though undeniable, cannot be treated as serious criticism. Of greater weight is the undoubted fact that both Philippon and Lamare considered the front next to the castle as the weakest point in the defences, and that Burgoyne both before and after the siege maintained that, by opening a parallel four hundred yards from the castle wall, the place might have been taken in eight or ten days.

But, assuming that the first parallels were opened at the most advantageous point, was it reasonable to hope that the fortress could be stormed after the fashion prescribed to the Fourth and Light Divisions? Wellington was aware that the breaches had been retrenched; and it is probable that at the moment of the assault they were the strongest part of the lines. But as a matter of fact, not a single British soldier passed the summit of the breaches, so that the strength of the retrenchment was never tested. How was this? All who took part in the assault declared that the *chevaux de frise* of sword-blades moored fast to the ground made an impassable obstruction. The British engineers on the contrary declared that, having been erected after dark, these barriers could only have been attached to the earth by the extreme ends, and that consequently they could not have been firmly fixed and might have been swept away by the determined rush of any solid mass of men.

These officers seem to have been unaware that the *chevaux de frise* had been first placed on the breaches on the night of the 4th, carefully removed at dawn, and replaced after dusk of every subsequent day; so that the French workmen must have been expert in planting them rapidly and stably in position. To me, therefore, as to a far better judge, Napier, before me, this contention of the British engineers appears unsupportable. Whether these obstacles could have been blown to pieces by a continuous fire from the batteries, or by field-pieces, brought up to the glacis for the purpose with the storming party, is another question. All authorities agree that the British cannon were silent after four o'clock in the afternoon of the 6th; and many maintain that this respite enabled Philippon to make his breaches impregnable. Upon the whole, it should seem that neither Wellington nor his engineers appreciated the resource which a brave, highly-trained, and energetic commander might bring to bear upon the maintenance of his defences.

As regards the assaults of the Third and Fifth Division, it appears that neither Picton nor Leith were originally intended to deliver more than feint attacks, and that it was owing to their personal remonstrances that they were empowered to attempt a serious escalade. For some reason the credit of the fall of the fortress is generally assigned to Picton, but as a matter of fact quite as much praise, if not more, is due to Leith and to his gallant Brigadier, Walker. It was Leith who took the town, though it was Picton who, by mastering the citadel, frustrated Philippon's plans for prolonging the defence. In the matter of time it is certain that Picton's success came before Leith's; but the movements of the Third Division after they seized the castle are exceedingly obscure. Sometimes Picton appears to be in command, sometimes Campbell. Sometimes all the gates of the castle are so barricaded that the British cannot get out; sometimes they fly open by magic, the French come in and are driven out again; but the British never make an attempt to pursue them or to seize the gate, and the barriers once again are mysteriously closed.

All that is certain is that the Third Division after mastering the castle did not obey Wellington's orders to fall upon the rear of the defenders of the breach; and that, in fact, its influence upon the issue of the assault was moral and not physical. There may have been good reasons for this; for we know that Philippon had prepared the castle for isolated defence; and in the darkness and confusion outlets must have been troublesome to find and troops difficult to keep together. Still, after making all allowances, the comparative apathy of the Third Division in the castle is not easy to understand. In the matter of Leith's escalade, it seems clear that, but for the delay in bringing him his ladders, his attack would have weakened the defence at the breaches earlier and saved many hundreds of lives. That delay was due to carelessness, and that there should have been carelessness in respect of so important a matter is sufficient proof of the false calculations upon which the arrangements for the assault were founded.

But, after all has been said and all criticism has been passed, the storm of Badajoz remains and must always remain one of the great deeds of the British Army, one of those actions that show forth above others the might and prowess of the British soldier. Only those perhaps who have walked, whether within or without, round the ramparts of the fortress, little changed after the lapse of a century can realise how terrible must have been that struggle on the night of the 6th of April. The breaches have been long since built up, and the traveller sees only green turf on that space of one hundred yards square which in 1812 was red with British corpses.

But the grey walls of the castle and of the bastion of San Vincente still loom up stern and forbidding; and beneath them an Englishman may stand and picture, if he can, the wave of red-coats breaking against them under a hurricane of fire, leaping up in slender threads where the ladders were planted, falling back again shivered into spray, only to spring forward and leap up once more, and at the last to surge over the summit. And then he will marvel not less at the physical strength than at the desperate valour, which carried these soldiers over the wall. Their ladders were in most cases too short, and the stormers had to scramble up the masonry as best they could, hoisting each other upward from below, hauling each other upward from above by sheer muscular force, all under such a tempest of grape and musketry and bursting shells that a broken neck was the least of the risks to be run.

Only once before, perhaps, in the history of the army had British soldiers shown such utter contempt of death and such unconquerable resolution to master a hostile stronghold no matter at what cost; and that was at Ticonderoga in 1758. On that occasion their gallantry and devotion were expended in vain; at Badajoz they were seconded by a happier fortune, and victory was theirs, though at terrible cost. Small wonder that even the iron firmness of Wellington was broken down when he learned the number of the fallen, and that for the first time ever recorded of him he burst into a passion of tears.

CHAPTER 7

Hill and Almaraz

Wellington's original idea, in the event of the fall of Badajoz, had been to advance into Andalusia and drive Soult from that province; but the condition of Ciudad Rodrigo, thanks to Spanish procrastination and the advance of Marmont to the Coa, forbade him to indulge any such hope. It was a pity, for in the south matters were going well for the Allies. Soult's advanced guard had reached Villalba and Fuente del Maestre on the 7th, and his main body was actually on the march from Villafranca on the 8th, when tidings reached him from Philippon of the disaster that had befallen the French arms. Too weak in numbers to meet Wellington's army he fell back at once to Llerena, designing to retire still further towards Andalusia and choose a position where he could either offer battle, if the British should press him, or, in the contrary event, could recover the ground lost in the province. (Soult to Berthier, 8th April 1812. Ducasse, viii.)

Meanwhile he had heard that Penne Villemur and Morillo from Niebla and Ballesteros from Ronda were closing in upon Seville and had actually severed its communications with La Mancha, Granada, and Malaga. He therefore at once detached his brother's division of cavalry, two brigades of infantry, and the bulk of his artillery to cross the Guadalquivir at Lora del Rio; at the same time sending a brigade of dragoons, together with another of infantry, by a more direct route to Seville, in the hope of surprising the enemy before the city.

On the 9th, however, the Spaniards received warning of what was coming and withdrew, Penne Villemur and Morillo for Estremadura by Wellington's orders, and Ballesteros south-eastward upon Setenil de las Bodegas, whence he sent detachments to assail two French posts to the north, both of which attacks were beaten off with some loss on either side.

Then suddenly hearing that General Rey lay isolated with three battalions twenty-five miles to eastward at Alora, Ballesteros fell upon him by surprise on the 14th, and drove him back to Malaga with a loss of over one hundred men and two guns. The town of Malaga was in a high state of excitement, which might have proved fatal to Rey had not Maransin and Pierre Soult hastened to aid their comrade. Thereupon the Spanish commander retired once more to the mountains of Ronda.

Soult meanwhile had hurried to Seville, which he reached on the 11th; and d'Erlon was left with his own and Darricau's divisions of infantry and a division of dragoons at Llerena to screen the marshal's movements and observe those of the enemy. Wellington had every wish to impress his adversary with the idea that he meant to invade Andalusia; and accordingly Ponsonby's, (formerly Anson's; but Anson was at home on leave). brigade of Light Dragoons was pushed forward upon the heels of the retreating French, with the brigades of Le Marchant and Slade in support, the whole being under the command of Cotton. (*Slade's Brigade*: Royals; 3rd and 4th D.G. *Le Marchant's*: 3rd and 4th D.; 5th D.G. *Ponsonby's*, late Anson's: 12th, 14th, 16th L.D.). Graham received orders to bespeak rations for forty thousand men at Zafra and to spread reports everywhere of Wellington's coming; for a false rumour that Ballesteros had captured Seville had sent the whole country into transports of delight and even Graham nourished hopes that an energetic demonstration might compel the raising of the siege of Cadiz.

On the 10th, therefore, the brigades of Slade and Ponsonby being at Villafranca and Ribera and that of Le Marchant at Los Santos, Cotton rode out to Bienvenida, and, mounting the steeple of the church, ascertained that d'Erlon still occupied Llerena in force, having a strong body of cavalry bivouacked in a wood at Villagarcia some four miles in rear, that is to say to northward, of Llerena. After careful reconnaissance he directed Ponsonby to move forthwith on Usagre with the Twelfth and Fourteenth, and made arrangements for the concentration of all three brigades at Bienvenida one hour before daybreak of the morrow. Ere night, however, Cotton learned that the French had evacuated Villagarcia; whereupon, much troubled lest the enemy should escape him, he ordered Ponsonby to push two squadrons into the village next morning, and to send out patrols from thence to look for the French towards Berlanga, on the road to Cordova.

The two heavy brigades and the Sixteenth Light Dragoons were punctually assembled at Bienvenida before dawn of the 11th; and it then occurred to Cotton that, by deferring the advance of Ponsonby until Le Marchant's brigade should have had time to move round the enemy's rear, he might cut off the French cavalry from Llerena, and annihilate it. He sent an *aide-de-camp* to Ponsonby with instructions not to march until further orders, but too late; for Ponsonby's advanced squadrons had already driven in the French picquets from the hill before Villagarcia. Pushing back the enemy through the village, these squadrons came upon the main body of the French horse in the plain beyond, and were promptly chased in turn; whereupon Cotton sent Ponsonby forward again with the remainder of the Twelfth and Fourteenth, making six squadrons in all, to skirmish with the enemy in front, while he prepared a movement against their flank.

The French general, Lallemand, unable to see more troops than Ponsonby's six hundred sabres, joyfully fell into the trap; and, while he was manoeuvring against them, the Sixteenth rode forward to form on Ponsonby's right; Le Marchant's brigade passing over the hill still further to the right so as to come down unperceived upon Lallemand's left flank. As the reinforcements topped the rising ground, they perceived the Twelfth and Fourteenth on the plain retiring into a narrow defile between some stone walls, with Lallemand's horsemen about a quarter of a mile beyond them briskly advancing. The Sixteenth inclined to their left to join Ponsonby, who had faced his brigade about; but before they could attack, the Fifth Dragoon Guards came galloping up in single file across a ravine upon the left flank of the French, and, hastily reforming in a grove of olives, delivered their charge.

With horses weary after a long march and blown by a rapid movement over fully four miles of ground, the first onslaught of the Fifth was fruitless. The French, much superior in numbers, appear to have received them at the halt and to have beaten them back by the fire of carbines and pistols from the saddle. But the Fifth speedily rallied for a second charge; and now, to the amazement of Lallemand, who had counted upon a low stone wall to protect his front, the Sixteenth came trotting steadily down the hill, broke into a gallop at its foot, leaped the wall in line, and crashed straight into his ranks from the north, just as the Fifth sprang upon them from the west.

Utterly broken the French turned and fled with the British in pursuit; but Cotton presently halted his men to restore their formation; and Lallemand seized the opportunity to rally his troopers in rear of a wide ditch about two miles on the road to Llerena. Cotton thereupon detached two squadrons of the Sixteenth to turn the enemy's left, and charging their front with the Twelfth for the second time dashed them into headlong flight.

After this charge the pursuit was not checked until the British dragoons actually entered Llerena, when a few round shot from the French artillery which, with the whole of d'Erlon's infantry, was drawn up on the hill beyond the town, warned Cotton to retire. The loss of the French in prisoners alone amounted to four officers and one hundred and twenty-four men, so that their casualties altogether can hardly have fallen below two hundred. Those of the British did not exceed fifty-eight killed, wounded, and missing, forty of whom belonged to the Fifth Dragoon Guards, and the remainder to the three regiments of Light Dragoons; the Fourth Dragoons having but one man wounded, and the Third and Slade's brigade no losses at all.

Altogether it was a brilliant little affair, though less effective than it should have been. Cotton unjustly blamed Ponsonby for having marred a plan which was not communicated to him until too late; and experienced officers judged that Cotton himself was wrong to check the pursuit after the first charge, when the enemy, being in hopeless confusion, might have been far more heavily punished. But, it should seem that Wellington's scathing rebuke of the Thirteenth Light Dragoons after the affair of Campo Maior had made all his cavalry officers somewhat nervous about following up a success. (See Tomkinson; *Memoirs of Viscount Combermere*, i.; Cannon's *Records of the 5th D.G.*, and *Memoirs of a Dragoon*, a MS. sent to me by an officer of the 5th D.G. I have failed to find any French account, d'Erlon's report, Ducasse, viii., having gone astray. The French regiments engaged were the 2nd Hussars, 17th and 27th Dragoons. They lost, by Martinien's lists, three officers killed and wounded).

After the action d'Erlon retired with all his troops on the road to Cordova, whence Soult summoned him to join the main army. For the Marshal still expected Wellington to invade Andalusia, though he could hardly believe that the British Commander would commit the mistake of entangling his army in the Sierra Morena. Wellington, however, was for the present fully occupied with the movements of Marmont, who, as we have seen, had advanced upon Ciudad Rodrigo at the end of March with some twenty-six thousand men, carrying with him fifteen days' supplies, scaling ladders, and the material for making a bridge. Pursuant to Wellington's orders Trant and Wilson had some days earlier marched down with some six thousand militia to Lamego, so as to be ready to protect the magazines of the Allies on the Douro and Mondego; and Silveira with as many more was advancing slowly towards the same quarter.

But Wellington's directions had been drawn up on the assumption that both Almeida and Ciudad Rodrigo were proof against a sudden attack; and that Marmont, if faced by a respectable body of militia, would not venture to cross the Coa leaving these two strong places behind him. Herein the British general was deceived. The defences of Almeida were still so far from complete that the governor, Colonel Le Mesurier, in justifiable anxiety begged Trant to come to his assistance. Meanwhile on the 30th the French approached Ciudad Rodrigo, and on the following day reached the Agueda, when Marmont summoned the fortress, but, after throwing a few shells into it, and making some menace of an escalade, decided to leave a force to blockade it and to pass on.

But now happened an incident which Wellington could hardly have foreseen. Victor Alten, to whom together with the 1st German Hussars he had entrusted the delicate task of maintaining contact with Marmont's army and delaying its advance as much as possible, suddenly lost his head. Though the Agueda was passable at one ford only, Alten on the 1st of April deliberately abandoned that ford to two squadrons of French cavalry, and, retreating by rapid marches through Sabugal and Pedrogão, reached Castello Branco on the 6th of April. Carlos d'España, having only eight hundred infantry over and above the garrison of Ciudad Rodrigo, fell back at the same time to Fort Concepcion; but Marmont, having laid his bridge over the Agueda on the 3rd, pushed him out of this position and compelled him to retire upon Almeida. Near this place fortunately d'España ran into the arms of Trant, who had hurried down with a brigade of militia to the assistance of Le Mesurier; and Trant, dressing up some guides in scarlet coats, galloped with them to the fortress, whence, after a conference with the governor, he withdrew a troop of British cavalry which happened to be within the walls.

As night fell, he multiplied the fires about his bivouac, so as to give the impression that a large force was present; and Le Mesurier, making a sortie, drove in the French light infantry that encompassed him. As a matter of fact Marmont had despatched two divisions to storm Almeida without more ado; but the officer in command of this detachment, judging from all appearances that British troops were approaching, thought his position unsafe and moved up the Coa next morning to rejoin the marshal. Trant therefore sent back the troop of British cavalry to Le Mesurier, and proceeded towards Guarda to protect the magazines and hospital at Celorico.

Meanwhile Marmont, leaving one division to blockade Ciudad Rodrigo, had marched by Fuenteguinaldo for Alfaiates, where the two divisions from Almeida rejoined him, and thence pushed southward by Sabugal and Penamacor upon Castello Branco. While he was still from forty to fifty miles distant, Victor Alten again took the alarm; and, leaving Castello Branco on the 8th, he crossed the Tagus, in direct contradiction to Wellington's orders, on the following day at Villa Velha, and actually suggested the destruction of the bridge. Happily the Portuguese Colonel Le Cor, who was in command at Castello Branco, kept his wits about him. Driving back the advanced parties of the French, he withdrew the hospital and great part of the stores, and stood firm, until on the 12th he was compelled by an overwhelming force to evacuate the place.

Le Cor then destroyed such stores as had not been removed, and retired, not as had Alten to the other side of the Tagus, but a short seven miles along the road towards the river. He judged rightly, for on the morrow Marmont, having arrived at the fifteenth day since his departure from Salamanca, found himself in distress for supplies and began his retreat, scattering his troops far and wide to search for provisions. Trant, who since his arrival at Guarda had been joined by Wilson, now formed the bold project of surprising the marshal in his quarters at Sabugal, but was obliged to abandon it.

This was no misfortune, for Marmont had conceived the idea of surprising Trant at Guarda on the very same night, and indeed would have succeeded had he not been scared away by an accidental beating of drums. Trant therefore fell back; his militia, though raw levies, preserving good order in the face of the French cavalry, until the force began to cross the Mondego. At this point, however, the rear-guard, being hardly pressed and finding its cartridges useless owing to the pouring rain, took to its heels and carried panic and confusion into the main body, which none the less contrived ultimately to pass the river, though with considerable loss in prisoners, and to reach Celorico.

★★★★★★

Napier, doubtless following Trant, gives the number of the Portuguese prisoners at 200; Marmont states that they numbered 1500, that 5 colours were captured with them, and that 3000 men threw down their arms and ran. Napier adds that Marmont would not let his cavalry cut down the unhappy peasants, and that not a man was killed in the action.

★★★★★★

Here General Bacellar, who had now taken command, destroyed a quantity of powder and withdrew with Trant's people to Lamego. Wilson, on the other hand, remained at Celorico until his outposts were driven in by the enemy, when he gave orders for the magazines there to be destroyed; but this work had not been completed when the French retired, having news of the approach of a more formidable enemy.

Immediately upon ascertaining the retreat of Soult from Llerena, Wellington began on the 11th to set his army in motion for the north, taking first the precaution of sending Major Burgoyne to Villa Velha with orders to move the bridge of boats to a safe place, as soon as Marmont should reach Castello Branco. Victor Alten was also directed, not without rebuke, to recross the Tagus and return towards that place. On the 16th the Light Division, forming the advanced guard of the army, entered Castello Branco, by which time Marmont had concentrated the whole of his force, excepting the division left before Ciudad Rodrigo, between Sabugal and Penamacor. Heavy rains had flooded the Coa and the Agueda behind him, and had carried away his bridges over the latter river, which rendered his position far from comfortable; for now his only way of retreat was by the headwaters of the Agueda, and, while he was taking this circuitous route, Wellington might pass the bridge of Ciudad Rodrigo with superior numbers and cut him off from Salamanca.

He was, however, unaware of his danger, judging that the Allies were in no great strength in his front. Moreover, the weather affected the movements of the British as much as those of the French. Wellington was unwilling to allow his troops to bivouac in the incessant rain, and there was not space in the cantonments to north of the Tagus to shelter more than one division at a time. He therefore abandoned any idea of a rapid advance in force, and brought the rear divisions across the Tagus one at a time, frequently halting those in the front to accommodate this movement. Thus it was that on the 19th the Light Division was still but eight miles beyond Castello Branco, and the Third Division in line with it a little to the westward. On that day fugitive Portuguese militiamen brought in wild rumours that Trant had suffered a disaster at Guarda, which news was shortly afterwards corrected by a true report of his reverse from Trant himself.

Meanwhile Marmont had begun to retire; and on the 20th the outposts of the Light Division were at Penamacor. On the 22nd the British patrols entered Alfaiates and ascertained that the enemy had

143

left it on the same morning, pointing eastward for the headwaters of the Agueda and the bridge of El Villar. The leading divisions of the French had as a matter of fact already begun the passage of the river at those points; but in the course of the next day their bridge above Ciudad Rodrigo was repaired in time for the rear divisions to use it. By the 24th Wellington, being satisfied that Marmont was in full retreat for the Tormes, halted the whole army; and on the following day the marshal re-entered Salamanca. So ended with brilliant triumph for the British commander the spring campaign of 1812. (*Wellington Desp.* To Graham, 18th, 20th, 21st, 22nd, 24th April; to Liverpool, 24th April; to Alten, 18th April 1812. Ducasse. *Mém. du Roi Joseph*, viii.)

That the disasters of the French were due to Napoleon's perseverance in attempting to direct from Paris the operations in Spain, there can I think be no doubt, in spite of Napier's unconvincing declamation to the contrary. Orders which cannot reach commanders in the field until the conditions which they are designed to meet have ceased for three weeks to exist, must inevitably work mischief, were they issued by a hundred Napoleons. Napier defends the emperor's plan of weakening Marmont's army in order to strengthen Suchet's, on the ground that Valencia was the most important point at the moment, and therefore that upon which the main strength of the French should have been concentrated. But was Valencia the most important point at that or at any other moment after Wellington landed in 1809? Never. Wherever the British Army might be, there was the heart of the struggle in the Peninsula; and Napoleon was far too great a man to be unaware of it. But he had entangled himself in designs beyond full comprehension even by his gigantic intellect, and, being unable to make them square with existing facts, he sought to overcome the difficulty by substituting for facts such fiction as would best square with his designs.

And herein his greatest error lay, perhaps, less in the ascription of imaginary weakness to his enemy's force and of imaginary strength to his own, than in his assumption that war would everywhere support war. We have seen that in his sober moments he awoke to the fallacy of this postulate, so far at any rate as Portugal was concerned; but he suffered himself to be deceived by it once more whenever the truth proved inconvenient.

This was, after all, the system upon which the wars of the French Revolution at large had been carried out; and his own surpassing success in the field had been due chiefly to masterly reassembling of hosts, previously scattered for purposes of subsistence, upon the field of decisive combat. But, after the desolation wrought by four years of waste and warring in most parts of the Peninsula, concentration had become impossible without magazines, and advance in force impossible without means of transport. Wellington being aware of this took his measures accordingly, and was lord of the situation, for the simple reason that he could move and his enemy could not.

So much for the broad causes which brought about the early mishaps to the French arms in 1812. As to the minor details outside the scope of Napoleon's orders, it is unprofitable to discuss whether the responsibility for the fall of Ciudad Rodrigo should be fastened upon Dorsenne, owing to the weakness of the garrison and the inefficiency of the governor whom he had installed in the place; or upon Joseph, who, according to Marmont's statement, squandered provisions which should have filled magazines for the Army of Portugal and enabled it to take the field earlier. Beyond all question the storming of the fortress after twelve days of siege took every French general in Spain by surprise, and would probably have been equally unforeseen by Napoleon had he been in the country. It was a stroke after the Great Captain's own heart, swift, sudden, defiant of all rules, boldly sacrificing men in lieu of time. The loss of Badajoz stands in a different category. This misfortune undoubtedly would have been averted if Marmont and Soult had been left free to combine their operations without the emperor's interference.

But it is idle to contend with Napier that, if Marmont had followed Napoleon's orders, the disaster would not have occurred; for those orders presupposed either that the marshal had supplies and transport—which he had not—or that the country over which he had to advance was not a desert—which it was. Nevertheless it must be conceded that Marmont, to use Wellington's phrase, made but a feeble effort; and it is perfectly true that he disliked the advance into Beira, expected no good from it, and was not displeased when that expectation was realised. It is very probable that a bold assault upon either Ciudad Rodrigo or Almeida might have succeeded; but Marmont could not divine that neither fortress was in a condition to offer a stout resistance, any more than Wellington could have guessed that Badajoz might have been easily stormed on the first day of investment.

It is not true that, as Napier asserts, Marmont had at this crisis sixty thousand fighting men present with the eagles. He had only fifty-two thousand, of whom fifteen thousand were required for Asturias, for garrisons and for the security of the lines of communication. (Returns of 15th April 1812 in *Archives de la Guerre*. Where Napier finds his returns of the same date in the Appendix to his 4th volume I do not know. Neither these figures nor those of 1st Oct. 1811 agree with those which I transcribed in detail with my own hand in Paris).

Upon arrival at Salamanca Marmont again put his troops into cantonments, keeping them as closely assembled as difficulties of subsistence would permit. Foy's division was in the valley of the Tagus; Clausel's at Avila; Percy's at Valladolid and on the Douro; Sarrut's at Toro; Maucune's at Salamanca; Brenier's at Medina del Campo; Thomières's at Zamora; Bonnet's in Asturias; the light cavalry division between the Tormes and the Douro; and the division of dragoons at Rio Seco. By this arrangement Marmont reckoned that the entire force, excepting the divisions of Foy and Bonnet, could be concentrated at Salamanca within five days. Soult likewise cantoned his army, keeping his head-quarters at Seville, and d'Erlon's division in the district of La Serena, with its right flank resting on the Guadiana at Villanueva. He was still wholly impotent from want of provisions for his army.

Wellington followed the example of his enemies, dispersing his army over an immense front from São João da Pesqueira on the Douro in the north almost to the Sierra Morena in the south; his head-quarters from the 25th of April onwards being fixed at Fuenteguinaldo. The troops were drawn back as close to their magazines as possible, so that the transport of the army might be devoted wholly to the replenishing of the magazines and strong places with supplies. The disposition was, of course, vicious, and, as Wellington said, not such as could have been attempted in any other war; but it was excused, first, by absolute necessity, and, secondly, by the extreme improbability that the French would ever find out anything about it.

It seemed now more than ever hopeless to count upon the Spaniards for any concerted operation, even for one so simple as the victualling of a fortress. Wellington had relied on Abadia to make some diversion in Galicia during his absence before Badajoz; but nothing appreciable had been done. He had definitely ordered Carlos d'España to break down the bridge on the Agueda if pressed back by the French; but the Spanish general had omitted to obey, and through this neglect Marmont had gained two days on his march into Beira.

The advantage of these two days, heightened as it was by the misconduct of Victor Alten, had led to the evacuation of Castello Branco and the destruction of the magazines there, which now of course must be refilled. Finally d'España's slackness in repairing and revictualling Ciudad Rodrigo proved to be part of a general design of the Spanish Government to make the British supply the garrisons and take responsibility for the safety both of that place and of Badajoz. Wellington firmly declined to spare a single man, British or Portuguese, for either stronghold, and clinched the matter by warning the Spanish Government that, unless they took suitable measures to furnish and maintain proper garrisons for these two fortresses, he would destroy them both. Yet even so it was not until the 9th of May that he heard that a regiment had at last arrived at Ayamonte to form part of the garrison of Badajoz. (*Wellington Desp.* To H. Wellesley, 3rd May; to Graham, 4th May; to Colonel Austen, 9th May 1812).

In the midst of these cares, however, there was still one project which he now thought ripe for execution, namely, the destruction of the French bridge and bridgehead at Almaraz, which he had prescribed to Hill so long ago as in January but had then been compelled to abandon. The enterprise was now the more desirable inasmuch as Soult's pontoon-train had been captured in Badajoz, so that to all intent the boat-bridge laid down by Marmont at Almaraz furnished the only communication between the French armies north and south of the Tagus between Toledo and the Portuguese frontier.

On the 30th of April warning was sent to Hill that this operation would shortly be expected of him; and on the 4th of May Wellington ordered the First and Sixth divisions under Graham to Portalegre to avert any possible dash of the enemy upon Badajoz. On the 12th of May Sir Rowland marched with Howard's brigade of infantry, part of Wilson's brigade, Ashworth's Portuguese brigade, and the Thirteenth Light Dragoons, in all some six thousand men, leaving the rest of his division under the command of Sir William Erskine at Almendralejo.

★★★★★★

Oman conjectures that an intercepted letter of Marmont to Jourdan, dated 30th April, prompted Wellington to press this operation at this moment, but the date seems to vitiate this conjecture. Unfortunately none of Wellington's papers bear the date of their receipt, so that certainty upon this point is impossible.

Howard's Brigade: 50th, 71st, 92nd, 1 co. 5/60th.
Wilson's Brigade: 28th, 34th, 1 co. 5/60th.
Ashworth's Brigade: 6th and 18th Portuguese inf.; 6th Caçadores (5 batts.).

★★★★★★

On the same day he was met at Merida by two companies of artillery, British and Portuguese, from Elvas, with six heavy cannon and three fieldpieces, and by a party of engineers with a train of pontoons. Crossing the Guadiana at Merida, where the bridge had been repaired by the British engineers, he entered Truxillo on the 15th, and, dropping all baggage at that place, proceeded next day to the foot of the Sierra de Mirabete near Jaraicejo. Soult, having early tidings of his advance from d'Erlon, and being positively informed by his officers that most of Wellington's troops—and in particular Wellington himself—had returned to Elvas, made up his mind that the long-threatened invasion of Andalusia was coming at last.

Reckoning that he would be inferior to his enemy by twenty thousand men, and that Ballesteros would move out from the mountains of San Roque immediately his back was turned, Soult became seriously alarmed, and appealed to Joseph that he should send reinforcements to the Army of the South, and should give orders to Marmont to manoeuvre in the valley of the Tagus against Wellington's left flank. On the 16th d'Erlon reported that Hill was advancing with fifteen to eighteen thousand men and eighteen guns upon Miajadas, pointing for Almaraz; from which Soult inferred that, as soon as Sir Rowland had mastered the bridge at that point, Wellington would come down with all his force upon the Army of the South. The marshal felt confident, however, that Marmont would have marched with all his troops for the Tagus, as he ought, in Soult's opinion, to have done long ago, so that he had some hope of a decisive battle which would settle the fate of Spain for ever. These speculations form an instructive commentary upon Wellington's assurance in scattering his army along a front of nearly two hundred miles. (*Arch. de la Guerre*. Soult to Joseph, 15th, 19th May 1812).

The fortifications constructed by Marmont for defence of the bridge of boats at Almaraz were formidable. On the north bank of the river stood Fort Ragusa, a pentagonal work containing a magazine of supplies and stores, which though unfinished was exceedingly strong, having in its centre a kind of citadel in the form of a loopholed stone tower, twenty-five feet high, and being flanked by a field-work near the bridge. On the south bank was the bridge-head itself, revetted with masonry; and upon a height overlooking it was Fort Napoleon, a redoubt constructed for four hundred and fifty men, of which the ditch was deep, but with a scarp which rose by two steps instead of sheer to the summit, and consequently was not difficult of ascent.

The rear of the redoubt was strongly retrenched, with a palisaded ditch and a loop-holed tower, as in Fort Ragusa, for citadel, so that this inner fortification was still capable of resistance after the outer enclosure had been captured. The principal approach to the bridge by the main road from Truxillo had likewise been placed in a state of defence. About six miles south of the bridge this road climbs the Sierra de Mirabete, a range so rugged that wheeled vehicles cannot move except on the highway; and at the summit of the pass the French had surrounded an old castle with a rampart twelve feet high, and had mounted seven or eight guns within it.

Beyond this again were two small works connecting the tower with a large house close to the road, which the French had likewise fortified, so that the whole formed a strong line of defence across the pass. There was another pass, that of La Cueva, two to three miles to east of Mirabete, with a fair road up the southern slope, which degenerated into a mere goat's path as it descended upon the village of Romangordo on its way to Almaraz. The problem set to Hill was to overcome all these difficulties and to destroy the bridge.

Having halted near Jaraicejo till the evening of the 16th, he marched off at nightfall in three columns. The left or westernmost of these three, consisting of the Twenty-Eighth, Thirty-Fourth, and the 6th Caçadores under General Chowne, (formerly Tilson), was to carry the castle of Mirabete; the centre column, made up of the two remaining Portuguese regiments and all the artillery, was to follow the main road and attack the defences of the pass; and the right column, Howard's brigade under command of Hill himself, was to bear eastward and descend by the pass of La Cueva upon Almaraz. The first and last of these columns were both of them provided with scaling-ladders, axes and petards, and it was hoped that they would reach their destination before dawn. This hope was frustrated. So long and difficult were the roads that the coming of day found all three of the columns still far from their striking points; and Hill realised that all idea of a surprise must be abandoned.

Throughout the 17th and 18th Sir Rowland sought in vain for some other passage by which he could bring his artillery down to Almaraz, for the castle and its dependent works were situated upon a hill so precipitous that it was hopeless to think of taking them by storm. Then, finding that the garrisons were still quiet and unsuspicious, he decided to leave his guns on the mountain for a false attack on the castle, and attempt to escalade Fort Napoleon and the bridge-head with his infantry only. Accordingly at nine o'clock on the evening of the 18th Howard's brigade, reinforced by the *Caçadores* and a single company of the Sixtieth, began their march over the pass of La Cueva, carrying their ladders, now shortened to sixteen feet, with them. The head of the column halted before dawn behind some heights half a mile from Fort Napoleon; but such were the difficulties of the road that the men were scattered over the hill like sheep, and the rear did not close up until eight o'clock.

Meanwhile as soon as it was light Chowne, according to preconcerted arrangements, had opened a cannonade at long range upon the castle of Mirabete; and the entire garrison of Fort Napoleon was crowded on the parapet watching the proceedings with no apparent suspicion of any nearer danger. Yet the French had had warning of the approach of the British; and Major Aubert, who was in command, had strengthened the garrison of the fort and taken up two of the centre boats of the bridge. Hence when the Fiftieth and a wing of the Seventy-First suddenly sprang into sight and came rushing over the plain, the enemy was ready for them, and the guns of Fort Ragusa and the musketry of Fort Napoleon made havoc in their ranks. Undismayed, the assailants in three several columns flew upon their prey, and leaping into the ditch found their ladders too short for the escalade. Under a shower of missiles of every description they spliced two ladders together; scrambled up the first step of the scarp, which by chance was unduly broad, pulled their ladders after them, ran up to the rampart and closed hand to hand with the garrison.

Aubert was wounded; the French gave way before stress of numbers; and the whole struggling mass of assailants and defenders surged into the retrenchment. The enemy, now panic-stricken, made no attempt to defend the tower, but fled to the bridge-head. Yet here also their pursuers were as quick as they, and driving them from this stronghold as well, hunted them on even to the gap in the bridge and so to a watery death. For a few minutes Fort Ragusa opened fire upon Fort Napoleon; but the British gunners speedily answered with the captured cannon; and the garrison on the other side of the river, catching the infection of panic, streamed hurriedly out of the entrenchments and retreated in disorder upon Naval Moral. The whole affair had lasted little more than forty minutes.

Immediately after the evacuation of Fort Ragusa some men of the Ninety-Second swam the river, and brought back boats for the repair of the bridge, which enabled that work to be occupied forthwith.

The fortifications were abundantly furnished with supplies; and Hill's soldiers, who for three days had received only double allowance of beef in lieu of bread, feasted sumptuously upon every kind of delicacy washed down with abundance of wine. The towers and magazines were then blown up, a German officer of artillery unfortunately perishing in the explosion through some accident; and, the troops having recrossed the river from Fort Ragusa, the bridge was hauled over to the southern bank and burned.

The store-houses were likewise set on fire, and, before night fell, the force retired to the pass of La Cueva, leaving only a small party to complete the work of destruction, which was accomplished on the following day. Two hundred and fifty-nine prisoners were taken; and the total loss of the French can hardly have fallen below four hundred. That of the assailants amounted to thirty-three killed and one hundred and forty-four wounded, twenty-eight of the killed and one hundred and ten of the wounded belonging to the Fiftieth Regiment alone. The whole enterprise was brilliant in the audacity alike of its conception and of its execution, and highly creditable both to the troops and to Hill. (Narratives of the affair of Almaraz will be found in Hill's despatch, *Wellington Desp.*, v.; Jones's *Sieges*, i.; *Adventures of Capt. Patterson*; and *Journal of a Soldier of the 71st*).

Sir Rowland now prepared to reduce the works of Mirabete with his heavy guns, there being to all appearance nothing that could hinder him. Foy, warned of the danger of Almaraz on the night of the 17th, had ordered General Chemineau to march thither in all haste with the 6th Light; but that officer, meeting the fugitives as he was leaving Naval Moral on the evening of the 19th, took fright and fell back to Oropesa. Soult, again, was so convinced that he would shortly be attacked by Wellington in force that he could think of nothing else. But d'Erlon, acting upon his own responsibility, had pushed in the British outposts at Medellin and Robera on the 17th and 18th; and Erskine, losing his head, cried out that Soult's entire army was upon him.

Graham thereupon marched his two divisions into Badajoz; Hill, fearful of being cut off, on the 21st retired to Truxillo; and the works of Mirabete were left unmolested. Marmont moved Clausel's division to the Tagus to enable Foy to relieve the garrison at the castle, which that officer duly did on the 23rd. Thus this isolated post, which, if Erskine had not given way to groundless panic, should in Wellington's view have been swept away with loss to the enemy, was left intact. The commander-in-chief was intensely annoyed, he wrote:—

> Notwithstanding all that has passed, I cannot prevail upon the general officers to feel a little confidence in their situations. They take alarm at the least movement of the enemy; and then spread the alarm and interrupt everything.

It is not surprising that Erskine's timidity, following immediately upon that of Victor Alten, should have drawn from Wellington this scathing criticism. (*Wellington Desp.* To Liverpool, 28th May. *Archives de la Guerre*. Soult to Joseph, 26th May; Girod de l'Ain, *Vie du General Foy*).

Still the bridge had been destroyed, and thereby the communication between the Armies of Portugal and of the South had been thrust back to the bridge of Toledo—a pretty stroke to finish off the work that had been begun at Ciudad Rodrigo and Badajoz. It may be imagined that the French commanders were profoundly affected by this succession of misfortunes; but they were helpless against them. Foy wrote:—

> I know that in case of an attack by the enemy the place for my division is in the vicinity of Almaraz. But how can I move my troops in a desert, when for several days they have not received even half a ration of bread, and when the prospect of seeing bread come to us grows more remote?

The complaints of Marmont and Soult were precisely the same. Their men were in the greatest distress for victuals, and could only be kept alive by dispersion over a wide area until harvest should come. Meanwhile Wellington, having both supplies and transport, could march about the country and work mischief practically without hindrance. He had triumphed, in fact, less by the art of war than by the science of organisation; and he had every intention of pushing the system further. The possession of Ciudad Rodrigo and Badajoz enabled him, though his main source of supply was still the sea, to push his advanced bases forward to the Portuguese frontier; and, since he could not spare his transport always to fill the magazines at these bases, he decided to facilitate communications by improving the navigation of the Douro and the Tagus. After many difficulties the channel of the former was opened as far as the Spanish frontier at Barca d'Alva, and of the latter as far as Alcantara; and, one hundred miles of dreary hauling over bad roads being thus avoided, supplies and stores were brought through Portugal to Spain at an immense saving of labour and expense.

This most important work Wellington supplemented by another, purely military rather than administrative, for shortening the line of communication between his own corps and Hill's by the restoration of the damaged bridge of Alcantara. The height of the bridge being fifty yards and the width of the gap thirty yards, the task was one of great difficulty; but all obstacles were overcome by the ingenuity of Major Sturgeon of the Royal Staff Corps. (I may repeat here that the Royal Staff Corps were the Engineers of the commander-in-chief, as distinct from the Royal Engineers, who were the Engineers of the Master of the Ordnance). This very remarkable officer, of whom we shall see more, conceived the idea hitherto unknown in Europe, though long converted into practice in the East of stretching cables across the chasm, and laying upon them a network of stout ropes, strong enough to bear the weight even of heavy cannon. In other words he improvised the first suspension-bridge ever seen in Europe out of materials found in the fortress of Elvas. The whole of these materials were transported in sections to Alcantara in seventeen carts, before any one could guess at their significance, and were there put together under his direction, with perfect success. Thus the long march to Villa Velha was avoided and the distance from Estremadura to Beira shortened by the best part of one hundred miles.

With these facilities and with Ciudad Rodrigo and Badajoz at his back, Wellington could choose for himself whether he should move against Salamanca in the north, against Madrid in the centre, or against Seville in the south; and could keep his enemies in doubt to the last moment as to the line that he should select. But before following him through the campaign of the summer of 1812, it is necessary to take note of affairs in other parts of Europe, and in other quarters of the Peninsula.

CHAPTER 8

The Peninsula 1812

On the 9th of May, 1812, Napoleon left Paris for Dresden, the first stage of the journey which was to end at Moscow. A general account has already been given of the arrangements which he had made for the prosecution of his affairs in Spain during his absence, and in particular of the committal of the chief command to his brother Joseph; and, since his orders had by the end of April had time to take effect, it will be convenient at this point to examine them in closer detail.

First, as to the reorganisation of the armies, all Polish troops and the greater part of the Imperial Guard were, as we have seen, withdrawn from the Peninsula for service in the Russian campaign; and the remainder were re-grouped as follows:

The Army of Aragon was reconstituted as the Third Corps or Army of Valencia, and was reduced to three divisions of infantry—those of Musnier, Harispe, and Habert—together with Boussard's brigade of cavalry, and a due proportion of artillery; the rest being transferred, as will be seen, to the Ebro. It numbered close upon twenty-two thousand men, exclusive of four thousand sick, and was entrusted to Suchet.

The Army of Catalonia was also reduced at first to fifteen thousand effective men, but was eventually increased, by the addition of Reille's division from Suchet's army, to twenty-five thousand; and the supreme command, civil and military, in Catalonia was vested in General Decaen.

A more ambitious change was the formation of a new corps called the Army of the Ebro, under the command of General Reille, with a nominal strength, on paper, of forty-three thousand men. For this purpose the reserve was moved from France into Spain, and raised, by the incorporation of Severoli's Italians and Frere's French division from Suchet's force, to a total of thirteen to fourteen thousand effective men. But this army was broken up almost as soon as created. The number had been reduced by the transfer of Reille's division to De-caen, and of Palombini's to the Army of the North, and it can hardly be said to have enjoyed an independent existence at all. Still the duties prescribed to it were sufficiently onerous, namely, to keep order in Catalonia, to look to the victualling of Barcelona, to protect Aragon, and to maintain communication through Valladolid with the Army of Portugal, through Madrid with the Army of the Centre, and of course southward with the Army of Valencia.

The Army of the North was likewise remodelled. It was ordained that this should consist, besides cavalry, of three divisions of infantry, namely, that of Caffarelli, a second to be taken from Marmont, and a third drawn in part from regiments in France and in part from the Army of the Centre, with a total strength of some thirty-five thousand nominal, or thirty thousand effective men. Marmont, on receiving the order to detach a division, selected that of Bonnet, for which Napo-leon took him sharply to task, ordering that these troops should be sent to Asturias. Ultimately the emperor decided to weaken Marmont no further; and Suchet was directed to send Palombini's Italians to the Army of the North instead of to Reille; whereby Caffarelli's force, be-ing allowed also to retain two regiments of the Guard and some Na-tional Guards under Dumoutier, was raised to its appointed numbers. (*Arch, de la Guerre.* Berthier to Dorsenne, 18th Feb.; to Suchet, 18th Feb. 1812. *Corres. de Napoléon).*

After all these arrangements, Marmont was left with about fifteen thousand effective men for the Army of Portugal; Joseph with about eighteen thousand—one third of them Spaniards—for the Army of the Centre; and Soult with about fifty-six thousand for the Army of the South, (after the fall of Badajoz, 51,000), making a general total of about two hundred and thirty thousand troops fit for duty in the French armies at large.

★★★★★★

I am aware that these numbers do not quite agree with those given by Napier in his appendix to vol. v.; but mine are drawn, as were his, from the Imperial muster rolls, copied with my own hand in detail. The figures given by Ducasse, viii. confirm mine. The details of reorganisation are drawn from returns in the *Ar-chives Nationals*, and from Berthier's letters to Suchet, Dorsenne, and Reille, of 26th Jan. 1812, in *Arch, de la Guerre.* See also *Cor-res, de Napoléon.*

★★★★★★

The purport of these dispositions was evidently to secure the line of communication with France, and to extinguish the insurgent bands which threatened it; no fewer than ninety thousand men being assigned practically to this duty alone from Tarragona to Oviedo. In fact Napoleon's parting message to Joseph prescribed the maintenance of the most direct communications with France as his most important duty, and forbade any offensive entry into Portugal unless rendered absolutely necessary by circumstances. The preservation and extension of conquests (such was the drift of this final instruction) was of course to be a principal object; but continued warfare upon the guerilla-bands was still more imperative, and the attitude of the French troops towards the British Army was to be a strict but imposing defensive. The emperor's idea appears to have been that Joseph should content himself merely with minor operations, for the purpose of establishing such security as would ensure a victorious advance of the Grand Army into Spain upon its return from Russia. (Clarke to Joseph, 12th May 1812. *Arch, de la Guerre*, partly printed in Ducasse, viii.)

The plan, supposing it to have been practicable, was no doubt a sound one; but it was utterly upset by Wellington's assumption of the offensive. The dislocation of the French armies, which was not accomplished without innumerable orders and counter-orders, came just at the wrong time, and was, as we have seen, in itself a source of embarrassment to the generals. The guerillas in the north did not fail to take advantage of the opportunity, being encouraged by the active help of Sir Howard Douglas, the British commissioner at Coruña. It was indeed the principle of that very able officer to aid the guerillas rather than the Spanish regular troops with arms and money; and with the assistance of a small squadron under Sir Home Popham, which had been sent at his request to the coast, he maintained the various bands in high activity. He was confirmed in this course by the discovery that the Spaniards contemplated embarking part of their regular force at Coruña for the reconquest of South America, and sending with them the muskets and artillery which had been supplied by England for the defence of their hearths and homes.

Douglas intervened effectively to put a stop to this folly; and meanwhile Mina and other chiefs gained success after success in Navarre, the Basque provinces and Upper Leon. On the 11th of January Mina and General Mendizabal overthrew a column of two thousand men under General Abbé at Sanguesa, killed six hundred men—having sworn to give no quarter—and captured two guns. At the end of February Don Benito Marquinez killed two hundred French dragoons and captured fifty more, at a point lest than forty miles north-east of Valladolid. On the 11th of March Mina met a French column of over two thousand men, once again at Sanguesa, and defeated it, inflicting a loss of nine hundred men. On the 9th of April he crowned all previous efforts by surprising at Arlaban a large convoy which was going north under escort of a Polish regiment of fifteen hundred men and four hundred French from various corps, destroyed or captured four to five hundred of the troops, and carried off two colours and every waggon of the convoy.

★★★★★★

Mina in his letter of 11th April to Howard Douglas (Record Office, W.O. i. 262) gives the French casualties at 600 killed, 500 wounded, and 150 prisoners. Dorsenne (Ducasse, viii.) states them at 150 killed and 68 wounded. A letter from General L'Huillier to Berthier of 16th April (*Arch, de la Guerre*) numbers the officers at 11, a figure confirmed by Martinien's list, and the men at 365. The regiment was the 7th Polish.

★★★★★★

Shortly afterwards he narrowly escaped death owing to the treachery of a subordinate; and towards the end of May his activity was checked for a time by a wound received in action against General Abbé.

In Santander, Biscay and Guipuzcoa such leaders as Longa, Porlier and Campillo wrought mischief on a smaller scale but continuously upon the French; and about Burgos the priest Merino was indefatigably energetic and troublesome. It was said that no reinforcements on their way to the Armies of the North or of the Centre entered the town without being employed against Merino and his band before they were allowed to proceed. It was he who, just a week after Mina's victory at Arlaban, rivalled it by surprising a French column of about a thousand men at Peñeranda de Duero, and routing it completely; after which he hanged sixty of his prisoners in revenge for the execution of members of the Junta of Burgos by the French. (These troops again seem to have been Polish, for Martinien gives a list of 10 officers of the 4th Regiment of the Legion of the Vistula wounded in this affair).

Still further to the east, General Duran on the 28th of May swooped suddenly upon Tudela, destroyed a number of guns which had been sent there by Suchet, and captured a quantity of arms and one hundred prisoners. Moreover on the 14th of June (to anticipate matters a little) he escaladed Aranda de Duero, and drove the French from it with the loss of three hundred killed and wounded.

In Lower Catalonia, as we have seen, the French gained a signal victory over Eroles at Altafulla on the 28th of January; but that indomitable leader, together with his companions Sarsfield, Milans, and Rovira, soon made his presence felt in spite of the defeat. Twice towards the end of January Rovira beat off with considerable loss the attacks of French columns on the upper waters of the Fluvia. On the 30th of the same month General Milans threw himself across the front of a French column, five thousand strong, under General Lamarque, which was marching from Barcelona by the coast for the Ampurdan. Four British ships cannonaded the French from the sea as they moved, but Lamarque, notwithstanding some loss, forced his way into Mataro, where he halted for two days in the deserted town under continual fire from the British squadron.

On the 2nd of February he resumed his northward movement, turned inland to avoid the broadsides of the British cruisers, and found himself harassed on the other flank by Milans. With great difficulty he struggled on for yet forty-eight hours, when, the Spanish commander being obliged to return to Mataro for supplies, he was at last left free to continue his advance, having lost five hundred killed and wounded in the five days of fighting. In the course of this same week, moreover, one of Rovira's lieutenants surprised and almost annihilated a column of five hundred French between the frontier and Figueras.

On the 14th of February Sarsfield made a raid into France from Puigcerda, overthrew a French battalion which tried to check him, and, after levying contributions on the towns of Tarascon and Foix on the Ariège, returned on the 19th to Puigcerda with two thousand head of cattle and sheep, having suffered no further loss than that of a few men wounded. He had intended to come back by the valley of Aran, some seventy miles to westward as the crow flies; and to ensure his safe retreat Eroles had been sent up with a thousand men between the two rivers known as the Noguera Pollaresa and the Noguera Rivagorzana.

Finding that a strong column of over three thousand French under General Bourke was in search of him, Eroles took up a good position at Roda, (about forty-five miles due north of Lerida), and there awaiting Bourke's attack beat him off on the 5th of March after a fight of ten hours with the loss of over two hundred and sixty killed and wounded. (Napier says 150 killed and wounded; Arteche, no doubt following Eroles, 1000; my figures, 60 killed, 209 wounded are taken from a letter of Suchet to Berthier, 23rd March. *Arch, de la Guerre).*

Such were the more important successes achieved by the various bands, regular and irregular, in Spain during the first five months of 1812; and they were supplemented by thrice as many petty engagements equally damaging on their own scale. (Suchet to Berthier, 23rd March, mentions that Palombini had lost no men in a small affair against Villacampa). They were of course chequered from time to time by defeats more or less severe; but such reverses were comparatively rare; and the exertions demanded of the French, often to no purpose, in the chase of these elusive enemies, wasted their ranks little less than actual overthrow in the field. There was therefore ample employment for the armies of Catalonia, of the Ebro and of the North, even if they should devote their whole time and energy to the security of their communications, as Napoleon appears to have desired. But it was obviously impossible that they could do so unless the British and Portuguese could be compelled to stand on the defensive.

The task set to Joseph, then, was so to adjust the movements of the armies placed under his command as to fulfil this condition. It must be confessed that the emperor had not made it easy for him. In the first place the king, when he received on the 28th of March his commission as commander-in-chief, had not the slightest idea as to the numbers, composition, locality, and designs either of his own armies or of his enemy's. Moreover, all the generals had been irritated by the amazing confusion and absurdity of Napoleon's plans for the relief of Badajoz. Napoleon had counted upon Marmont's advance into Beira to raise the siege, and had informed him that Soult would send twenty thousand men under d'Erlon to the Guadiana. Imperative orders to that effect were actually sent to Soult on the 19th of February, with a further instruction that the corps under Drouet was to invade the Alemtejo. The despatch ended with a sharp intimation that Ballesteros was an enemy who might be ignored, since Suchet would suffice to keep him employed; and that Soult and no one else was responsible for the country to south of the Tagus.

This absurd missive did not reach Soult until the third week in April. In answer, he quietly explained that it was quite impossible for him to spare twenty thousand men for d'Erlon; but meanwhile Napoleon on the 3rd of April had hinted that a junction of the armies of Marmont, of Soult, and of a detachment from the Army of the Centre on the south of the Tagus, would confront Wellington with a force twice as numerous as his own, and compel him to raise the siege of Badajoz. On the same day Joseph heard from Marmont that, if his manoeuvres on the Agueda had no effect as a diversion in favour of that fortress, he should move southwards and send a division to join Foy's in making a raid into the valley of the Tagus.

Joseph therefore sent a large supply of provisions to Talavera to victual these two divisions, and despatched General Darmagnac with three battalions and two regiments of horse to occupy that place, and so to release Foy for active operations. These dispositions, however, compelled him to apply to Suchet for a reinforcement of one division from the Army of Valencia; and, before he could adjust himself any further to the situation, there came the news that Badajoz had fallen. (Berthier to Soult, 19th Feb. 1812. *Arch, de la Guerre*, Napoleon to Berthier; Jourdan to Berthier, 3rd April 1812, printed in Ducasse, viii.)

Here therefore was a new complication which, in the dearth of intelligence respecting any of the armies excepting that of Portugal, rendered the existing obscurity doubly obscure to Joseph. He had sent letters to all of the commanding generals, but so far without receiving any answer except from Marmont; wherefore, thinking the re-establishment of communications with Soult to be of the first importance, he ordered Darmagnac's detachment and one brigade of Foy's division to enter La Mancha so as to regain touch with the Army of the South at Andujar. Joseph also announced his intention of sending to the same quarter any troops which he might receive from Suchet, so that there might be a corps ready to help Soult in case Wellington should invade Andalusia. At last there came a despatch from Dorsenne, which said nothing as to his own situation, but gave Joseph to understand that the Army of the North was not under the king's command but under the immediate orders of the emperor. This was unpleasant for the unfortunate monarch; but it was only a beginning of mortifications.

A few days later arrived a letter from Marmont deprecating the idea of transferring any part of his force to the south of the Tagus. He admitted that possibly Wellington might have designs upon Andalusia; but in that case the British general would, at most, only drive the French from that province without occupying it permanently, whereas, if he should learn that the Army of Portugal had made strong detachments to the south, he might double back and overwhelm the remnant left in the north before it could be succoured. On the whole, therefore, Marmont announced that he should stay in the vicinity

160

of Salamanca, hinting with little disguise that the Army of Portugal could best be turned to account by placing the whole of it, without any deduction whatever, at the disposal of its proper commander, so that he might establish himself firmly and in strength upon the Zezere. (*Archives de la Guerre*. Jourdan to Berthier, 27th April 1812; Ducasse, viii. Dorsenne to Joseph, 19th April; Marmont to Jourdan, 29th April 1812).

By this time May was come, and during its early days Joseph received a series of messengers. First came one from Napoleon conveying orders to see that Marmont acted in concert with Soult for the relief of Badajoz, and to take care that his royal commands were obeyed. Secondly, Suchet sent one to express his regret that he could not spare the division required of him. Thirdly, there arrived an *aide-de-camp* from Soult who reported that, when he left Seville on the 23rd of April, no information had reached the Marshal that he was under the king's command at all, and that consequently he, the *aide-de-camp*, would not allow his chief's reports to Berthier to be opened at Madrid. Fourthly, a letter from Marmont announced that Wellington had certainly five divisions on the north bank of the Tagus, and that all indications pointed to an advance of the British upon Salamanca.

At last, therefore, Joseph and Jourdan ascertained enough concerning the forces under their control to frame some kind of plan for employing them. Supplies and transport were absolutely wanting, so that there was no prospect of operations on any great scale before harvest; but at least something could be done towards making the various commanders work for a common object. Rightly concluding from Marmont's reports that Wellington's next movement would be in the north, Jourdan cancelled his instructions respecting La Mancha, ordered Darmagnac to keep his detachment at Talavera, and released Foy's troops for the exclusive service of the Army of Portugal. Marmont was directed to stand fast at Salamanca unless he should find three or fewer British divisions opposed to him in that quarter, in which case he was to march with four divisions to Almaraz.

Suchet was bidden to make some kind of diversion in Murcia, so as to keep the Spaniards there from annoying the Army of the South; and Soult, having been first informed that this was no time for trifles such as the siege of Tarifa, was positively commanded to reinforce d'Erlon's corps on the Guadiana, so that it should either be able to beat Hill, if that commander remained on his front, or to march rapidly for the bridge of Arzobispo in order to cover Madrid, if Hill should cross to the right bank of the Tagus. Intimations to the same effect were sent directly to d'Erlon. "The success of the French armies in Spain". (such was the close of Joseph's letter to Soult) "depends henceforward on the concert of the Armies of the South and of Portugal; and I am placed in the centre to ensure that concert." (Ducasse, ix. *Arch, de la Guerre*; Jourdan to Marmont, 4th May 1812).

These commands blew the smouldering fires of insubordination into full blaze. Marmont in his answer began by reporting that three of the five British divisions before him had disappeared, he knew not whither, and that therefore he could not tell what Wellington's plans might be. He then proceeded to observe that unless Dorsenne gave him a division—which that officer had refused to do—he could not send more than three divisions to the Tagus; and he ended by declaring that he should think himself criminal if he obeyed Joseph's latest instructions. Caffarelli, who had succeeded Dorsenne in command of the Army of the North, replied after the fashion of his predecessor that he was not under the king's orders.

Soult after considerable delay urged persistently that Wellington was beyond doubt contemplating the invasion of Andalusia, and that Marmont ought to place his army about the pass of Baños so as to be ready to cross the Tagus at a moment's notice. Poor Joseph, much bewildered, suggested to Marmont that Soult after all might be correct; but he weakly conceded that, in such an event, it would suffice for three divisions of the Army of Portugal to cross the Tagus. Soult now followed up his first letter by two more, one of which added to his reiterated opinion a vehement attack upon Marmont, while the other declared that, if Joseph were going to issue orders direct to subordinate generals, such as d'Erlon, he, Soult, would not be responsible for the Army of the South, but would be glad to be relieved of his command.

D'Erlon, for his part, wrote loyally that he knew not how to act between the conflicting instructions of the marshal and of the king, since obedience to either might bring about disaster. Joseph thereupon informed Soult that he might resign his command to d'Erlon if he so wished; but the offer was not accepted. So matters stood at the end of June, long before which the general confusion had been worse confounded by Hill's destruction of the bridge of Almaraz. Joseph and Jourdan were in despair. All the commanders of armies without exception defied them. Soult studiously abstained from announcing in orders to his corps that it was subject to the direction of the king; and

Suchet had gone to the length of proclaiming to his troops that th were under his own sole command. The headquarters staff at Madrid could not even obtain returns of the strength of the forces which they were supposed to govern, much less of their dispositions.

Meanwhile starvation reigned in that capital; bread cost eighteen-pence a pound; an insurrection was daily expected; and guerilla-bands made depredations up to the very gates. Utterly powerless to mend matters, Joseph and Jourdan addressed complaints to the Minister for War at Paris; but he could give no help. They also appealed to Napoleon himself; but the emperor was twelve hundred miles away. After declaring war against Russia on the 22nd of June he had set four hundred thousand men in motion to cross the Niemen, and could spare no attention for lesser campaigns.

★★★★★★

Ducasse, ix. Ducasse has a maddening habit of leaving many letters imprinted which are referred to in the rest of the correspondence. I have, however, found most of them in *Arch, de la Guerre*, notably Marmont to Joseph of 7th May, and Soult to Joseph of 26th May 1812. Many parts of the former letter are obscure, having been either ciphered or deciphered incorrectly.

★★★★★★

Compared with Joseph's position, therefore, that of Wellington was comparatively easy. As to his plans for the future he had already made up his mind. The Spanish Government was pressing him to invade Andalusia; but for that the time was now past. The harvest in that province would begin in June, and then Soult would be able to assemble and to move his army, living on the country. Moreover, the crops in Estremadura would also be reaped by the second week in June, so that, if the British should turn southward, Marmont would be able to march into that province and strengthen Soult's army to a number far exceeding that of the Allies.

On the other hand, the harvest in Castile did not ripen until August, so that there were still two months during which Marmont would be helpless in that quarter from want of victuals. The marshal, indeed, with much misgiving recognised the fact, (Ducasse, viii.), which was the more galling since he had just received some heavy cannon which, if he could but have collected supplies, would have enabled him to attack Ciudad Rodrigo. The arrival of these guns furnished an additional reason for Wellington to remain in the north; and in spite of his bitter railing against Carlos d'España and the Spanish

Government for their neglect (which was culpable enough) to repair and revictual Ciudad Rodrigo, it may be doubted whether he had ever seriously contemplated the invasion of Andalusia at all. The risk of such an operation even in the most favourable circumstances must have been very great, while avowedly the only object that would be attained by it was the raising of the siege of Cadiz and the evacuation of Andalusia by Soult.

But such evacuation would naturally have tended to concentrate the French armies, whereas Wellington's sole hope of success lay in keeping them dispersed. Now, as Wellington himself confessed, Soult, so long as he remained in Andalusia, was obliged to blockade Cadiz, and to that end was bound to keep garrisons in Seville, Granada, Malaga, and other places. But this in turn signified that he could not venture to withdraw his army for long from that province without leaving a sufficient force to hold Ballesteros in check. In other words, so long as Soult occupied Andalusia, at least twenty thousand good French soldiers could be paralysed by about fifteen thousand Spaniards, poor troops under a poor commander; and it is difficult to see what object there could be to the British General in ending so advantageous a state of affairs.

Having, therefore, rightly resolved to carry his operations into Castile against the Army of Portugal, Wellington took measures for diverting the attention of the remaining French armies. The destruction of the bridge of Almaraz had done very much to secure his right flank; but Hill must none the less be left to guard it against a large proportion of Soult's forces. It was therefore arranged that Ballesteros should pursue his old game of threatening Seville; while Hill, who had already nineteen thousand British and Portuguese, should be further strengthened by the Spanish troops under Penne Villemur and Morillo. Knowing by intercepted letters that Joseph had ordered Soult to give a full third of his army to d'Erlon, but unaware of Soult's disinclination to obey, Wellington surmised that the Duke of Dalmatia would probably manoeuvre by Hill's right.

In this case Sir Rowland was to assemble his force in the position of Albuera, making a better use of it than had Beresford, or cross the Guadiana and place himself about Juromenha. If, on the contrary, Soult should manoeuvre by Hill's left,, Sir Rowland was to retire to Badajoz and post his army on the heights of San Cristobal; taking care, if the marshal should still advance, to call out the Portuguese militia to Elvas, Campo Maior and Ouguela. Should Soult cover the movement of d'Erlon across Estremadura, Hill must not attempt the impossible task of preventing it; but if d'Erlon's detachment alone should march across Hill's front through Estremadura, then Sir Rowland should be able to make matters very uncomfortable for him. Any further complications, such as an advance of the Army of the Centre, would be dealt with as occasion might arise. Meanwhile the *Empecinado* had received orders to make demonstrations near Madrid so as to alarm King Joseph for his capital.

So much for the Armies of the South and Centre: there remained still that of Suchet, which, on the strength of information from Downing Street, Wellington hoped might be effectually occupied by Bentinck with his troops from Sicily. The siege of Tarragona was the operation which he had prescribed as most desirable for Bentinck's force, and he had taken great pains to provide a battering-train for that purpose, drawing ammunition for the heavy guns even from Cadiz, when Gibraltar was found unable to supply it, rather than suffer Lord William to be ill-equipped.

Finally there was the Army of the North, for which Popham's naval squadron was already furnishing employment by raids on the coast, but which was to be still further harassed by an advance of the Army of Galicia, under Castaños, upon Astorga. Moreover four battalions of Portuguese militia and three regiments of cavalry under d'Urban were to move from Braganza along the Douro, so as to sever communications between Zamora and Astorga, or in other words between Marmont and Caffarelli; while Mendizabal had been entreated to give all the trouble that he could to Marmont himself. Altogether it seemed unlikely that in the north at any rate the French would be able to assemble in superior strength. (*Wellington Desp.* To Hill, 6th, 10th June; to Liverpool, 18th June 1812).

Nevertheless Wellington was not without his doubts and anxieties. In the first place he had based all his plans upon the presumption that Soult could dispose of only forty-five thousand men; and not till the 9th of June four days before he designed to set his troops in motion did he discover that the true numbers of the Army of the South were fifty-two thousand. This rendered Hill's position more hazardous than Wellington had contemplated, the more so since Penne Villemur was inclined to wander off "plundering corn and crimping recruits," instead of attending to legitimate business in Estremadura. To make matters worse, Ballesteros, on learning that Soult was fortifying the line of the Guadalete at Bornos, forsook his shelter at San Roque to attack him, and was beaten back on the 1st of June with the loss of fifteen hundred men and three guns.

Within his own army also there was much to annoy Wellington. Colquhoun Grant, the prince of intelligencers, had by ill-luck fallen into the hands of Marmont during the French raid into Beira; the marshal had refused to exchange him; and there seemed no hope of recovering him except by forcible recapture. Marvellous to say, Grant, even when a prisoner at Salamanca, managed to furnish Wellington with good information; and on reaching Bayonne he escaped to Paris, sent valuable reports to his chief from there for some weeks, and finally making his way to England, rejoined from thence the British headquarters in the Peninsula within four months of his capture. All this, however, could not be foreseen by Wellington, who deeply lamented the mishap, declaring that the loss of a brigade could scarcely have been more sensibly felt by him than the loss of Grant. (Accounts of Grant's marvellous adventures will be found in Napier, iv.; and in *Autobiography of Sir J. M'Grigor*).

But misfortunes never come singly, and within a few days Wellington learned with regret, which was at first not unmingled with wrath, that General Murray, the Chief of his Staff, was about to leave Spain immediately to take up another appointment in Ireland. The Duke of York proposed to send Colonel Gordon, reputed to be one of the ablest officers at the Horse Guards, to succeed him; but for the present Murray's place was taken by his deputy-quarter-master-general, De Lancey. Within less than a week after this second blow Dr. M'Grigor came to report that General Graham would be obliged to go home very shortly in consequence of a disorder in his eyes; so that practically within two months Wellington was deprived of his best intelligence-officer, of the chief of his staff, and of his ablest divisional general. But it was never one of his failings to repine over the inevitable, and while returning thanks for the appointment of Gordon, he begged that no fresh general should be sent from home of equal rank with Graham. (*Wellington Desp.* To Graham, 18th April; to Murray, 28th May; to Liverpool, 3rd June 1812).

More serious than any embarrassment on account of officers was the continuance of outrages by British soldiers when employed with small detachments, an evil which, to use Wellington's own words, had become so enormous as to be dangerous alike to the common cause and to the army itself. The general attributed it in part to the fact that the pay of non-commissioned officers had not been increased in proportion to that of the men; but its real root lay in the sudden change in the regulation of regimental courts-martial, which had been forced upon the army by the House of Commons. The new system had raised so rank a growth of legal technicalities that it was impossible for courts-martial to see their way through them; and it was necessary to send home the proceedings of every court for confirmation before sentences could be executed.

Hence, as Wellington reported, the guard-rooms were crowded with prisoners, but the guilty remained unpunished, to the destruction of all discipline and the general injury of England's reputation for justice. This, no doubt, was a result which had not been contemplated; but it cannot too strongly be impressed upon the reader that the misbehaviour of the army in the Peninsula was due chiefly, if not entirely, to the interference of a small body of pedantic and sentimental members of the House of Commons. The only remedy which Wellington could suggest was that a legal assistant should be sent out, to convert, if it were possible, the folly of Parliament into wisdom; and this was accordingly done. In November there came to headquarters as Judge-Advocate-General Mr. Francis Seymour Larpent, a high wrangler and a respectable lawyer, but, more than this, a man with a seeing eye and an understanding heart, whose private journal is one of the most valuable documents that we possess concerning the later period of the Peninsular War.

Yet another difficulty was less easily overcome, namely the old trouble of want of specie. In May 1812 the pay of the troops was three months, and of the Staff five months, in arrear; the Spanish muleteers, upon whom the entire organisation of the transport depended, had not been paid for twelve months; and there were outstanding bills for meat alone amounting to £200,000. The Treasury itself, at its wits' end for coined money, had negatived—rightly or wrongly—all Wellington's plans for raising the sums that he needed; the remittances of precious metal from South America had been disappointing; and, worst of all, Lord William Bentinck, with the characteristic selfishness of the enthusiast, had outbidden Wellington in the purchase of a large hoard of dollars at Gibraltar.

The dearth of money was the more exasperating inasmuch as the partisans of the British in Castile had given him assurance of concealed granaries, great part of which would be thrown open to his army on credit, if only cash could be paid for the remainder; and, though Wellington had taken what measures he could to meet such a contingency, the failure of this resource might be dangerously embarrassing, he wrote:—

> I cannot reflect, without shuddering upon the probability that we shall be distressed, nor upon the consequences which may result from our wanting money in the interior of Spain.

However, in spite of all obstacles, he began to concentrate his troops at the beginning of June, and by the 10th had collected the whole of them on the Azava. (*Wellington Desp.* To Liverpool, 12th, 26th May; to C. Stuart, 10th May, 15th July 1810).

Hill, meanwhile, after his raid upon Almaraz had retired first to Truxillo, and thence to Merida, leaving Foy, as has been told, to relieve the garrison of Mirabete unmolested. Upon the recall of Foy from the valley of the Tagus by Marmont at the end of May, Joseph, supposing d'Erlon to have been heavily reinforced by Soult, ordered him to march after Hill on the left bank of the Tagus and if possible to fight and defeat him. As a matter of fact d'Erlon had only six thousand men with him, for Soult, in spite of Joseph's commands, had not yet sent him a single soldier; whereas Hill had, including the garrison of Badajoz, nineteen thousand British and Portuguese, besides three thousand Spaniards under Penne Villemur and Morillo. None the less, on receiving a copy of Joseph's letter, which had been intercepted by Wellington, Hill judged it prudent to contract his cantonments; and on the 3rd of June he collected his corps at Almendralejo, Villafranca, Fuente del Maestre, and Los Santos, with his cavalry in advance at Ribera, and his Spaniards at Zafra.

On the 4th Sir Rowland heard of the relief of Mirabete; and a few days later d'Erlon fell back from his advanced positions at Medellin and Don Benito south-eastward to Fuenteovejuna. Hill thereupon followed him up; and Penne Villemur arranged to make a reconnaissance from Llerena towards Azuaga on the 12th, in order to collect the harvest of Estremadura. With the object of covering Villemur's northern flank Slade with his brigade, about six hundred strong, was sent out to Llera on the 11th, with orders to proceed towards Granja, but on no account to commit himself to any serious engagement.

It so happened that d'Erlon had likewise sent forward Lallemand's brigade of dragoons, about eight hundred strong, from Granja on the 10th, with instructions to march by Maguilla upon Llera; and by the morning of the 11th Lallemand had passed Valencia de las Torres on his way to the latter place. Slade, having information of the movement early on the same day, formed his two regiments, the Royals and Third Dragoon Guards, before a wood; and the advanced parties of both brigades presently engaged each other in a skirmish. Lallemand, however, who had only one of his regiments, the 17th Dragoons, with him, and could not tell what might be behind the wood, presently turned about and retired at a sharp pace. Slade thereupon followed him at a canter, and at length, after missing many favourable opportunities, charged with three squadrons of the Royals, supported by the Third.

The attack was completely successful. Many of the French were cut down, over one hundred prisoners were taken; and the British dragoons, with Slade at their head, galloped in wild disorder after their flying enemy, and hunted them into a defile near Maguilla. Upon emerging from this, however, Lallemand's second regiment, the 27th was seen drawn up on their flank in the plain beyond; whereupon the British, stricken with sudden panic, turned round and flew back as fast as they had previously dashed forward. (Such is the account given in Soult's report and by Tomkinson. Ainslie, *History of the Royal Dragoons,* declares that it was not the whole regiment, but one squadron only, this I doubt). Lallemand seized the moment to launch the 27th at them; and, though a reserve squadron of the Royals strove gallantly to stem the attack, the remainder of the British dragoons could not be induced to rally in support of them. The French, therefore, enjoyed an exciting chase for some eight miles until at last pursuers and pursued, overcome by the heat and choked with dust, came to a standstill at Valencia de las Torres.

In this very disgraceful affair the Royals and Third Dragoon Guards lost twenty-two men killed, twenty-six wounded, two officers and one hundred and sixteen men prisoners, and over one hundred and thirty horses killed and taken; two-thirds of the casualties falling upon the Third. The loss of the French did not exceed fifty-one, including three prisoners. (The French account slightly exaggerates the British losses to 3 officers, 127 men, and 150 horses taken, so that their own losses may be slightly understated). The whole course of the action was exactly what might have been expected from Slade, who was always rash when he should have been cautious, and timid when he should have been bold. His first report of the mishap was so absurd that the entire army laughed at it, and his second report still left the greater part of the unpleasant story untold. Wellington was furious.

The whole affair was occasioned, as he said, "by the trick our officers of cavalry have acquired of galloping at everything, and then galloping back as fast as they gallop on the enemy"; and it was the more vexatious for him inasmuch as the two regiments engaged were the best of the British cavalry in the Peninsula. It must, however, be conceded that the French had not much to boast of, and that their commander in furnishing his report was little more ingenuous than Slade; for he said nothing of the action previous to the scare at the defile of Maguilla, and wholly ignored the fact that the British had in the first place hunted him for eight miles and taken from him a great number of prisoners. Upon the whole, therefore, though the advantage was decidedly with the French, the action cannot be called creditable to either party. Happily two days later Lieutenant Strenowitz, Sir William Erskine's *aide-de-camp*, attacked eighty French dragoons at Maguilla with fifty-six of the Royals and Third Dragoon Guards, killing several and taking twenty-one of them, besides releasing many of the British prisoners captured on the 11th. This brilliant little enterprise did something to redeem the fame of the British horse.

★★★★★★

The authorities for this affair are Ainslie's *History of the Royal Dragoons*, which gives interesting details; "*Rapport historique de l'Armee du Midi*," for 30th June 1812 in *Arch, de la Guerre*; Tomkinson's *Diary of a Cavalry Officer*, and see *Wellington Desp.*, to Hill 18th June; to Liverpool, 18th, 30th June 1812. The losses given in Soult's letter of 15th June (*Wellington Supp. Desp.* xiv.) are plainly absurd.

★★★★★★

On the 11th Hill fixed his headquarters at Zafra, his own troops occupying Los Santos, Bienvenida and Usagre, and the detachment of Spaniards Llerena; and now at last Soult consented, though with a very bad grace, to reinforce d'Erlon, sending him Barrois's division of foot and Pierre Soult's of horse. He announced that these troops, about five thousand men in all, would leave Seville on the 14th, and d'Erlon begged that they might join him by way of Constantina so as to gain touch with his cavalry at Berlanga; but Soult did not despatch them until the 16th, and then sent them due north by Monesterio, obliging d'Erlon to move with his whole force south-westward to meet them, and thereby to endanger his communications with the Tagus.

★★★★★★

The returns of 1st March 1812 give Barrois's division at 7776, and Soult's at 2338, all ranks, or 11,114 of all ranks; but d'Erlon writing to Joseph on 3rd July (*Arch, de la Guerre*) gives the strength of the reinforcement at 3 500 infantry and 1500 cavalry. D'Espinchal (*Souvenirs militaires*, i.) who was in P. Soult's division, says that Barrois's division was 12,000, and P. Soult's 3000 strong, and speaks of d'Erlon's complete force as numbering 20,000 men, which is self-contradictory; for the above figures added to the force of d'Erlon's and Darricau's divisions (11,000 men) would make 25,000. But d'Espinchal is manifestly untrustworthy throughout, and his "journal" contains so much embroidery, evidently added after the event, that I have little faith in him. Still Napier gives d'Erlon 21,000 men, no doubt on the faith of Soult's papers, whereas d'Erlon gives himself barely 17,000. The discrepancy is curious; but it is not clear why d'Erlon should lie about a point which could be instantly refuted by Soult. Hill's information likewise bears out d'Erlon.

★★★★★★

The junction was, however, safely effected at Bienvenida on the 19th, for Hill had already begun to withdraw his troops northward; and on the 18th Sir Rowland retired to the position of Albuera, which he occupied on the 21st with some twenty-two thousand men, of whom over eight thousand were British. (This does not include the Spaniards (3000 to 4000) under Morillo and Penne Villemur.) Soult's orders to d'Erlon were to keep Hill constantly employed, to invest Badajoz if a favourable opportunity should present itself, and to prevent the advance of any English corps by the valley of the Tagus, but on no account to take the divisions of Barrois and Pierre Soult across the Guadiana. The Duke of Dalmatia, even on the day when Wellington marched from the Agueda upon Salamanca, still clung obstinately to the opinion that the British intended to invade Andalusia.

Looking to the numbers on both sides, it seems remarkable that Hill should have displayed such extreme caution in dealing with d'Erlon, he wrote on the 25th:—

My information leads me to believe that the enemy's force does not exceed twelve or thirteen thousand infantry; and, if I were certain of that, I should be prepared to move against them.

But, as Wellington confessed, the quality of great part of Hill's troops was such that they could not be trusted to manoeuvre in face of the enemy; and moreover, Sir Rowland, not being admitted to Wellington's secrets, hesitated to take any risk by which his chief's ulterior intentions might possibly be frustrated. Even a decisive victory over d'Erlon, by calling Soult in force to the north, might derange Wellington's combinations. D'Erlon on his side was not less cautious, for, according to his intelligence, Hill had no fewer than thirty-three thousand men with him, exclusive of the Spaniards; this result being arrived at partly by exaggeration of the strength of the corps actually present, but chiefly by the addition to them of the Seventh Division, which as a matter of fact was with Wellington, one hundred and fifty miles away. Incidentally this computation, in conjunction with a report that seven thousand British had landed at Lisbon and were marching to join Hill, gave Soult an excellent excuse for reiterating his former opinion that Andalusia was Wellington's true objective. To d'Erlon this same report was a source of perpetual anxiety. He therefore felt his way very carefully to Hill's front, and did not venture until the 1st of July upon a reconnaissance in force.

On that day General Lallemand attacked Penne Villemur's Spanish cavalry, and routed them with a loss of two hundred men, which would have been still greater had not a squadron of the Third Dragoon Guards interfered to save them. (The French report was that the Third Dragoon Guards on this occasion lost 2 officers and 30 men killed; the true numbers were an officer and 4 men killed). On the 3rd Hill, having received discretionary orders from Wellington to fight, advanced, and d'Erlon falling back took up a position at Valencia de las Torres to await attack; but finding that he was unmolested he retired a few miles to Berlanga and Azuaga, while Hill established himself over against him at Llerena. There for the present the two commanders remained; d'Erlon occasionally despatching parties towards Merida, but failing to cajole Hill into sending a detachment to watch them; from which, as usual, Soult drew the inference that the invasion of Andalusia was imminent.

Once only the monotony was broken on the 24th of July by a small engagement between Erskine's division of horse and Lallemand's brigade of dragoons near Ribera, wherein the British gained some advantage. At length on the 28th of July Hill moved to Zafra, as a healthier station during the hot weather, whither d'Erlon followed him, having positive orders from Soult not to let the British general out of sight but to attack him in whatever position he might take up. The reinforcements sent to d'Erlon for the purpose, however, were not such as to warrant him in attempting so hazardous an adventure, as they probably did not exceed three thousand men.

★★★★★★

I can discover nothing about the reinforcement in the Archives de la Guerre, nor in any French authority. But Hill writing to Wellington on 21st July speaks of two columns joining Drouet in the third week of July, the one by Constantina, the other by St. Olalla and Monesterio. Of the first he gives no details, but he states that the second under General Bonnemain consisted of 3 battalions of the 9th Light and 250 horse, say 2000 men altogether. Hill to Wellington, 21st, 23rd July, 14th Aug. 1812. *Hill MSS.*, Brit. Museum.

★★★★★★

The French general therefore stationed his troops along the Sierra de Hornachos, extending his cantonments from Guareña on the north to Valencia de las Torres on the south. For the second time Hill felt greatly tempted to attack him, being heartened by the news of a great victory—presently to be described—which had been won by Wellington near Salamanca on the 22nd of July; but d'Erlon's position was strong, and there was neither hope of a decisive success nor prospect of being able to hold any country that might be gained. Sir Rowland therefore remained steadfast in his cantonments about Zafra, until towards the end of August came the news that Soult was evacuating his sick and his stores from Seville upon Cordova, and evidently preparing for a great movement.

In the circumstances Hill judged that it was time for him to thrust d'Erlon back, but that it would be imprudent to follow his adversary far while Soult, disembarrassed of all encumbrances, lay with his army concentrated about Seville. Accordingly on the 26th Sir Rowland advanced, and on the 28th found that d'Erlon had fallen back from Hornachos. On the 31st d'Erlon's rear-guard was reported to have passed through Velmez; but Hill saw no object in pursuing him. "It seems to me," he wrote to Wellington, "that I ought to close up towards you"; and accordingly on the 31st he turned northwards from Berlanga through Campillo and Castuera to the Guadiana at Villa Nueva de la Serena.

His information was that Soult was making for Granada and d'Erlon for Jaen, and that King Joseph was retiring southward by the pass of Despeñaperros to join them, from which it was plain that the Army of the South was not going to traverse La Mancha. Hill decided, therefore, that he must march no further northward, and halted at Villa Nueva in some uneasiness, for he had received no orders from Wellington for several days. At last on the 13th of September came the welcome command to cross the river at Almaraz; and the British troops bade farewell for ever to the south bank of the Tagus. (See Hill's letters to Wellington in August and September 1812. *Hill MSS.*)

The great English historian of the war has commended Hill not a little for refraining in the month of June from a general action which promised him unbounded fame, because he was loath to risk the possible undoing of Wellington's operations in Castile. No one will hesitate to grant that with Sir Rowland selfish considerations counted for nothing and personal ambition for less than nothing, or to join in encomiums upon a character which contained such excellencies. But Napier's estimate of d'Erlon's force is so utterly incorrect as to vitiate his comments beyond remedy. He assumed that Hill had twenty-two thousand men, and his adversary twenty-one thousand, whereas the latter in reality had but sixteen to seventeen thousand. It should seem then that probably a great opportunity of striking a telling blow was lost, and lost through Wellington's fault.

Napier, it is true, mentions that Hill had discretionary orders to fight, but omits to point out that he did not receive them until he had informed Wellington of the weakness of the force opposed to him, and had hinted at his eagerness to take the offensive. The fact is that Wellington never dreamed that Soult would calmly sit still at Seville, as he did during the whole of June, July, and August, averring to the last that the principal design of the British was aimed against Andalusia and declining to interest himself in anything external to that province.

Nor indeed can Wellington be blamed for failing to foresee such culpable apathy and selfishness in a good and able soldier. It was supposed that Soult had taken offence because he had not been appointed chief of the staff to Joseph—to all intent, that is, commander-in-chief—in place of Jourdan. It may be that herein he was unworthily treated; but nothing can excuse his deliberate exposure of d'Erlon's detachment to the chance of overwhelming defeat by a force which, as he believed—or at any rate professed to believe—counted over fifteen thousand British and Germans, over thirteen thousand Portuguese, and from three to five thousand Spaniards, including four thousand cavalry and over thirty guns. That Hill, but for Wellington's orders, would have engaged d'Erlon at the outset and probably have handled him very roughly appears certain; and in that case Soult would have been obliged to collect his forces hastily as best he could, leaving Ballesteros, who had recovered from his defeat and was eager for revenge, behind him. Seville would then have been lost with all the sick and the stores deposited in it; and there is no saying where the mischief would have ended.

By good fortune rather than by his own deserts Soult escaped the disgrace which would have been attached to his name by the defeat of d'Erlon, and by the consequent exposure of his own misconduct; but it remains none the less true that, whether it were dictated by jealousy or cupidity, by resentment against Joseph's command or by love of the good things of Andalusia, his behaviour during the summer months of 1812 was little else than infamous.

The Battle of Salamanca

Having secured his advanced bases at Ciudad Rodrigo and Bada-joz, and reduced the French north and south of the Tagus to the bridge of Toledo as their one channel of communication, Welling-ton on the 13th of June crossed the Agueda with an army of about forty-three thousand of all ranks, (British and Germans: 1315 officers; 26,879 N.C.O. and men. Portuguese: 13,051 rank and file; say 14,682 all ranks. See Appendix for composition of brigades and divisions), over and above from three to four thousand Spaniards under Carlos d'España. His divisional leaders at the outset were almost unchanged, but in the course of a few weeks the First Division fell to Campbell, the Third to Pakenham, the Sixth to Henry Clinton, who had lately joined the army, and the Seventh to John Hope. (John Hope the less; not the greater, who later became Lord Hopetoun). Advancing in four columns Wellington reached the Valmusa rivulet, within six miles of Salamanca, on the 16th, where after a trifling skirmish his cavalry drove that of the French across the Tormes.

Having but two divisions in the town, Marmont retired in the night north-eastward towards the Douro, whither he had already sum-moned the remainder of his army, including Bonnet's division from Asturias and as many troops as Caffarelli could spare him. The bridges over the Tormes being all broken down excepting that of Salamanca itself, which was commanded by the guns of the French forts, the British Army on the 17th forded the river above and below the town; and on the same day the Sixth Division invested the forts. A detach-ment was pushed on to keep Marmont under observation, and the main army took up its position on the heights of San Cristobal, some six miles to the north of the town. Extravagant demonstrations of joy from the people of Salamanca showed how eagerly they welcomed deliverance from the French after three years of oppression.

The forts, which had been erected by Marmont in obedience to Napoleon's orders, were three in number. The first and most important had been developed out of the convent of San Vicente and bore its name; it stood on a perpendicular cliff above the Tormes at the south-western angle of the town, (in Jones's *Sieges* the north point is misplaced in the plan of the forts, and the orientation in his text is consequently incorrect), and was connected by lines of works with the old wall of Salamanca. Two hundred and fifty yards south and east of it, and on the other side of a deep ravine, stood the two remaining forts, San Gaetano and La Merced, both of them likewise founded upon convents, but of much smaller size, and square instead of polygonal in form. All three of these strongholds were formidable; but report had unfortunately represented them as of small account, and Wellington had accordingly brought with him only four heavy guns, with such a mere handful of trained sappers and miners as to be quite inadequate to the business of a regular siege. Three heavy howitzers were borrowed from the field-train, and on the night of the 17th Colonel Burgoyne began the construction of a battery for seven pieces at a distance of two hundred and fifty yards from the northern front of San Vicente.

But every circumstance militated against the besiegers. The ground was so much encumbered by ruins that it could not be excavated; and it was necessary to bring earth from a distance. The moon was nearly at the full, and the workmen, being thereby exposed to a destructive fire of the enemy and being moreover inexpert, made very little progress. An attempt to blow in a part of the counterscarp on the same night was frustrated with some loss; and altogether the operations began badly. On the 18th eight hundred German Light Infantry were brought up, who taking cover among the ruins kept down in great measure the French fire; and two more batteries were begun to right and left of the first; that on the left, consisting of two field-guns, being placed in the upper windows of the convent of San Bernardo to ply that of San Vicente with shrapnel shell. On the 20th six large howitzers arrived from Elvas; the new batteries opened fire from twelve heavy pieces; and a part of the convent's wall was at last overthrown, falling like an avalanche upon the French sharpshooters and crushing the life out of many of them.

The British followed up this achievement with a shower of carcasses, and it was only by great exertions that the French prevented the convent from being burnt down; but there the success ended. The enemy still maintained a destructive fire from seven pieces of ordnance, whereas the ammunition of the British was exhausted.

On the same day Marmont, having collected five out of his eight divisions, in all about twenty-five thousand men, was reported to be advancing from Fuente Sauco. Wellington thereupon withdrew one brigade of the Sixth Division to the main army, sent his heavy guns to the south of the Tormes and, suspending the siege, formed his troops in order of battle in an exceedingly strong position on the heights of San Cristobal. Towards evening there was a slight skirmish between the cavalry of both sides; and at five o'clock Marmont advanced to the very foot of the heights within short cannon-shot of the Allies. Wellington watched him with intense earnestness, saying now and again, "Damned tempting! I have a great mind to attack 'em", (Colonel James Stanhope's *Journal*); but he restrained himself, and allowed Marmont to throw shells on the hill with impunity for some time after dark.

The Allies slept by their arms, and in the course of the night Marmont was joined by the rest of his force, Bonnet's division excepted, which was thus raised to a total of about thirty-five thousand men.

★★★★★★

There are considerable discrepancies among the authorities as to the time when Marmont's whole force was assembled, and as to its numbers. Napier says that he started with four divisions of infantry, and was joined by three more and a brigade of cavalry on the 22nd. Belmas agrees with him as to the arrival of the divisions but not as to the time, which he gives as the night of the 20th to 21st. Marmont says that he started on the 20th with the 2nd, 3rd, 4th, 5th, and 6th divisions, but omits to mention when the three remaining divisions joined him. I have followed Marmont as to the strength with which he advanced, and Belmas as to the date when the rest of the army joined him, which is by implication confirmed by Girod de l'Ain, *Vie Militaire du General Foy*. As to the number of the force, Girod de l'Ain says 30,000, which is certainly too low, Napier close on 40,000, which I think too high, and Belmas 32,000, which again I think too low. My own numbers are arrived at by deducting the strength of Bonnet's division and of 7000 for garrisons (including those of the forts at Salamanca) from the total shown in the returns of 15th April 1812.

★★★★★★

178

The day of the 21st, however, passed quietly until evening, when Wellington sent the Sixty-Eighth to take a village on the right of his position, which had been occupied by the French, a task which was not accomplished without a sharp skirmish. On that night Marmont held a council of war, having some idea of attacking the Allies, but found that the opinion of his generals was unanimous against so hazardous a venture; though Foy and Clausel urged that he should stand his ground and manoeuvre east and west on the right bank of the Tormes until his reinforcements should arrive.

On the morning of the 22nd the marshal reconnoitred Wellington's position from a point so close to it that an unsuccessful effort was made by two squadrons to cut him off; but he attempted no further movement than to seize a height before the right of the Allies, from which the Seventh Division promptly dislodged him. Thereupon he abandoned the forts to their fate and withdrew in the night to Aldearrubia, nine miles east and north of Salamanca, from which station he commanded the ford of Huerta on the Tormes, and thus could cross to the left bank to threaten Wellington's communications. The loss of the British from the 20th to the 22nd was one hundred and thirty-one killed, wounded, and missing.

Upon realising Marmont's new position Wellington on the 23rd made a corresponding change of front to his right. The Tormes, which flows from south to north as far as Huerta, makes at that point a sudden bend from east to west, so that it was in his power to act along the chord of the arc, while Marmont was obliged to move round the curve. Wellington therefore shifted his left to Morescos, his centre to Aldea Lengua, and his right to the ford of Santa Marta, ready to cross there at any moment; while Bock's German brigade of heavy dragoons was pushed over the water to observe the French at Huerta.

The enemy remained quiet on this day, but at dawn of the 24th two French divisions together with twenty guns and a body of cavalry forded the Tormes, and advanced southward upon Wellington's communications. Bock, though hard pressed, fell back with admirable steadiness and order; Graham led two divisions and Le Marchant's brigade of cavalry to his support; and Marmont, perceiving that Wellington was fully prepared for him, hastily faced about and retired by the way that he had come.

He had in fact exposed himself to a formidable counterstroke, for it was open to Wellington to reinforce Graham and overwhelm the French detachment on the left bank of the Tormes, while either hold-

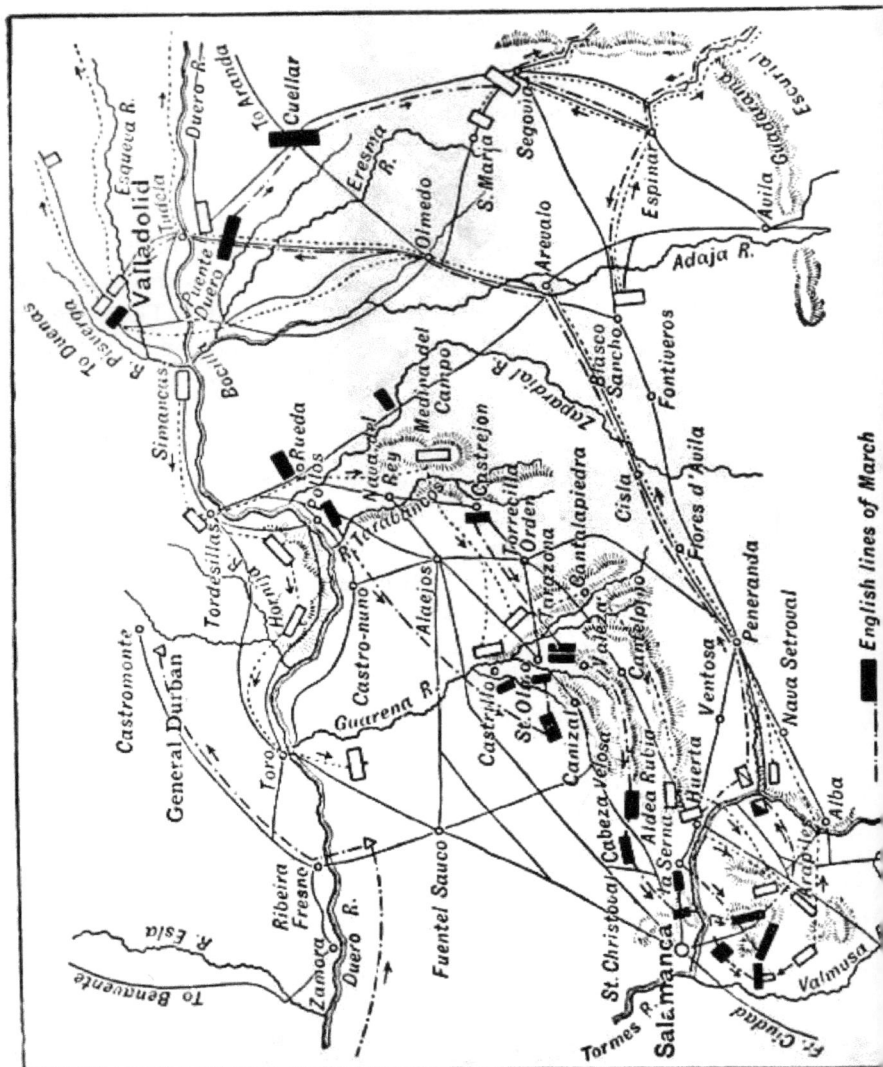

English lines of March

Battle of SALAMANCA with operations before and after the Action.

Legend:
- ▮ Cavalry
- ┄┄ French lines of March
- ▯ Cavalry

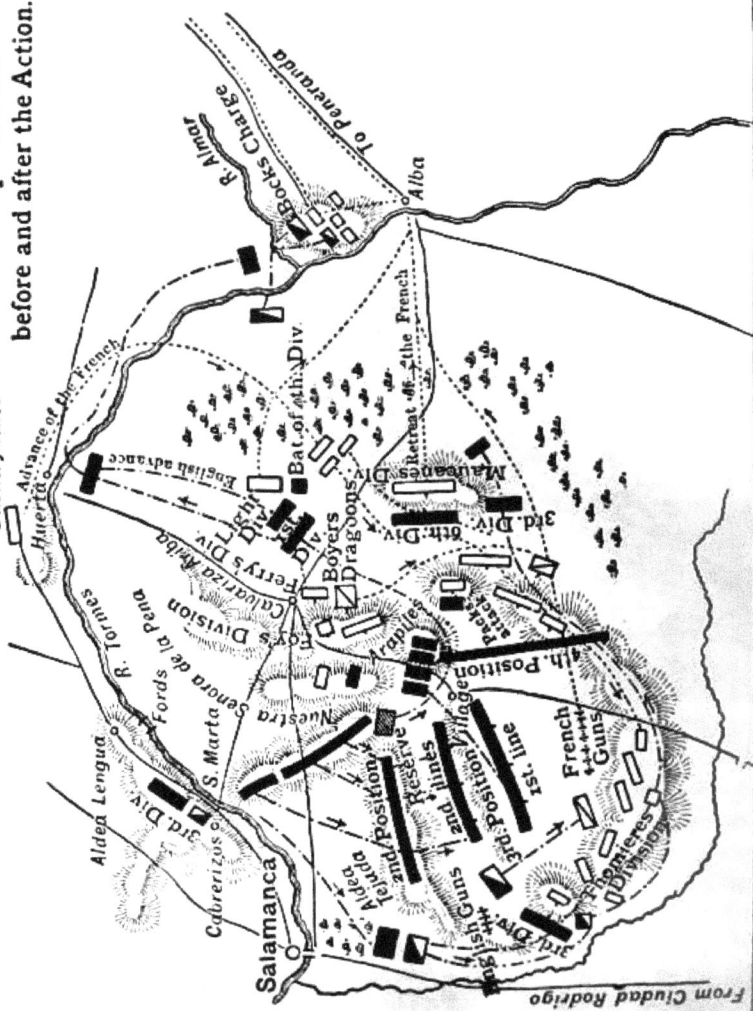

To Penaranda

R. Almar

Bock's Charge

Alba

Retreat of the French

Bat. of 4th Div.

English advance

Advance of the French

Babila fuente

Huerta

1st Lt. Div.

Calvarizza Ariba

Maucune's Div.

3rd Div.

4th Div.

Boyer's Dragoons

Ferry's Div.

Pack's

Cole's Division

Pakenham's

R. Tormes

Maples

4th. Position

French Guns

Nuestra Senora de la Pena

Fords

S. Marta

Aldea Lengua

3rd Div.

French Guns

2nd Position

Reserve and lines

3rd Position Village

1st. line

Thomiere's Division

Cabrerizos

Salamanca

Aldea Tejada

Spanish Guns and lines

3rd Div.

From Ciudad Rodrigo

ing the rest of Marmont's army engaged on the right bank, or falling upon their flank if they attempted to go to the assistance of their comrades. The fact that the only retreat of the detachment lay over the river by the ford of Huerta made such an enterprise particularly tempting, but Wellington abstained from any aggressive movement and allowed his enemy to withdraw unmolested.

Meanwhile four heavy guns had on the 23rd been brought back and placed in battery to play, with such scanty allowance of ammunition as still remained, upon the north-west front of San Gaetano; and after an ineffective cannonade an attempt was made to escalade that fort and La Merced at ten o'clock that night. The troops of the Sixth Division, appointed for the attack, evinced no great alacrity in what seemed to them a desperate venture. Only two ladders were planted; no one mounted them; and in half an hour the assailants were beaten off with a loss of one hundred and twenty killed and wounded, chief among the slain being General Bowes who, though hurt early in the engagement, returned to the fight when he heard that the soldiers were yielding, and met—he if no other—with a glorious death.

On the 26th fresh ammunition arrived; the guns were replaced in the bastions; San Vicente and Gaetano were plied with red-hot shot; and on the morning of the 27th the convent of San Vicente was kindled beyond the power of the garrison to extinguish the flames. Moreover, a practicable breach was made in Gaetano. The latter fort then hoisted the white flag, and the commandant offered to yield it and La Merced, if two hours were granted to him to consult his brother commandant at San Vicente, who presently also sent out a flag of truce, proposing to surrender in three hours. Wellington, suspecting a trick to gain time, allowed only five minutes, and then gave the order to assault, when the forts were carried against little resistance, with the loss of seven hundred prisoners and thirty guns taken from the enemy. So far the operations had cost the Allies five hundred and ten of all ranks killed, wounded, and missing, seventenths of whom had fallen in the siege.

Thus without any great credit to the Allies was gained the first object of Wellington's campaign. He has been blamed for not assailing Marmont between the 20th and 22nd when the marshal, with an inferior force, lay well within his reach. His answer was that the forward movement of the French seemed to indicate an intention to attack, that a defensive would have better suited him than an offensive action, that his numbers were not so superior as to make an offensive action decisive, and that, in case of defeat, he had the Tormes in his rear with no bridge whereby to cross it. (The criticism of Napier, who condemns him for not attacking on the 21st before the whole of Marmont's troops had joined the French Army, is vitiated by the fact that the whole of the French force was actually present on the 21st). The truth is that at the outset Wellington had been confronted with two unpleasant surprises. In the first place the Army of Portugal was much stronger than he had expected, and in the second he had thought it impossible that Marmont, in the face of Napoleon's orders (a copy of which had been intercepted), could recall Bonnet's division from Asturias. Taking into account these disappointments he expected no great results from his campaign, and, though he adhered to his determination to invade Castile, was inclined to husband his strength for some better opportunity.

Marmont has likewise been blamed for advancing to beard his enemy and yet lacking courage to fight him; for making an initial blunder in locking up eight hundred men in the forts of Salamanca, and for then wanting the strength of mind either to rescue or to sacrifice them. It should seem further that his march to San Cristobal on the 20th and his thrusting of two divisions in isolation across the Tormes on the 24th were operations alike aimless and dangerous. For all the good that he accomplished he had better have remained in his original station by the Douro. Marmont said indeed that he had intended to cross the Tormes on the night of the 28th, (see not following), so as to threaten Wellington's communications; and it is a fact that he issued orders to that effect, though he recalled them later because the fall of the forts on the 27th had rendered such an enterprise useless. But, if he had really formed serious designs for this manoeuvre, he would best have executed them on the night of the 22nd, before Wellington had changed position. Altogether it is plain that he was not at his ease in Wellington's presence, and was unwilling to run the hazard of such a reverse as Vimeiro or Bussaco.

★★★★★★

Note:—Napier's story, founded on "confidential official reports obtained from the French War Office," is hardly borne out either by Marmont's narrative, or by the letters published in Marmont's *Mémoires*, or by Marmont's official despatch published in Belmas, iv. Napier's account is that Marmont would have fought on the 23rd, had he not heard on the 22nd that Caffarelli was sending him a strong reinforcement; and that the marshal learned by the evening of the 26th that Caffarelli's reinforcement was not to be expected. In an intercepted letter from Marmont to Jourdan (kindly communicated to me by Oman from the *Scovell MSS.*) there occurs the following passage: "I suspended my projected operations on the left bank of the Tormes because Caffarelli on the 10th, 14th, and 20th of June had promised me reinforcements immediately (*m'avait annoncé des renforts immédiates*)." This letter of the 20th of June is the last that could have reached Marmont before the 26th, and it was the first in which Caffarelli threw any doubt upon the arrival of his reinforcements. Marmont, however, evidently did expect them still on the 26th, and he says as much not only in his *Memoirs* but also in his despatches of 30th June and 1st July. It was not until the 26th that Caffarelli wrote definitely that he could send no infantry; and that letter evidently did not reach Marmont for a week.

★★★★★★

On the night of the 27th Marmont withdrew his garrison from Alba de Tormes and retreated in three columns, the 1st and 7th Divisions with Carrié's brigade of dragoons upon Toro, and the remainder upon Tordesillas. Reaching the Trabancos on the 29th he halted for a day; but finding that Wellington was following him, he pushed on to Rueda on the 1st of July, and on the 2nd began the passage of the Douro by the bridge of Tordesillas. The Allies meanwhile had marched in three columns before dawn of the 29th, their advanced guard gaining contact with Marmont's rear on the 30th, and reaching Nava del Rey on the 1st of July.

Having received a false report that the bridge of Tordesillas was destroyed, and knowing from intercepted letters that Marmont intended to take up a position near that place, Wellington made up his mind that the French had already passed the Douro, and ordered the forward movement to be continued on the 2nd in two columns, the right upon Medina del Campo, and the left upon Rueda. To his surprise his advanced guard found a strong force of infantry as well as cavalry in Rueda, which was driven back in some confusion by the British dragoons and horse-artillery. The main body of the French Army was still filing across the bridge, so that, had some British infantry been at hand, the rearguard might have been almost annihilated. In the circumstances, however, Wellington refused permission to the cavalry to charge; and the enemy escaped with little loss.

Marmont, having broken down all the bridges over the Douro

except that at Tordesillas, made that place the centre of his line; his left being at Simancas where the unfordable River Pisuerga protected his flank, and his right at Polios, about nine miles, as the crow flies, to west and south of Simancas. Wellington on the 3rd marched the Third Division over to the ford at Polios, and actually sent some riflemen of the Sixtieth across it; but the water was found to be too deep for any large number of men, while the ground on the north side was commanded by a large body of French troops. He therefore gave up for the present all idea of passing the river, and sent out his cavalry to explore the fords of the Douro generally.

Meanwhile he disposed his troops over against Marmont's: the Third Division opposite to Polios; headquarters at Rueda; and the bulk of the army in rear of it at Medina del Campo. The soldiers of the two armies, where they came into contact, were on most friendly terms, bathing in the same streams, sharing comforts and exchanging rations, but never firing a shot. The weather was extremely hot and there was not a single tree to give shade from the sun; but wine was abundant in the immense vaults of Rueda, and altogether the rank and file found life not unpleasant during the deadlock on the Douro.

Far otherwise was it for their commanders. Marmont was joined by Bonnet on the evening of the 1st of July; but Caffarelli, who had at first been so free with promises of reinforcements, had declared on the 26th of June that, what with Popham's raids on the coast and the activity of the guerillas all round him, he could spare no infantry, though he would send both cavalry and guns. Nevertheless not a man had arrived at Valladolid on the day when Marmont crossed the Douro; and the marshal did not fail to apprise his colleague of the fact in extremely bitter terms.

Sharp words, however, did not mend matters, and Caffarelli's subsequent letters were simply variations on a single theme—that the desire of his life was to send troops to the Duke of Ragusa, but that untoward circumstances forbade him to gratify it. Having foreseen from the first that little help would be forthcoming from this quarter, Marmont turned to Joseph and the Army of the Centre for reinforcements. The king, to do him justice, was anxious to strengthen the Army of Portugal, and had sent Caffarelli express directions to do so, though of course with no result. On the 29th of May Joseph had ordered Suchet to send him six thousand men so as to release that number from the Army of the Centre; but Suchet had produced a despatch from Berthier bidding him use his troops as he thought best, and had added to it a letter of his own to the effect that he would resign rather than obey His Most Catholic Majesty.

Soult, as we have seen, not only slighted the king's commands, but insisted that all Wellington's operations were designed against Andalusia; and the unfortunate Joseph, excusably swayed by so strong an opinion, could devise nothing better than to scrape together four thousand men of his own little Army of the Centre and place them under General Treilhard in the valley of the Tagus, with orders to follow d'Erlon's Corps wherever Hill's movements might lead it, whether to Castile or to Andalusia. Up to the end of June the king declared that he could do no more; but on hearing that Marmont had retired behind the Douro, he despatched an urgent message on the 6th of July to Soult bidding him move ten thousand men at once to Toledo, no matter what places such a detachment might compel him to evacuate. Soult answered on the 16th with an uncompromising negative; and before his letter could reach Joseph, Marmont, as shall be seen, had taken matters into his own hands. (Ducasse, ix. Joseph to Soult, 6th July; to Clark, 17th July; Soult to Joseph, 16th July; *Mémoires du duc de Raguse*, iv.; *Archives de la Guerre:* Jourdan to Suchet, 29th May 1812).

On Wellington's side matters, though more cheerful, were not without anxiety. After much pressure Castaños had at the end of June set in motion fifteen thousand men of the Galician Army under General Santocildes to invest Astorga, the process being appreciably hastened by Bonnet's withdrawal from Asturias. But the operations went forward slowly from want of means; and, though the Spanish batteries opened fire on the 2nd of July, their effect whether physical or moral was very slight. Popham had sailed from Coruña on the 18th of June, and had attacked several small places on the coast with varying success; but little or nothing of his doings was known at headquarters, albeit they were sufficiently energetic to distract Caffarelli.

The advance of the Portuguese cavalry and militia upon Marmont's right was visibly disquieting to the marshal; but all Portuguese affairs were uncertain at the moment, owing to the dearth of specie. Moreover, Wellington had as yet no knowledge of the insubordination of the French generals. He had intercepted more than one of Joseph's orders from Madrid; but these told him only that d'Erlon had been instructed to leave troops enough to contain Hill on the south of the Tagus, and to cross to the north bank with the rest of his force. He had also captured a letter from Marmont summoning Palombini's division to his assistance, so that the increase of the Army of Portugal seemed to be endless. To make matters worse Wellington received just at this time Bentinck's report that he was renouncing the east coast of Spain to return to Italy, and was taking away with him all the specie that was at Gibraltar.

As shall be seen in due time, Bentinck, distraught by the many opportunities for the work of liberation which appeared to offer themselves on all sides, had decided most wrongly to divide his force, and had actually shipped seven thousand men for Alicante on the 26th of June. But Wellington did not yet know of this and was in despair, he wrote to his brother:—

> Lord William Bentinck's decision is fatal to the campaign, at least for the present. If he should land *anywhere* in Italy, he will, as usual, be obliged to re-embark, and we shall have lost a golden opportunity here.

Finally it was in these same weeks that Graham and Picton were obliged to go home through ill-health, leaving their divisions to H. Campbell and Pakenham. James Stanhope, when presenting Graham's letter on the 3rd of July, said that he ought to accompany him to England, being on his staff, as a mark of respect. Wellington said:—

> I think you have seen the end of it, if Marmont destroys the bridges and throws back his right on the Pisuerga, he is safe unless I can cross at Tudela de Duero. I shan't fight him without an advantage, nor he me, I believe. Therefore go, and if you come out again, I will take care of you.

From the 3rd until the 16th of July the two forces remained in view of each other inactive; Marmont merely shifting troops from end to end of the line and repairing the bridges of Toro and Puente Duero at the extremities, so as to keep his adversary in continual suspense as to his designs. But before the 14th Wellington's anxiety had been considerably allayed by the knowledge that neither Caffarelli nor Palombini were likely to add any strength to the Army of Portugal, though he was still in doubt as to the movements of d'Erlon and of the king. Meanwhile it was quite certain that he must not dream of attacking the French in their present advantageous position; and he could conceive of no method of disturbing Marmont except by asking Santocildes to reduce his force before Astorga as low as possible consistently with safety, and to send the remainder down the Esla upon the marshal's right rear.

Wellington was not aware that there was much discontent in the

French Army over the feeble demonstration before San Cristobal in June, and a strong feeling in favour of a bold offensive. Marmont was a good and accomplished soldier and a skilful tactician; but he was not, in the presence of difficulties, a resolute man. In the actual circumstances of the moment he dominated the situation. He had the entire harvest ready to his hand to furnish supplies, and needed only to sit still patiently for yet a little while; for, whatever the apparent vacillations of Joseph, it was plain that at Madrid the reinforcement of the Army of Portugal was regarded as of the first importance to the campaign. It is true that Marmont's officers complained of his inaction and want of enterprise; but Wellington's officers were equally crying out against their chief for precisely the same reason; and Marmont's spies cannot have failed to apprise him of the gossip in the Allied camp. Yet, while Wellington treated such clamour with contempt, the marshal writhed under it with all the sensitiveness of a man who was less master of himself than slave of his reputation. He had injured his fame by the loss of the forts of Salamanca; and he felt impelled to do something—he knew not clearly what—in order to redeem it.

This impatient impulse was strengthened by the fact that his last letters both from Jourdan and Joseph held out no hope of aid from the Army of the Centre, and urged him to fight a battle at once before Hill should join Wellington and raise the Allied Army to overpowering strength. Such counsel, being founded upon the false assumption that Wellington had only eighteen thousand British troops with him instead of thirty thousand, might well have been disregarded by a commander of clearer insight and greater force of will.

By a strange irony Joseph, on the 9th of July, had finally made up his mind to evacuate the greater part of New Castile and to march with fourteen thousand men to the assistance of the Army of Portugal; but both the original and the duplicate of his letters to Marmont were intercepted and brought to Wellington, so that the marshal had nothing to guide him but the earlier instructions. Interpreting these with the impetuosity which so often accompanies weakness the Duke of Ragusa resolved to take the offensive. (Ducasse, ix. *Mémoires du duc de Raguse*, iv. *Wellington Desp.* To Graham and Clinton, 16th July 1812. The letter last quoted shows that Wellington had received Joseph's intercepted letter by the 16th of July. Oman was the first to discover this lost letter in the *Scovell MSS.*)

On the morning of the 16th Marmont with much ostentation shifted a body of troops to Toro and sent Bonnet's division across the bridge. Wellington accordingly made a corresponding movement to his left. Then under cover of night Marmont recalled Bonnet, broke down the repairs of the bridge at Toro, and, massing the whole of his army at Tordesillas, crossed the Douro at that point on the morning of the 17th, finally halting at Nava del Rey after a long and exhausting forced march. On the night of the 16th Wellington had issued orders for his centre and left to concentrate on the Guareña about Cañizal; but, from some suspicion of the enemy's real intentions, he directed the right, which consisted of the Fourth and Light Divisions and Anson's brigade of cavalry under Cotton, to halt some ten miles east of Castrillo at Castrejon. Having encountered advanced parties of the enemy about Rueda on his march, Cotton sent out patrols before daylight of the 18th, which were at once driven in by the French horse; and a skirmish ensued between the cavalry and horse-artillery of both sides, Cotton holding his ground stubbornly.

Meanwhile Wellington, being apprised of Marmont's arrival at Nava, had ordered Bock's, Alten's, and Le Marchant's brigades of cavalry to Alaejos, and the Fifth Division to Torrecilla de la Orden to extricate Cotton; and he came upon the ground himself at seven o'clock in company with Beresford. Very shortly afterwards a small body of French cavalry under a very brave leader advanced upon a couple of British guns. Some of Beresford's staff, alarmed for the safety of the pieces, assumed the direction of two British squadrons which were present, and by dint of giving them the wrong word of command threw them into hopeless and abject confusion. (See Tomkinson. When staff officers try to take the place unnecessarily of regimental officers, mishaps nearly always follow.) The French cavalry galloping on not only overpowered the guns for the moment, but swept away Wellington, Beresford, and their staff, who were obliged to draw their swords and only escaped with difficulty. Shortly after this incident Marmont, having ascertained that only part of the Allies were before him, brought forward his infantry to Alaejos; and Wellington, seeing that his left was turned, gave the order to retire by Torrecilla de la Orden.

The three divisions of infantry therefore marched off, each battalion in close column so as to form square readily at any moment if the enemy's cavalry should attack, while the British horse covered the flanks and rear. The French infantry on their side strained every nerve to cut off the Allies; and for ten miles the two hostile columns strode on through stifling heat and clouds of dust in two parallel lines, not more than five hundred yards apart, (Napier, who was present, says "half musket shot," whatever that may mean, Simmons says five hundred yards, which appears to me nearer the truth, but no doubt the distance constantly varied), each continually quickening its pace in the hope of outstripping the other, yet neither losing for a moment the perfection of its order.

The officers of both armies exchanged signals of courtesy; from time to time the French guns unlimbered, and thundered out a sterner salute; and once at least a body of French infantry ran forward and forced the Light Division to leave the road and strike through the plains of standing corn. All was to no purpose. The British reached the Guareña first; and there was a general rush for a draught of muddy water. Instantly the French guns appeared on the heights above, unlimbered, and poured such a tempest of shot upon the Fifth Division that Leith deployed his brigades, and in that order ascended the rising ground on the other side of the stream, while the Light and Fourth Divisions were fain to leave the water and hurry on.

★★★★★★

Napier says that the Fifth alone halted to drink, and that the Light Division drank as they marched. Leith admits that he halted the Fifth; but Leach of the Ninety-Fifth and Cook of the Forty-Third agree that the Light Division made a general rush for water; Cooke adding words which imply that thirst for once prevailed over discipline; while Leach says that he can never forgive the French for not permitting him to drink without the accompaniment of a nine-pound shot. Grattan confirms the story of the rush for water.

★★★★★★

Arrived at the summit of the heights, all three divisions faced about, the Fourth on the left of the new front about Castrillo; the Light Division in the centre; and the Fifth on the right about Cañizal; the remaining divisions, by Wellington's orders, forming still farther to the right at Vallesa. Meanwhile the French came up in two columns, and Clausel, who commanded that on the right, seeing few troops before him, pushed Carrié's brigade of dragoons, (German authorities, Beamish and Schwertfeger, say that it was not Carrié's brigade only but Boyer's whole division), over the ford near Castrillo with a battalion of infantry and three guns in support. Victor Alten met the dragoons with his brigade of light cavalry, and after a confused fight amid blinding dust succeeded in driving them back to the refuge of their infantry, with a loss of ninety-four prisoners, including Carrié himself. Reinforced by the Third Dragoons, Alten appears next to have essayed a second attack, which was unsuccessful; but the Twenty-Seventh and Fortieth coming up from the Fourth Division soon swept the isolated battalion away with the bayonet, and a squadron of German hussars, pursuing, captured about one hundred and fifty prisoners.

The loss of the cavalry in this affair amounted to one hundred and forty five killed, wounded, and taken; and the casualties of the Allies for the day reached the total of four hundred and forty-two of all ranks, of whom one hundred and forty fell in the Twenty-Seventh and Fortieth, and one hundred and thirty in the Portuguese. Those of the enemy can hardly have been fewer.

★★★★★★

It is difficult to know what to make of this little action. The German authors represent Victor Alten's conduct as brilliant; Napier, who never grudged praise to the German Legion, takes a contrary view; and his account is supported by the fact that Alten lost twelve prisoners, which points at any rate to a moment of ill-success. The account given by Grattan (not a very trustworthy author) differs altogether from the others, and brings two French divisions instead of a single French battalion of infantry into action.

★★★★★★

During the night Wellington threw up some fieldworks for the defence of his position; and on the following day the two armies looked at each other until the afternoon, the heat being intense and Marmont anxious to give his troops some rest and to collect his stragglers.

The marshal, however, knowing the country intimately, had matured his design to ascend the eastern branch of the Guareña until it became a mere rivulet, to cross it at Cantalapiedra, and to occupy in considerable force a high plateau which extended from that point without an undulation almost to Salamanca. Accordingly at four o'clock he started on the first stage of his journey with a short march to his left as far as Tarazona, upon which Wellington made a corresponding movement on his right to the heights of Vallesa. On the 20th Wellington expected to be attacked, but found to his dismay that the French were speeding up the river and had actually passed it before any dispositions could be made to oppose them.

Marmont in fact had turned the Allied right flank; and Wellington had no alternative but to follow him in a parallel line but on lower ground. Both armies were formed in parallel columns, the French in two and the Allies in three, with cavalry in the van and rear; and both preserved their distances and intervals so exactly that either could be brought at a moment's notice into battle array by the simple word "Right (or Left) wheel into line." Between them was a slight hollow, so that they could see each other perfectly; and being within cannon-shot the French artillery from time to time unlimbered and fired a few rounds, which did little or no damage. So the two hosts strode on in a vast interminable cloud of dust; racing, yet with all the superb order of a parade-movement, for the Tormes; while the two commanders with a nerve more surprising even than their consummate mastery of their art, each watched coolly, though in vain, for some technical blunder on the part of his rival.

By noon the rear of the Allies had dragged itself out into a long tail of straggling vehicles; and Bonnet, it is said, begged Marmont's permission to fall upon this disorderly crowd, but was sternly refused. The marshal had gained the lead and intended to keep it. Wellington made a strenuous effort to cross his line of advance at Cantalpino but failed, for the French were the better marchers; and he now forsook the parallel line, detained the Fifth Division to gather up the baggage and stragglers, and then bore away more to westward upon Aldear-rubia, intending to halt his main body there, while sending the Sixth Division and Alten's cavalry to Aldea Lengua. Before evening the two armies had lost sight of each other; but at nightfall the gleam of camp-fires revealed the presence of the French at Babila Fuente, where they commanded the ford of Huerta on the Tormes.

As they had marched for a greater distance than the Allies, Wel-lington had not expected them to push on to the river that even-ing; and he now saw to his disgust that he had been outmanoeuvred. Without delay he brought forward his second line to join the first at Cabeça Vellosa, where the troops bivouacked for the night, having lost in the course of the march some four hundred stragglers cap-tured by the French dragoons. (So Marmont says, though no English historian mentions the fact; but a private letter from an officer in the 79th mentions that his battalion, or his brigade, for the context is not very clear, lost 100 prisoners. I have to thank Mr. A. G. M. Mackenzie, A.R.I.B.A., for a copy of this letter).

The troubles of this day did not end without the further mis-hap that d'Urban's Portuguese horse, being mistaken for French, were fired on by the Third Division and suffered appreciable loss both in men and horses.

At dawn of the 21st the Allies moved up to the position of San Cristobal; and there Wellington wrote a letter to Castaños and another to the Secretary of State, acquainting them that he could not hold his ground. Marmont, as he pointed out, was manoeuvring to cut him off from his lines of supply, and he himself was unable to retaliate; for the French armies, under their system of plunder, had no such lines. He was therefore determined to cover Salamanca for as long as possible, but not upon any account to sacrifice his communications with Ciudad Rodrigo, nor, except under very advantageous conditions, to engage in a general action. In fact Wellington had realised that his offensive movement was to all present appearances doomed to failure, and that, without some unexpected stroke of good fortune, he must retire to Portugal and resume the waiting game once more. His mortification cannot but have been aggravated by the despondency which was visible among all classes in Salamanca, and by the remembrance that on that very ground only one short month before, he had reluctantly permitted a great opportunity for a favourable attack to escape him.

Marmont, on the other hand, in spite of his success, had not laid aside his diffidence and irresolution. At ten o'clock, though the Allies had been in motion since dawn, his army was still stationary; and, when at last his orders came round at that hour, they were based upon a fortuitous circumstance which had just come to his knowledge. Upon marching northward from Salamanca Wellington had left Carlos d'España in garrison at Alba de Tormes; and that officer, seized with panic, had not only evacuated the place but, worse still, had, from dread of Wellington's wrath, omitted to inform him of the fact. Marmont accordingly issued directions for his army to march up the Tormes to Alba, intending to hold the town with his left, so that his front would face to the west full upon the flank of Wellington's line of communications. Foy combated this project, because it would not only reveal the marshal's plans, but give Wellington an opportunity of foiling them. If, he argued, the intention was to cross the Tormes, it would be better to do so at once while there was no enemy in the way, instead of allowing Wellington a full day to occupy the plateau of Calvarrasa de Arriba, from which position he could make the passage a very difficult and hazardous operation.

Clausel seconded the arguments of Foy; Marmont yielded to them; and at noon the French troops traversed the Tormes by the fords of Huerta and Encinos de Abajo, about three miles farther up the river, leaving one division behind them on the heights of Babila Fuente.

Wellington made no effort to impede their march; and at nightfall they bivouacked between Alba and Salamanca, with their advanced parties occupying Calvarrasa de Arriba, (*i.e.* Upper Calvarrasa, as opposed to Calvarrasa de Abajo or Lower Calvarrasa. Arriba and Abajo correspond to the French *amont* and *aval*), and Nuestra Senhora de la Pena, a short distance to the west of the former village.

On learning of the movement Wellington left the Third Division and d'Urban's Portuguese cavalry entrenched at Cabrerizos, as a counter to the French detachment at Babila Fuente, and towards evening passed the rest of the army over the bridge of Salamanca and the ford of Santa Marta. The new position marked out for the army was with the left resting upon the Tormes near the ford of Santa Marta, and with the right upon a rugged hill, of which more shall presently be said, near the village of Los Arapiles, the advanced cavalry being pushed forward to Calvarrasa de Abajo.

The movement was not complete until after dark, when the sultry weather broke up in a thunderstorm of appalling violence. With such rapidity were the upper waters of the river swollen by the rain that the Light Division passed the ford almost shoulder-deep, while the lightning played on the muskets of the marching columns in sheets of fire so dazzling as to hinder the progress of the men. Many horses both of French and English broke away in terror and galloped furiously they knew not whither; and some of those of the Fifth Dragoon Guards even tore their bridles out of the hands of the men, who were sitting on the ground at their heads, and injured many soldiers as they rushed through the bivouac. Then the rain came down with such violence that the Third Division, which was throwing up field-works at Cabrerizos, was obliged to desist, the trenches being full of water.

All night long the deluge continued, with furious gusts of wind, forbidding all sleep and drenching both armies to the skin. But the darkness brought something worse than discomfort to Wellington in the form of certain intelligence that General Chauvel with seventeen hundred horse and twenty guns from Caffarelli's army had reached Polios on the 20th and would join Marmont on the 22nd or 23rd. By a curious fatality Joseph also—though Marmont and Wellington knew it not—was marching the self-same evening with thirteen thousand men for the Tormes. The dawn of the 22nd broke cloudless after the storm; and soon after light appeared Marmont rode up to the heights of Calvarrasa de Arriba to reconnoitre his enemy.

Within cannon-shot to his front a single scarlet division—the Seventh—lay astride the road to Salamanca; three to four miles beyond it a smaller body, evidently part of the escort to the retreating baggage-train, was visible ascending the hill of Aldea Tejada; and far to the right the heights of San Cristobal showed signs of a small occupying force.

★★★★★★

Both Foy and Marmont speak not of Aldea Tejada but of Tejares, which is three miles north-west of the former place, and six miles from where they were standing. Arteche accepts their statements literally, and goes wrong in consequence. Tejares is obviously a mistake for Aldea Tejada.

I am unable to divine what these latter troops can have been, possibly a detachment of D'Urban's cavalry from the other side of the river, or a flanking party of the escort to the general hospital which was evacuating at this time.

★★★★★★

All the rest of the British Army was hidden by a range of hills which runs due south from the village of Santa Marta for over three miles, and is then broken for the space of a mile into the two flat-topped isolated hills known as the Arapiles. Only on the summit of the range was a little knot of horsemen, grouped about a central figure in a blue frock-coat and low-crowned hat, who could be no other than Lord Wellington.

Marmont concluded that the Allies were about to retire to the position of Tejares, there to join the road to Ciudad Rodrigo; and it occurred to him that the Seventh Division must be the rear-guard and that, unless he assailed it at once, it might escape him. He had already brought up Foy's division to the west of Calvarrasa de Arriba, and Foy's skirmishers were engaged in a lively bicker with the British Sixty-Eighth; but the marshal refrained from a general attack, and after long hesitation decided to move his army southward so as to turn Wellington's right. The French officers who recommended this course appear to have hoped that Wellington would thus be manoeuvred out of his position without fighting, and would then find his retreat to Ciudad Rodrigo a very difficult operation; but Marmont had accepted their advice with a vague lurking desire for a battle.

Nor perhaps was he unduly bold herein, for he had with him on the field some seven and forty thousand fighting men, good soldiers of one nation, with seventy-eight guns; whereas Wellington had not above fifty thousand, British, Germans, Portuguese, and Spaniards, with sixty guns.

195

I give the returns upon which I base my calculations in the Appendix; but I suspect that the numbers upon both sides should be lower. Napier gives what purports to be a morning state of the sabres and bayonets of the army on the 22nd, amounting to 25,381 British, 17,517 Portuguese, and 3500 Spaniards, or 46,398 in all. Adding one-eighth for officers, sergeants, and drummers, the total would be roughly 52,000 of all ranks; which by the addition of 2000 for artillery would be increased to 54,000. On the other hand Tomkinson summarises the Allied force on the 18th of July as roughly 40,000 rank and file of all nations, or say 45,000 of all ranks. I do not know where Napier obtained his returns, for I have been unable to find a morning state of the 22nd July; but I believe his summary of it to be worthless.

Be that as it may, the marshal summoned to him the detachment that he had left at Babila Fuente and set his whole army in march to southward.

To understand his movements aright it will now be necessary to consider more closely the nature of the ground over which the two armies were manoeuvring, its general character the country greatly resembles Salisbury Plain, being unenclosed although cultivated, and therefore favourable for cavalry, but nevertheless diversified by undulations which make it far blinder than the inexperienced would suppose. Two conspicuous features, however, strike the eye immediately, namely the two flat-topped hills already mentioned as the Arapiles. The more northerly of these, known as the Lesser Arapil, rises abruptly to a height of about one hundred feet; and its summit, which is about two hundred and fifty yards long by seventy-five broad, is as flat as a billiard-table. It is so closely connected with the main ridge as to form a part of it, and was the feature upon which Wellington had rested his right flank.

The second or Greater Arapil lies about a thousand yards to south of it and is far more isolated from the adjacent heights. Its summit is over two hundred yards long, and it rises to rather greater elevation than the Lesser Arapil. Both of these hills are exceedingly steep to climb, and in both of them the grey stone crops out thickly near the top, forming a little wilderness of rocks. (The Greater Arapil is now a quarry). These two Arapiles, to use Napier's phrase which is no less correct than graphic, form the door-posts to a basin of apparently level plain, about two miles north and south by one mile east and west, the northerly boundary being marked by a bold round hill called the Teso of San Miguel.

At the foot of this hill stands the little village of Arapiles on the left bank of a tiny brook; and to south of the village again the ground rises to the height of La Cuquera, which forms the western border of the basin. As a matter of fact the plain slopes gently upward for a mile to west of the two Arapiles, until it culminates at La Cuquera, from which point it declines as gently northward to yet another basin, which Napier has omitted to mention, although it was the scene of great exploits. Speaking generally, one standing on the summit of either of the two Arapiles can command singularly little ground, though the prospect may seem wide to him; so many are the folds and hollows in which troops can be hidden away.

For Marmont, who designed to march round the southern flank of the Allies and then either to attack them or turn westward upon their line of communication, the two Arapiles were two little fortresses which would serve admirably to protect his army while it changed position; and he accordingly ordered Bonnet to seize them at once. Bonnet thereupon detached troops for the purpose; but Wellington being apprised of the movement sent the 7th Caçadores to be beforehand with them. At this the French broke their ranks and raced for the two hills. The Lesser Arapil, being close to the Allied position, was seized by the *Caçadores* without difficulty; but the French were the first to gain the Greater Arapil, which they occupied at once with a battalion.

Being the higher and more important of the two, this was sufficient for Marmont's purpose; and having ordered guns to be brought to the summit, (the guns were dismounted and carried up by hand, the hill being too steep to permit them to be drawn up), and massed Bonnet's division in rear of it, he proceeded with his further arrangements. Foy's division he left on the plateau of Calvarrasa de Arriba, very advantageous ground, with Ferey's to support it in second line, and Boyer's cavalry in rear of all, the whole amounting to some ten thousand infantry and thirteen hundred cavalry.

On the left of Foy the divisions of Clausel, Sarrut, Maucune, and Brenier, together over twenty thousand men, were ordered to march along the edge of the great forest which lay in rear of the French line, and to mass themselves south-east of the Greater Arapil, from which point they could move in any direction. Thomières's division, about forty-five hundred strong, was directed to move to a steep height, named El Sierro, somewhat farther to the south, with Curto's light cavalry upon its outer flank.

★★★★★★

Marmont himself says only that he placed Thomières's division on a steep height on "the left of the wood," but its position is correctly shown in Wyld's *Atlas*. Arteche, basing his opinion apparently upon a map in the War Office at Madrid, places it at Nuestra Señora de la Pena—a most astonishing blunder.

★★★★★★

In their essence these dispositions were defensive, for Marmont was only waiting for the Allies to retire westward, when he hoped to inflict some damage upon their rearguard.

Upon seeing Marmont's movements Wellington at once took steps to counter them. He therefore threw the light companies of the Guards into the village of Arapiles; stationed Cole's division *en potence* on the Teso de San Miguel immediately behind it, and on the Lesser Arapil, which was occupied by Anson's brigade; brought up Bradford's Portuguese and d'España's Spaniards to the right rear of Cole near the village of Las Torres; and sent orders to Pakenham to cross the Tormes with the whole of his force and take post in rear of the village of Aldea Tejada, nearly three miles to the north of Arapiles.

At the same time Wellington posted the Light Division to confront Foy's troops opposite Nuestra Senora de la Pena, with the First Division in support. Thus a new line was formed, extending from the Lesser Arapil in the east to Aldea Tejada in the west, with its face towards the south; but the Fifth, Sixth, and Seventh Divisions were still hidden away on the reverse slope of the ridge which the Allies had occupied on the preceding night.

While these movements were going forward, Leith brought Lawson's battery within range to play upon the French columns as they marched southward; but his guns were soon silenced with some loss by the superior cannon of the French. All was then again quiet until eleven o'clock, when Wellington, observing the accumulation of the enemy in rear of the Greater Arapil, decided to assault and take that hill, and actually brought the First Division forward for the purpose. Marmont, who was himself on the summit, anticipating a general attack, came down hastily and galloped to his main body; but the troops of the Allies presently halted and faced about, Beresford having dissuaded his chief from venturing as yet upon the offensive.

This sudden retirement was not lost upon Marmont; and about noon another sign convinced him that Wellington had begun his retreat upon Ciudad Rodrigo. A glorious sunny morning had already dried up the rain of the previous night; and a huge cloud of dust was visible moving steadily from north-east to southwest. The marshal inferred that Wellington meant to retire by his right, and was therefore reinforcing that wing to the utmost. As a matter of fact the dust had been raised by Pakenham, who, instead of making for the bridge of Salamanca, had passed the Tormes by the ford of Cabrerizos, and was striking across country, little more than a mile in rear of the Light Division, towards Aldea Tejada. (See Cooke's *Memoirs of the late War*, i. I imagine that he took the route by Sta. Marta and Carbajosa. Grattan, who might have informed us, wastes his space in inaccurate descriptions of what he did not see, instead of telling us what he did see).

Certainly Wellington had not sent Pakenham thither without an eye to the general retreat of his entire host; but Marmont's imagination magnified the movement of one division of infantry and one brigade of cavalry into the march of half an army.

Since Wellington was thus strengthening his right—so the marshal reasoned—he himself must strengthen his left; and accordingly at about two o'clock orders were sent to Maucune to lead his division forward to the ridge next in front and to the left of him, known as the Monte de Azan, and to draw the men up on its eastern extremity with the division of Thomières in second line, and Clausel's as reserve in rear of all; while Brenier's division was to take the place of Thomières's on the height of El Sierro. Further, the whole of Boyer's dragoons, except one regiment, were withdrawn from Foy and stationed on the flank of Clausel; and finally one regiment of Bonnet's division—the 122nd—was directed to occupy an intermediate height between the Greater Arapil and the new position, so as to make the new line coherent. By this manoeuvre Marmont judged that towards evening he would be able, if he wished, to cut off the communications of the Allies with Tamames and Ciudad Rodrigo.

Accordingly Maucune and Thomières set their troops in motion, while Clausel toiled after them far in rear; Maucune covering the entire movement by a heavy cannonade and a bold advance of sharp-shooters upon the village of Arapiles. In due time Maucune and Thomières reached the Monte de Azan, when for some reason the former, after a short halt opposite the village, extended his division far to westward, while the latter, instead of forming in rear of Maucune, not only came up to the same level but actually took the lead of him, hastening still farther to the west. Whether through their own fault or through Marmont's, both evidently imagined that the race of the previous days was to be resumed. Wellington, who had left his point of observation on the Lesser Arapil and was at dinner in a farm-house, came out at once on receiving the reports of his staff, turned his field-glass upon the French columns and ejaculated, "By God! that will do." Then hastening to the Lesser Arapil, he surveyed the scene with grim content. The whole of the Monte de Azan was covered with the horse, foot, and artillery of Marmont's left wing, all marching steadily away from any support of their right and centre.

"M. d'Alava," Wellington is said to have exclaimed to his Spanish *aide-de-camp*, "Marmont *est perdu*." He at once brought up the Fifth Division to the right of the Fourth, with the Seventh and Sixth Divisions in support of them, leaving Beresford's Portuguese and Le Marchant's brigade of heavy cavalry to the right rear of the Fifth. Then for the first time Marmont from the top of the Greater Arapil saw the larger portion, though still not the whole, of the British forces, and sent an urgent message for the divisions of Ferey and Sarrut to march with all speed to the help of his left. But Wellington was already galloping at the top of his speed to Aldea Tejada, where Pakenham's troops, unseen and unsuspected by Marmont, were hidden behind the hill. Those who saw the commander-in-chief arrive thought that he looked paler than usual; but his orders to his brother-in-law were terse—"Ned, move on with the Third Division; take the heights on your front; and drive everything before you."

Pakenham had already called his men to arms and reformed his columns. "I will, my lord," he said, "if you will give me your hand"; and Wellington having gravely offered his hand galloped back again to the centre.

Pakenham then marched off his troops in four columns. On the right was Alten's brigade, commanded in his absence by Arentschild, which consisted of the Fourteenth Light Dragoons, and the 1st German Hussars, together with five hundred of D'Urban's Portuguese horse; on the right centre Wallace's brigade of the Forty-Fifth, Seventy-Fourth, and Eighty-Eighth; on the left centre Champalimaud's Portuguese brigade; on the left Campbell's brigade of the Fifth, Eighty-Third, and Ninety-Fourth. The distance to be traversed was about two miles and a half, for the greater part of which the force was concealed by the intervening hills; and the advance in spite of the dust appears to have been for some time unnoticed. (Wrottesley's *Life of Burgoyne*, i.)

D'Urban, riding a little distance ahead with his two *aides-de-camp*, came upon the leading battalion of Thomières's division, marching very fast in column of companies, and uncovered by any mounted advanced party or scouts of their own. Stealing back unperceived, he realised that this battalion had already passed across Pakenham's front, wherefore wheeling his Portuguese cavalry into line, with two squadrons of the Fourteenth Light Dragoons in support, he ordered them to attack it at once. The French, taken by surprise, had no time to do more than close the second company upon the first, which enabled them to repel the Portuguese that fell upon their front; but a single squadron charging upon their left flank broke them up completely and drove them with heavy loss up the hill. (These details are drawn from D'Urban's MS. Diary, as quoted by Oman).

Then Thomières suddenly became aware of his danger. His division was drawn out in a long string over a distance of more than a mile, the head of it far in advance of the rest and inclining towards the summit of the ridge, while the bulk was still on the reverse side. (Grattan says that behind the artillery Thomières's division was seen "endeavouring to regain its place in the combat"—a vague phrase which may mean anything, but which, when read with Burgoyne's account, seems to mean a farther extension to the west).

In this desperate situation he appears to have hurried his men to the extreme western eminence of the plateau, so as to gain it before the Allies; at the same time ranging twenty guns along the crest, and throwing out a cloud of skirmishers to his front in order to cover the formation of his main body. (Burgoyne is the authority for this, and as he repeats the statement twice over with comments upon its bearing on the fate of the day, I cannot doubt that it is correct. Wrottesley, *Life of Sir John Burgoyne*, i.)

He also sent six squadrons of Curto's light horse round the western base of the ridge to threaten the right flank of Pakenham's advance. (I deduce this from the narrative in Beamish, ii.; but Curto's movements are very difficult to follow, and I cannot be sure that this account of them is correct).

Arentschild, whose function it was to protect that flank, came upon these horsemen drawn up on the farther side of a deep and high-banked ravine. Always bold and enterprising, he ordered his Hussars to file from the centre of squadrons over this formidable obstacle, holding the Fourteenth in reserve; and the gallant Germans, reforming on the farther side, charged and broke the enemy's first line. A second line of the French advanced upon them, however, while they were in confusion; and it seemed as if nothing could save them from being driven headlong over the precipitous sides of the water-course. With admirable presence of mind their officers galloped with all possible speed to the brink of the ravine, faced about there, and rallied their men under the protection of a part of the Fourteenth, after which the entire brigade charged, broke the French for the second time, and pursued them, taking many prisoners.

Meanwhile the British infantry continued its steady forward march, heedless of the showers of grape rained upon it, while the French sharpshooters awaited the moment of deployment in order to pour in a destructive fire. But Pakenham, taking advantage of the oblique movement of the division upon the front and flank of the ridge, gave the word, when within two hundred and fifty yards of the enemy, to deploy without halting; whereupon, each company brought up right shoulders, and the three brigades formed three lines to their left, Wallace's leading, the Portuguese next in rear of it, and Campbell's brigade in reserve. The British skirmishers now ran forward and engaged those of the French, who, though greatly superior in number, made no effort to check the advancing array, or to gain time for their main body to order itself on the crest of the ridge. There was in fact confusion, natural enough in the circumstances, and possibly aggravated by the fate of Thomières, who fell early on this day. The Third Division therefore climbed the hill against but feeble opposition, and on the summit found the French still only half formed.

The enemy met them with one effective volley, which inflicted some loss; but, when Wallace's brigade continued to press on without discharging a shot, the French fire became wild and the men began to waver.

★★★★★★

Grattan draws a sensational picture of five thousand muskets belching forth a torrent of bullets "which brought down almost the entire of Wallace's first rank and more than half of the officers." This is mere Milesian boasting. Wallace's brigade went into action at least 1600 strong, and lost 237 killed, wounded, and missing. Of 81 officers, 2 were killed and 11 wounded, of whom 4 slightly.

★★★★★★

Their officers sprang forward to rally them, and the colonel of one regiment, snatching a musket from one of his men, shot Major Murphy, the commanding officer of the Eighty-Eighth, dead. A single bullet from the British ranks took vengeance for his fall; but the Eighty-Eighth, seeing the major's corpse dragged along by his terrified horse, became uncontrollable. Pakenham shouted to Wallace to "let them loose." The brigade instantly charged, and the French columns dissolved into a mob of panic-stricken fugitives.

Meanwhile the struggle had begun also in the centre, though Wellington held back the divisions in that quarter until Pakenham should be fairly engaged. The cannon had been busy upon each side with fortunate results for the Allies, for Marmont was almost immediately badly wounded by a shell; Bonnet, the next senior officer, was also disabled; and until Clausel could be found, the French were without a commander-in-chief. The Fifth Division lay down on the open plain, exposed to a very heavy fire of artillery from the Greater Arapil and from the guns on the height beyond it, Leith riding slowly up and down on their front to encourage them; while the French sharpshooters delivered attack upon attack against the village of Arapiles.

At last Wellington came up and directed Leith to form two lines, the first made up of the Royals, Ninth, Thirty-Eighth, (1st Batt., which had reached the army on the previous day to take the place of the 2nd Batt., its colonel, Greville, commanded the 1st Brigade), and part of the Fourth; the second of the remainder of the Fourth, the Thirtieth, Forty-Fourth, and Fifty-Eighth (the last three being very weak battalions), together with Spry's brigade of Portuguese. The men leaped gladly to their feet, but they had still to wait for some time before Bradford's Portuguese brigade came up on their right.

Then Leith at last gave the signal, and the whole strode forward in beautiful order, Wellington himself riding with them for a time between the first and second lines. The French artillery continued to play upon them; and as they drew nearer to the heights the fire of the French skirmishers became destructive, until Leith's light infantry drove them back and forced the guns also to retire to a new position. From their saddles the mounted officers could observe the hostile array, Maucune's battalions being massed in contiguous columns, (Leith Hay describes them first as squares and afterwards as columns), with the front rank kneeling, on the heights just fifty yards in rear of the brow where the British would first come into sight. The French were calm and confident, brave men under a brave officer; and not a musket was discharged until the whole burst out in a single volley. A moment later, having gained the crest, Leith gave the order to fire and charge; and with a great shout the British dashed through the smoke with the bayonet. Whether owing to heavy losses or to panic the French columns once again melted into a disorganised mass of flying men.

During this time Pakenham, pushing on after the defeated fragments of Thomières's leading battalions, found himself in the presence either of that general's second brigade or of a part of Maucune's division, which menaced him in front, while some of Curto's squadrons threatened his flank.

★★★★★★

Two of Thomières's regiments, the 62nd and 101st, were almost annihilated. The third (1st Line) escaped with the loss of at most no more than one-seventh of its numbers, and, singularly enough, of only four officers. It cannot therefore have been very heavily engaged, and must have escaped the onslaught of the cavalry.

★★★★★★

In the heat of pursuit Wallace's brigade had out-marched its supports and was now brought to an abrupt halt. Pakenham and Wallace, dreading an onset of cavalry, rode up and down the line helping their officers as they told off the men to form square. Arentschild was still following up the body of horse which he had defeated; but one of D'Urban's Portuguese regiments attempted a charge upon the French infantry and was repulsed. For a brief space Wallace's brigade was utterly at a loss. The dry grass, kindled by innumerable cartridge papers, had burst into flame, turning the warm air of summer into scorching heat, and rolling up dense clouds of suffocating smoke. Tremendous firing could be heard in front. Scattered soldiers of the Fifth Division, lost in the blinding vapour, had blundered into their ranks; and no man knew what might come next.

Presently loud cheering and trampling of horses was heard to the left rear, and the brigade turned half round, expecting an attack, when the smoke rolled away and revealed Le Marchant's heavy dragoons advancing at a canter, with Cotton at their head. They had been ordered to charge as soon as a favourable opportunity should offer itself. Wallace opened his line to let them pass; the dragoons formed line to their front; and the French hastily ran to throw themselves into square. Before the evolution was half completed the trumpets sounded the charge, and the heavy brigade crashed down upon the 66th Line of

Maucune's brigade. Huddling themselves together as best they could, the French opened a sharp though ineffective fire, but in an instant the British troopers broke into them and hewed them down with terrible slaughter. Leaving the prisoners to the care of Leith's division, Le Marchant rallied his brigade and led them against the regiment next in rear, the 15th Line. These troops had had more time to collect themselves, and met the onset with a volley that emptied many saddles; but they likewise were utterly dispersed, and fled the way of the 66th.

Still insatiate, Le Marchant pressed on against Brenier's leading regiment, the 22nd, which had just come upon the ground and was forming to cover Maucune's retreat. Though not in square, the 22nd was in good order and reserved its fire until the dragoons were within ten yards, when they poured in a volley which wrought havoc in the leading squadron. But they had waited too long. The dragoons might fall, but their horses could not be stopped; and after a desperate encounter of sabre against bayonet these brave Frenchmen also were driven into flight. Many of the helpless fugitives, spent and bleeding, flung themselves into the ranks of Wallace's brigade for safety and were spared. Hundreds more ran headlong to the shelter of a thin wood on the reverse side of the ridge, which could not, however, protect them. Cotton and his victorious dragoons thundered on, breaking through everything that stood in their way; and one squadron of the Fourth Dragoons under their colonel, Lord Edward Somerset, captured single-handed five guns.

Le Marchant himself was killed on the edge of the great forest in rear of the French position. At last with horses blown and exhausted, Cotton left the pursuit to be finished by the Eleventh and Sixteenth Light Dragoons, who had followed the Heavy Brigade over the hill, and by the cavalry of Arentschild and D'Urban. Two squadrons of the French 3rd Hussars endeavoured to impede the chase; but with great difficulty men enough of the German Hussars, Fourteenth, and Portuguese were collected to drive them off, and the French horse was seen no more on that quarter of the field. Anson's brigade pressed on so eagerly that, wreathed in a cloud of dust, they approached within close range of a large body of hostile infantry and artillery, but fortunately escaped without loss.

The entire attack, as thus far related, occupied less than an hour, and at its close the left wing of the French had been utterly overthrown. The 7th and 5th divisions were for all fighting purposes destroyed, and the 2nd much damaged; the three of them having lost some four thousand men. Moreover, Pakenham (for Leith had been wounded) with the Third and Fifth Divisions and the whole mass of Wellington's cavalry—one regiment excepted—was reforming line to sweep the entire field from west to east.

It was at the crisis of such a disaster that Clausel was summoned to take the command of the French army; but fortune had already offered him a chance to save something from the wreck, and he was now to show how great a French general could be in adversity. Simultaneously with the advance of the Fifth Division Wellington had launched Cole's into action immediately upon the left of Bradford's brigade, at the same time ordering Pack's Portuguese to assail the Greater Arapil, so as to relieve Cole of its fire upon his flank during the advance. The Fusilier brigade on the right and Stubbs's Portuguese on the left, making a single line of seven battalions, filed through the village of Arapiles under a terrible cannonade, threw out their markers on the farther side, and having reformed line moved forward steadily against Clausel's division, which was by this time arrayed upon the right of Maucune.

Upon reaching the low ground at the foot of the French position Cole perceived on his left front the detached regiment—the 122nd of Bonnet's division—which Marmont had stationed on a low ridge to connect the troops on the Great Arapil with those on the Monte de Azan; and he noticed also the bulk of Bonnet's division drawn up within supporting distance of it. Stubbs's Portuguese thrust aside the 122nd towards Bonnet's main body; and Cole, detaching the 7th Caçadores to hold it in check, pushed on with the remainder of his line against Clausel, his battalions suffering much from the enfilading fire of the French guns on the Great Arapil.

They pressed on, however, unwaveringly to the summit, where they met the first line—five battalions—of the French, and after a savage duel of musketry drove them back upon their reserves. But meanwhile Pack's attack upon the Greater Arapil had failed. His Portuguese had scrambled up the choking ascent of the hill and were within thirty feet of the top when they were checked by a perpendicular bank. The French then suddenly poured a volley upon them from the rocks, and closing upon them in front and flank with the bayonet, dashed them down to the plain with very heavy loss.

The situation became for a time serious. Cole had been wounded as he reached the crest of the ridge; his troops were blown and disordered by their attack; and now three out of four of Bonnet's regiments—the 118th, 119th, and 122nd—sallied out from behind the Greater Arapil upon his left flank. The 7th Caçadores strove gallantly to stem their advance, but were swept away by superior numbers; and Clausel, having rallied his five defeated battalions upon their reserves, led the whole ten forward to charge the front. The Fourth Division, thinned and exhausted by its effort, was in no state to await the shock. The Portuguese gave way first; the Fusiliers followed; and both brigades ran down headlong from the plateau into the plain. Pursuing his success without hesitation, Clausel developed a powerful counter-attack upon Wellington's centre. To Sarrut he committed the task of rallying and shielding the three beaten divisions; and then summoning Bonnet's three regiments to form upon his right, six squadrons of Boyer's dragoons to cover his right flank, and Ferey's division to advance in his support to the crest of the hill which he had regained, he pushed on in pursuit of Cole's defeated division.

The Fortieth, which had come forward to protect Pack's routed Portuguese, was thrust back by Bonnet to the Lesser Arapil, but was delivered from further pressure by the British guns on the summit of the hill. The Fusiliers and Stubbs's Portuguese were steadily borne down, and the latter suffered some loss from a charge of Boyer's dragoons, which, however, were beaten off by a square of the 11th Regiment. Some of the French horse even assailed the left flank battalion—the Fifty-Third—of the Sixth Division, which was now advancing to the support of the Fourth, and were not repelled before they had inflicted some damage. But the tide was soon about to turn. Beresford, catching up Spry's Portuguese brigade from the second line of the Fifth Division, turned it against Clausel's left flank; and though Beresford himself was wounded in the conflict, he brought the French counter-attack to a standstill.

And now the Sixth Division came striding over the plain to recover the ground that had been first won and then lost by Cole. Hinde's brigade on the right and Hulse's on the left made up the first line, and Rezonde's Portuguese the second line of Clinton's advance; and first the red-coats engaged the nine battalions of Bonnet in a bitter contest of musketry. As usual the British fire prevailed; and presently Bonnet's troops ran back discomfited to the hill in their rear, having lost, since they first came into action, some fifteen hundred men. Their retreat, by uncovering the right flank of Clausel's division, compelled that also to retire; and Wellington now directed his First Division to strike in between Foy and the Greater Arapil, so as at once to cut off Foy's troops from the main body, and to menace the right flank and retreat of Ferey's division on the Monte de Azan.

The order, however, was for some reason not obeyed by General Campbell, who appears to have pushed forward only his sharpshooters of the German Legion. Their advance, however, on the east and the retirement of Clausel's division to west of the Greater Arapil warned the 120th French regiment, which occupied that height, that it was in danger of being isolated; and these three last battalions of Bonnet's division hastened to rejoin their defeated comrades, not a little galled as they went by the fire of the Germans upon their flank.

Thus Clausel's counter-assault had been disastrously repulsed, and the plight of the French was rapidly becoming desperate. On the plateau Sarrut was fighting fiercely to save the shattered remnants of Marmont's left wing; but the Third and Fifth Divisions, now formed in one line, with the Seventh Division and Bradford's Portuguese in support, pressed him hard in front, while the cavalry of D'Urban, Arentschild, and Anson manoeuvred constantly round his left flank. Thus beset he could not, for all the valour of his troops, but give way, and it was only a question of time before his battalions would join the mob of the fugitives. Practically, therefore, only two divisions were left to Clausel, that of Foy which was fully occupied with the Light and First Divisions in its front, and that of Ferey which, with its face to the west, was holding the crest of a ridge a little to south-east of the Greater Arapil. Warned by Clausel that he must hold back the Allies in his front at all costs, Ferey formed seven of his battalions in line, and covering them on either flank with a single battalion in square, stood firmly at bay. He did not wait long before Clinton, having disposed of Bonnet, came up with his division, his left being now covered by the Fusilier brigade, which had speedily recovered itself and returned again to the front.

Without hesitation Clinton led his men up the glacis-like slope of the hill, to be met, when within two hundred yards of Ferey's line, by a deadly tempest of musketry and grape. The red-coats fell very fast but continued to press on slowly and steadily, closing in to fill up the gaps, and answering fire with fire. For an hour this murderous duel continued, the failing light being made good by the incessant blaze of the fusillade and the flames of the dry grass which had been kindled by the half-burned paper of the cartridges. At last the French gave way and Ferey withdrew his line, under the protection of the flanking squares, to the very edge of the forest, where his brave men turned and formed a new front.

Clinton's British battalions had suffered so terribly that he brought the Portuguese forward to drive the enemy from this last refuge, while the British guns, which had been unlimbered on the right or northern flank of Ferey's line, raked the French array from end to end. Ferey himself was slain by a round shot, but his men stood firm and repulsed Rezonde's battalions with very heavy loss. The British brigades then replaced the Portuguese in the firing line, but, before they could attack, the Fifth Division, which had been reforming after the dispersal of Sarrut's troops, came up on the enemy's left flank. This last stroke was decisive.

The 70th on the extreme French left broke and fled; the panic spread to the 26th and 77th; and only the 31st Light stood their ground for a time to cover the flight of their comrades, when they too retired into the forest and disappeared. The Sixth Division was too much exhausted to pursue; the Seventh, which had hardly been engaged, appears not to have been at hand; and the Light cavalry had, for some reason, been recalled by Cotton to the ground which it had occupied before the attack, so that no attempt was made to follow up the rout. Within the forest the confusion of the defeated was unspeakable.

Infantry, cavalry, artillery, waggons, carts, baggage-mules, and the reserve-pack, drawn by oxen, were all mingled together; the men shouting, swearing, running, beyond all control, everyone looking only to himself—a regular stampede.

There was no command and no commander, for Clausel, who had been wounded in the foot, was in the hands of the surgeons at Alba; and only the 31st Light, of the whole of the French centre and left, still bore themselves, to their undying praise, as soldiers. Had Carlos d'España but stuck to his post at Alba and barred the access to the bridge, the whole of this mass of fugitives must have surrendered.

There still remained Foy's division, which, half an hour before sunset, had been ordered by Clausel to cover the flank of the retreat and delay pursuit to the utmost of its power. Foy fell back accordingly, shielding the movement with a cloud of skirmishers, and turning to account every piece of advantageous ground with consummate skill. Wellington in person followed him with the First and Light Divisions and Anson's brigade of cavalry, but was unable to break his array.

At one moment it seemed certain that Foy must be cut off from the main body; but, on reaching the last point of vantage at the edge of the forest, he increased the number of his sharpshooters, and made a menace of counter-attack which caused the British artillery to un-limber and the infantry to form for an assault. Maintaining a heavy fire till the last moment he withdrew his men under cover of the smoke, and turning south-east retreated upon Alba de Tormes. Wellington, ignorant that Carlos d'España had evacuated that place, pressed the pursuit north-eastward to Huerta, where the Light Division bivou-acked at eleven o'clock at night. He sent a part of the cavalry down towards Alba nevertheless; and in returning from the river Cotton had the misfortune to ride into a Portuguese picquet, by the fire of which he was severely wounded. However Arentschild's brigade ascertained positively that the French had crossed the Tormes at Alba, and con-veyed the information to Wellington.

At daybreak the chase was resumed with the same troops, rein-forced by Bock's and Anson's brigades of cavalry. The Tormes was passed at Huerta; and the whole force, headed by the cavalry, was directed upon Peñeranda. The way lay along a bad stony road through a narrow marshy valley, and it was not until two o'clock that the advanced cavalry regained sight of the enemy's horse retiring from the village of Garcia Hernandez. A battery of French horse artillery, which was with them, unlimbered on a height to north-east of the village and opened fire on the Allied dragoons, while three battalions of the 76th Line and 6th Light formed squares on the slopes below. Wellington, at the first sight of the cavalry and before he was aware of the presence of infantry and artillery, ordered Anson and Bock to attack, which Anson at once did, driving back the enemy's left wing of horse, but leaving behind him two hostile squadrons, which were moving close to the heights and within range of the squares formed beneath them.

The German dragoons, who had only just emerged from a defile and were therefore still in column, now came galloping up, anxious not to be left out of the fight and hoping to complete their formation into line as they moved. The first squadron to come forward was that of Captain Haltorf, with Bock himself at its head, who seeing two squadrons of French before him charged at once without waiting for the rest of the brigade. The French, however, declined the combat and retired; and the Germans suffered some loss both from artillery-fire during their advance, and from the musketry of the squares of infantry upon their left flank, as they pursued. The attack therefore failed, but meanwhile the third squadron of the same regiment under Captain Gustavus van der Decken had galloped up; and he, finding himself likewise galled by the fusillade upon his left flank, wheeled instantly to the left, and bore down upon the nearest square to him—that of the 76th of the French line.

Within eighty yards the squadron received a first volley from the enemy. Several men and horses fell; and Decken himself, being struck by a bullet on the knee, after a desperate struggle to keep his seat reeled fainting from the saddle to the ground. Captain von Usslar Gleichen instantly took his place, and the squadron, unchecked and unbroken, thundered on. A second volley met them at close range; another officer and several more men dropped down; but one horse, stricken to the death, leaped high into the air and crashed down upon the bayonets. In a moment the dragoons had poured into the gap, huge men upon huge horses, and were hewing right and left with all the havoc of the sword. The square was transformed from an array of brave soldiers into a shrinking mass of terrified men, running frantically to escape one-sixth of their number of assailants.

★★★★★★

The returns of 15th July show the 1st battalion of the 76th as 29 officers and 671 men; those of the 1st of August at 18 officers and 313 men. It is impossible to say what may have been the loss of the battalion between the 15th and 23rd; but if the whole of it was in square on the 23rd it is plain that more than 50 (the number given by Schwertfeger) must have escaped.

★★★★★★

It is said that not above fifty men escaped death or capture; and the statement would seem to be true. (Oman has ascertained that practically every officer was captured).

While this slaughter was going forward the second squadron under Captain von Reitzenstein came up on the right of Decken, wheeled clear of him to its left, and galloped straight at the 6th Light, the two battalions of which were moving off in column to gain a more commanding position on the summit of the height. Their colonel appears to have lost his head; for, instead of giving the word to form square, he ordered the head of the column to increase its pace, an infallible expedient for widening the gaps between the sections, but a very uncertain method of evading an onslaught of galloping horse. Reitzenstein speedily overtook them, whereupon the two rear companies under Captain Philippe with great coolness faced about and fired a volley which killed or wounded two subalterns and several men. But the squadron was not to be stopped, and dashing into the flank of the disordered column overthrew or captured great numbers.

Many of the defeated ran to the top of the hill, where they joined the fugitives of the 76th and some of the French cavalry which had rallied; but by this time the leading squadron of the 2nd regiment of Hanoverian Dragoons had come up, which promptly dispersed the French horse and broke up the mass of infantry once more, before it could range itself in order. Meanwhile Foy had halted, formed part of his infantry into squares, and unlimbered some of his guns; and the broken remains of the 6th fled for refuge to the nearest square, which was composed of the 69th. Mad with success Marschalck led his Hanoverians, with ragged ranks and breathless horses, against this infantry also, but was beaten back with the loss of two officers and several men; and the action came to an end after lasting for about forty minutes.

The chase was then resumed by Anson's brigade, which gathered up several more prisoners; though on the following day Anson seems to have missed, through excessive caution, an opportunity for striking another telling blow. (Tomkinson). Then, however, the pursuit came to an end; for Clausel hastened his retreat with astonishing speed, and the Allies were so greatly exhausted that they could not hope to overtake him. Accordingly, on the 25th at Flores de Avila Wellington called a halt.

So ended the battle and pursuit of Salamanca, which General Foy in his journal characterised as sufficient to raise Wellington almost to the level of Marlborough, being the most skilful, the most considerable in point of numbers engaged, and the most important in its results that the British had won in modern times. Marmont always averred that he never intended to fight a general action, and that, had he not been disabled, there would have been no battle. Beyond question Marmont's wound, which came from a solitary cannon-shot fired almost at random, was a singular piece of good fortune for the Allies at the outset; but it cannot be accepted as exonerating Marmont from blame, nor as justifying the marshal in attempting to shuffle the responsibility of the defeat upon Clausel. Foy wrote:—

It was the Duke of Ragusa who began the battle, and began it against Clausel's advice. His left was already driven back when he was wounded, and from that moment it was impossible either to decline the action or to give a good turn to it. The only thing to do was to diminish the scale of the disaster, and that Clausel did. Things would have gone no better even if Marmont had never been wounded.

The fact seems to be that, though Marmont would not for the world have attacked Wellington on ground of Wellington's choice, he had no idea that the British general could do more than defend a position. The French Army and its officers flattered themselves that they alone understood how to manoeuvre; and Marmont, who could handle large bodies of troops with masterly skill, appears to have thought that, so long as he dazzled his adversary by brilliant movements, he incurred no danger. He did not deceive Wellington, who wrote contemptuously of Marmont's "manoeuvring all the morning in the usual French style, nobody knew with what object"; but he did deceive himself, for all this parade of tactical dexterity was simply a mask for his own irresolution. Wellington was of opinion that the marshal should have "given him a golden bridge" and have been content to see the Allies retreat to Ciudad Rodrigo; and this is what Massena in Marmont's place would undoubtedly have done.

The strength of the contending armies was too nearly equal to justify the commander of either of them in risking a general engagement, unless his adversary were guilty of some flagrant blunder. But Massena in adversity had the courage of his reputation, and Marmont had not. The Duke of Ragusa was not content to do the right thing. He wanted, as he himself says, a rear-guard action. This, though he did not confess it, meant some small affair wherein without any risk he could inflict a little damage, and which, by multiplying Wellington's casualties tenfold, he could expand into a victory that would make a figure in the *Moniteur*. He was therefore tempted on the 22nd to keep nibbling at the ground before him with his left wing, until he had committed that wing beyond rescue or recall, and was fairly caught in the act before he could correct the mistake. His generals also appear to have shared so thoroughly his opinion as to Wellington's impotence for the offensive that, even when Pakenham was in full march to the attack, they failed to realise his intention.

Once past the period of anarchy which intervened between the fall of Marmont and Bonnet, and the assumption by Clausel of the command, the French made a very fine fight; and no praise can be too high for Clausel's superb effort to change the fortune of the day. The weather was hot and dry, the sun and wind, as it chanced, were both in the faces of the French, and the troops were so choked with heat and dust that great exertions could hardly have been expected from them even with the certainty of victory, much less after one-fourth of their numbers had been ridden over and trampled under foot in the extremity of rout. Yet the 3rd, 4th, and 8th divisions fought with admirable tenacity; and the 1st, under the excellent leadership of Foy, showed perfect coolness and resolution when covering the retreat. Nevertheless the losses of the French were very heavy.

Comparison of the returns of the Army of Portugal on the 15th of July and the 1st of August shows a difference of over two hundred officers, over nine thousand men, over two thousand horses and twenty guns; but it is very certain that this does not represent the whole of the casualties. A return given by Napier states the loss between the 10th of July and the 10th of August at over twelve thousand men, nearly twelve hundred horses, and twelve guns; which, if fifteen hundred men be deducted as casualties before and after the action of the 22nd, will leave about eleven thousand for the battle itself.

★★★★★★

I cannot find the original of this return, and I imagine that it does not exist in the form in which he presents it, but was compiled from other returns; though as a rule these were made out fortnightly on the 1st and 15th of each month.

Killed or taken, 162 officers, 3867 men; wounded, 232 officers, 7529 men; stragglers (missing), 645. Total, 12,435 of all ranks. 1190 horses.

I can find no British return of the prisoners taken. Wellington talks vaguely of 7000, but says that he has no certain knowledge. This figure is certainly too high.

★★★★★★

But this figure is probably too low. The first account sent to Paris reckoned the losses in the week of the 22nd at fifteen to eighteen thousand, and Clarke, on the authority of a staff-officer from the Army of Portugal, reported them to Napoleon as at least twelve thousand. (*Arch. Rationales*. Comm. de Police Devillière, Bayonne, to Savary, 9th Aug.; Clarke to Napoleon, 22nd Aug. 1812). We shall be within the mark in accepting fourteen thousand as the least number. Among the wounded were Marmont, Bonnet, Clausel, and Menne; among the mortally wounded or killed Ferey, Thomières, and Desgraviers.

Thus the commander-in-chief and three out of eight divisional generals were slain or disabled; another was wounded, but not disabled, one general of brigade was killed, and another severely hurt. Among the trophies lost to the Allies were twenty guns, two eagles, the one belonging to the 22nd and the other to the 101st of the Line, and six other colours. (The number of captured guns once again is left vague, and is usually returned at 12; but I judge from the return already quoted. Some accounts give the numbers of eagles captured as 3, and one narrative specifies that of the 66th as taken).

The loss of the Allies on the 22nd amounted to over five thousand two hundred of all ranks killed and wounded and missing; (see list following), the proportion of Portuguese to British being as two to three, and the proportion of Spanish so minute as to be negligible. Among the general officers Le Marchant was killed, immediately after an angry altercation with Cotton; Leith, Cole, Cotton, Beresford and Victor Alten were wounded severely, Collins, who commanded a brigade in the Portuguese service, mortally; and Wellington at the end of the day was struck on the thigh by a spent bullet which had passed through his holster.

★★★★★★

Napier's return is incomplete and incorrectly added up.

	Killed.	Wounded.	Missing.		
British officers	28	178	0		
men	360	2536	74		
Portuguese officers	13	74	1		
men	291	1478	181		
Spaniards (men)	2	4	0		
Total	694	4270	256	=	5220

★★★★★★

Among the troops engaged the casualties of Hulse's brigade of the Sixth Division were incomparably the heaviest. The Sixty-First lost twenty-four officers and three hundred and forty-two men killed and wounded; the Eleventh sixteen officers and three hundred and twenty-five men, a proportion in each case of at least two in three; while the Fifty-Third lost eleven officers and one hundred and thirty-one men killed and wounded, or nearly if not quite one-half of the number present. (See list following). The casualties of the brigade therefore amounted at the very least to over four men in seven, and almost certainly to more; while those of the Eleventh and Sixty-First together rose to at least seven men in ten, or a trifle higher than that of the Fifty-Seventh at Albuera.

The following are the details :
Present 15th July,   11th, 34 off., 485 N.C.O. and men ⎫ all ranks,
              2/53rd, 25 „   316   „   „   ⎬ 1396
              1/61st, 29 „   507   „   „   ⎭
Casualties, 22nd July—
       11th,   killed,   1 off., 44 N.C.O. and men.
              wounded, 15 „   281   „   „
       2/53rd, killed,   26   „   „
              wounded, 11 „   105   „   „
       1/61st, killed,   5 „   39   „   „
              wounded, 19 „   303   „   „
    Total of all ranks, 849.

Napier indeed says that at the close of the day not above one hundred and sixty of all ranks of these two battalions were left standing, in which case they must have lost seven men out of every nine; but be it noted that in neither battalion was a man returned as missing. Full justice has not yet been done to these heroes of Gloucester and Devon. The remaining brigade of Clinton's division suffered far less severely; but the Royal Scots, Seventh, Thirty-Second, Thirty-Eighth, Fortieth and Eighty-Eighth all lost over one hundred officers and men. Many of the British and German battalions had hardly a man touched, and there were no fewer than twenty-seven which had been but lightly engaged, their aggregate losses being no more than half of those that fell in Hulse's brigade alone. In fact to all intents the whole of the work was done' by four divisions only of the infantry, aided by four brigades of cavalry and of course by artillery; or in other words the whole of Marmont's army, little inferior in numbers generally and with seventy-eight guns against sixty, was beaten by one-half of the Allies. The fact is so striking that it merits a little examination.

There is no occasion to dilate further on Marmont's tactical blunder in extending his left wing beyond reach of support, or on Wellington's swiftness in taking advantage of the fault; nor is it necessary to do more than mention the undoubted fact, admitted by Foy himself, that the fall of darkness alone saved the French Army from absolute destruction. It is very clear that at the first onset Wallace's brigade of the Third Division carried everything before it on the French left; that it far outstripped Ellis's brigade, which was in support of it; and that for a moment, upon finding itself confronted with Maucune's division, it thought itself lost. At the critical moment, however, the terrific onslaught of Le Marchant's heavy cavalry saved the situation, and elicited from Wellington the remark, "By God, Cotton, I never saw anything so beautiful in my life; the day is *yours*."

Leith's division made its attack in front simultaneously with Paken-ham's in flank; and here again the leading brigade, Greville's, did all the work, the five battalions of the rear brigade losing little more than seventy men out of some eighteen to nineteen hundred. Now, how-ever, came the check. Pack's Portuguese failed in their assault upon the Greater Arapil; and Cole's onset was in consequence beaten back for the time. It was the fashion among the British to blame the Portuguese for their defeat, and to declare that they were responsible for the incom-pleteness of the victory, (see the comments of Grattan and Cooke.); but Napier and Leith-Hay both acquit Pack's brigade of any misconduct—very justly, as it seems to me—and Napier goes so far as to say that the assault upon the Greater Arapil was of doubtful expediency.

There seems to be some force in the criticism, for the French guns on the hill were easily silenced by the troop of horse-artillery attached to the Seventh Division; and it is not clear why Dickson's brigade of heavy howitzers, which was close at hand and hardly engaged at all, was not employed to keep down the fire of the French infantry on the summit.

It is noteworthy that Wellington complained of the outranging of his guns by the French cannon, and wrote to ask for heavier metal; though, as a matter of fact, three long eighteen-pounders, which were with the army, were not brought to the front, but were held ready to be sent off early in case of a retreat. (*Dickson Papers*, chap. iv. *Wellington Desp.* To Bathurst, 24th July 1812).

To return, however, to the main point. After the repulse of Pack, Cole's first brigade was beaten back, and consequently his second bri-gade became seriously engaged; but his division was saved, as we have seen, by the withdrawal of Spry's Portuguese from the Fifth Division at Beresford's order. This points to the probability that the second line of the Fifth Division was not pushing on in support of the first line to complete the success, otherwise there seems to be no reason why it should not have acted with effect upon the flank of Maucune. The fall of Leith may perhaps account for this. However, Cole's leading bri-gade rallied, and presently it was relieved by the Sixth Division, which Wellington sent forward for the purpose.

Once again Clinton's British brigades did the whole of the work, losing twelve hundred out of twenty-eight hundred men; and, since Wellington had still three divisions of infantry and two brigades of cavalry ready to his hand, it is by no means easy to understand why he did not send at least a brigade to support Clinton.

At the same time it must be admitted that his contemplated stroke upon the French right, which he had committed to the First Division, may have been in his mind when he kept so large a body of infantry in reserve, and it has never been explained why Campbell did not act upon his orders. It is extremely probable that, had Graham been still in command of the First Division, the victory would have been far more decisive.

To sum up, the general result of our examination is that seventy-four French battalions and twenty-three squadrons with seventy-eight guns were utterly beaten by twenty-eight British battalions and as many Portuguese, of no greater average strength, and twenty-six squadrons with sixty guns.

★★★★★★

I have included among the British all that had 20 casualties and upwards; and among the Portuguese Bradford's and Pack's brigades, and the 4 brigades attached to the 3rd, 4th, 5th, and 6th divisions. Of the British thus included 5 battalions at least had only a few companies engaged; and the same is no doubt true of the Portuguese; but I am anxious to be guilty of no exaggeration.

★★★★★★

It is true that the French were taken at great tactical disadvantage, and that they were cruelly unfortunate in the fall of their chief and second in command; yet even so the fact is astonishing. But while Salamanca must remain a marvellous example of the powers of the British infantry in attack, there lies behind it always the question why, given such superiority of moral force, Wellington did not accomplish more.

The answer is, I think, to be found in the fact that rightly or wrongly, but in all likelihood rightly, he directed nearly every movement in person. We know positively that he himself galloped to Pakenham to give him his orders, instead of sending an *aide-de-camp*, that he not only gave Leith verbal instructions but rode with his division during part of its advance; and that he also spoke with his own mouth to Cole. It seems also that he was on the spot when Cotton delivered his charge, (*Memoirs of Viscount Combermere*, i.) and it is certain that he personally directed the advance of the Sixth Division, and took immediate command of the First and Light Divisions for their final movement at the close of the day, riding so far to the front as to be dangerously exposed.

It may be objected that these are not the duties of a commander-in-chief. That, in a general way, is true; but equally it is not the duty of a captain of a ship to stand by the side of the officer of the watch in mid-ocean, and yet very often he will find it prudent to do so. In the first place all accounts of the battle agree that the smoke and the dust, especially the latter, were blinding; and we have seen how Anson's brigade, even on the outskirts of the fight, was completely lost, and after halting found itself within easy range of a French battery. The ground had dried rapidly; troops were continuously in motion on both sides; and it must frequently have been impossible to make out at any distance what was going forward. Secondly, it must be remembered that this was Wellington's first offensive action against European troops; that he was meeting a great master of manoeuvre in command of soldiers who had conquered all other armies, and that by an unfortunate chance the best of his divisional commanders and brigadiers were absent through wounds or sickness

It is not surprising, therefore, that at the outset he should have taken upon himself the personal direction of every movement; and to judge by the use made by divisional leaders of their supports, it was a pity that he could not have kept his hand upon them throughout. At every crisis of the battle he was in the right place doing the right thing, even as he was three years later at Waterloo; but the general conduct of the action necessarily suffered in consequence. At Waterloo he was so busy superintending the work of others that he had not a moment to order up Hill's force from Hal; and at Salamanca for the same reason he had not leisure to turn a great success into a decisive victory.

A word must be added as to the part played by the cavalry in the actions of the 22nd and 23rd. Beyond question the attack of Le Marchant's brigade was a very brilliant stroke, produced great results, and was not marred apparently by the headlong galloping which had brought disaster in many minor actions, and was to be still more fatal at Waterloo. The three regiments suffered little, comparatively speaking, their losses amounting to just one hundred; but this was due to the vigour of their onslaught upon body after body of infantry, when the slightest hesitation would have been disastrous.

The day of Salamanca therefore rightly remains one of the great days in the history of the British horse; though their achievements must always sink into insignificance when compared with the performance of Bock's dragoons on the following day. The name of Garcia Hernandez will always be included among the great achievements of cavalry in the history of the world; and too much praise cannot be given to the brave Germans who made the combat a military classic. Four squadrons only, each about one hundred and ten strong, were engaged, though no two of them together; and three of them made successful charges, one upon a square fully formed of at least five hundred infantry; another upon a moving column of twice that strength; and the third upon a half-formed mass of beaten cavalry and infantry. The most striking point in the affair is the perfect control which the officers held over their men, the quickness with which they decided upon their attack, and the promptitude with which they translated decision into action.

An English squadron in the place of Decken's would probably have started off at twice the speed, and, when called upon to wheel suddenly to the left, would have squandered itself over three hundred yards of front, with the result that it would either have reached the square in disorder or must have reduced its pace and reformed its ranks, giving the enemy time to set their teeth, close their array, and probably to receive the troopers with three volleys instead of two. If Decken had failed it is likely enough that Reitzenstein and Marschalck would have hesitated to commit themselves, and then the French might have escaped with little difficulty or loss.

But in this famous brigade every officer of every squadron knew his business perfectly and could do it, while their men would follow them wherever they would lead; and hence this astonishing overthrow of some fifteen hundred infantry by less than one-third their number of horse. The losses of the four squadrons were heavy, amounting to six officers, one hundred and twenty-one men and one hundred and forty-four horses killed, wounded and missing; but it is reasonable to suppose that but for Marschalck's final attack upon the 69th, the casualties would have been less by fully one-fourth. Even as things were, however, it was not a very high price to pay for the destruction or capture of several hundred of the enemy.

★★★★★★

The number of prisoners taken by Bock's brigade is very uncertain. Beamish and Schwertfeger state it at 1400; but I think that this figure is too high. I may add that the number of casualties of the brigade as printed in the *Gazette* and by Beamish differ from that given by Schwertfeger. I have followed the last.

★★★★★★

Lastly, before taking leave of this great battle, one other small point must be noticed. In the despatch which reported the victory, Wellington as usual gave liberal thanks to all his principal officers, not excluding Carlos D'España who had so miserably deceived him as to Alba de Tormes; and ended with a commendation, hitherto unknown in documents of that nature, of the work of the civil departments. The good service of the Principal Medical Officer, Dr. M'Grigor, he had mentioned for the first time by M'Grigor's request in a supplementary letter after the fall of Badajoz; he now testified further to his attention and ability. But there is another sentence which probably gave to a few obscure individuals more intense pleasure than was felt by anyone else named in the document.

> Notwithstanding the increased distance of our operations from our magazines, and that the country is completely exhausted, we have hitherto wanted nothing, owing to the diligence and attention of the commissary-general, Mr. Bissett, and the officers of the department under his direction.

Wellington never used stronger words (except in wrath) than were absolutely necessary; otherwise diligence and attention might seem to be mild terms to explain Bissett's conquest of difficulties. With no fewer than thirty-seven separate depots in Portugal to be regulated; a larger commissariat establishment than had ever been known for a British army; Spanish muleteers who would not provide, if they knew it, for Portuguese troops at the front; Portuguese bullock-carts and worse still Portuguese roads in rear; a staff undermanned and overworked; accounts in consequence eighteen months in arrear; no power to promote or to punish (for he was not substantive Commissary-in-chief, but only acting until the return of his predecessor Kennedy); and above all the frightful gnawing anxiety over the dearth of specie, it seems wonderful that his brain should not have given way.

Yet he never lost his head. With a supply of Spanish couriers to ride on his errands, he maintained his hold upon every underling attached to the army and every clerk in charge of the depots; and by hook or by crook he kept the army supplied. It is well sometimes to turn from the man who fights—and gains all the glory—to the man who feeds him and gains none; to the man without whom, indeed, there can be neither marching nor fighting, but through whose patient indefatigable service a commander-in-chief may say in a barren country that his army has wanted for nothing.

The Investment of Burgos

On the 24th of July, 1812, Clausel brought his shattered troops into Arevalo; and on the same day Joseph, who had marched from Madrid with fourteen thousand men on the 21st, fixed his headquarters at Blasco Sancho, between ten and fifteen miles to south and west of him, being still ignorant not only of the Battle of Salamanca but even of the position of the Army of Portugal. On the 25th he received letters both from Marmont and Clausel, which revealed something of the truth. For the present, Clausel insisted, it was everything to him to reach Valladolid before the British, so as to evacuate the place of its hospitals and stores, and re-establish communication with the Army of the North; but if the English should march upon Madrid, he undertook to remain upon the Douro. Meanwhile he added the dispiriting remark that by the time that Joseph had assembled the Armies of Aragon and of the South, he hoped to have twenty thousand men fit for service.

Learning from the bearers of these letters that Clausel had already resumed his retreat northward upon Olmedo, Joseph made a rapid march to Espenar at the foot of the Guadarrama, so as to regain Madrid; but, on the representation of both Clausel and Marmont that the British pursuit had slackened, and that they were anxious for the junction of his force with theirs, he turned northward to Segovia, which he entered on the 27th. He gave the two commanders, however, to understand that he would go no further, and that if they wished for his help they must join him at Segovia, since he had no intention of abandoning the capital.

On the 29th he sent positive orders to Soult to evacuate Andalusia and move the whole of his force with all speed to Toledo; and on the 1st of August, having heard that the Army of Portugal had passed the

Douro, he quitted Segovia, regaining Madrid on the 5th.

Clausel, meanwhile, pursued his way from Olmedo to Valladolid, crossed the Douro, and ascending the Pisuerga, halted between Torquemada and Palencia, from whence he sent away his wounded and heavy waggons to Burgos under escort of one division, and pushed Foy's south-eastward to observe Aranda de Duero. He wrote to Clarke:—

I have been obliged to look for a position where I can restore the morale of the army . . . It is usual to see armies discouraged after a reverse, but it is difficult to find one in which the discouragement is greater than in this; and I must not conceal from you that there reigns and has reigned for some time past a very bad spirit in this army; our steps in this retreat have been marked everywhere by the most revolting disorders and excesses. (Ducasse, ix.; *Mémoires de Jourdan*).

It is hardly surprising in these circumstances that Wellington's halt on the 25th was criticised by one of his officers as "unlike a quick advance following up a great victory." (Tomkinson). A principal reason for the abandonment of the pursuit appears to have been the lagging of the supplies, which had been ordered back to Ciudad Rodrigo before the action of Salamanca, and were consequently far in rear. The recent scenes at Badajoz and Ciudad Rodrigo were evidently fresh in the commander-in-chief's mind, and he mistrusted the discipline of his troops unless he could deliver to them their rations punctually. Moreover, Cotton was disabled, and there was no other officer whom he could trust to lead his cavalry. It is humiliating to our national pride to confess the fact, but a fact it seems to be, that many a good opportunity in the Peninsula was thrown away because the higher commands were too often filled by incompetent men, and the rank and file, to use the general's own words, could bear neither failure nor success.

However that may be, Wellington resumed the pursuit on the 26th, having learned, through the capture of a small party of Joseph's cavalry near Arevalo on the previous day, that the king had advanced to Blasco Sancho and retired towards the passes of the Guadarrama. That he should desert Clausel puzzled Wellington somewhat; but he continued to follow the beaten army, the German hussars who led the way reaching Almenara on the 26th, and sighting the enemy's rearguard on the 29th at Aldea Mayor. The entire force of the Allies was now closing up in anticipation of resistance at the line of the Douro; but, as we have seen, Clausel's troops were in no condition for fighting, and on the 30th Wellington, amid loud acclamations from the people, entered Valladolid. Being still uncertain as to the movements of Joseph, he marched on the 31st south-eastward upon Cuellar, where on the 1st of August he fixed his headquarters; but hearing definitely on the 4th of the king's retirement to Madrid, he was free to make his decision concerning his future operations. (*Wellington Desp.*, to Douglas and Hill, 26th July; to Bathurst, 28th July; to Sir H. Popham, 4th Aug. 1812).

The state of affairs was briefly this. The armies of Clausel and Joseph were now separated, the former having fallen back to the vicinity of Burgos and the latter to Madrid. Furthermore, owing to the direction taken by Clausel in his retreat, the French posts at Zamora, Toro, Benavente, and Tordesillas were left isolated; and accordingly one of Wellington's first measures upon reaching Valladolid was to summon the Count of Amarante's Portuguese to beleaguer Zamora, while bidding the Spanish general Santocildes to look to Tordesillas and cover the blockade of all these places. The British Army, albeit in high spirits after its victory, was sickly; and many soldiers from the five battalions that had joined it since the opening of the campaign were already in hospital, their commanding officers, in spite of strict orders, having brought them up from Lisbon without any blankets. (2/4th, 1/5th, 38th, 1/42nd, 82nd. *Wellington Desp.* To Bathurst, 4th Aug. 1812).

On the other hand, the financial prospect, which Wellington on the 28th of July had summed up in the single word bankruptcy, was somewhat brighter, remittances of specie having lately arrived from England. Moreover, the demoralisation of Clausel's army was a matter of common knowledge, and Wellington had expressed his conviction that the French infantry would not stand against his own. In spite of the rapidity of his retreat Clausel had been unable to complete the evacuation of Valladolid; and seventeen guns, besides a large quantity of stores and eight hundred sick men in hospital, had been taken in the city. The guerilla-bands were showing renewed activity in every direction, and one of them under the leader Marquiñez had captured three hundred French prisoners on the 30th outside Valladolid.

Without rest and peace the Army of Portugal could not recover itself; and it was certain that, if pressed, Clausel would not wait at Burgos, but would be compelled to fall back behind the Ebro. It was open to Wellington to establish himself astride of the principal line of the enemy's communications at Burgos and lay siege to the fortress, which being of no great strength and unprepared for such a trial, would probably be taken without any great difficulty. The objection to this course was that Joseph might move up from Madrid against the British rear and communications with some eighteen thousand men, a force too great to be resisted by the Spaniards, even in combination with such small detachments as Wellington would be able to spare for their assistance. The alternative measure, namely, to march upon Madrid, was open to precisely the same danger as the first an advance of Clausel upon the rear and communications of the Allies. It was therefore necessary to choose between Madrid and Burgos as the more desirable acquisition; and the choice could only be determined by a review of the military situation in the Peninsula at large.

The Army of the North under Caffarelli had, as we have seen, been so much distraught by the operations of the guerillas inland and of Sir Home Popham from the sea, that no troops could be spared from it to reinforce Marmont. Caffarelli complained that he had but six thousand men at his disposal, and that the bands opposed to him numbered four times as many. The Army of the South, the most important in the Peninsula, was, as we have also seen, fully occupied with the siege of Cadiz, the repression of the guerillas and of Ballesteros, and the observation of Hill.

Wellington's most recent news of Ballesteros represented his position to be dangerous; but it was always possible to make a diversion in his favour by stirring up the garrison of Cadiz to activity. There remained the Armies of Aragon and of Valencia; for the Corps of the Ebro, which Napoleon had organised upon paper, had soon been broken up to reinforce the Army of the North. Joseph had long been clamouring for one of Suchet's divisions, and had actually received one of his regiments, though the Duke of Albufera was distracted by the activity of the Spanish bands in all quarters, and by the menace of a descent of the British upon the coast.

Suchet was obliged to go north to Reus to concert operations with Decaen on the 10th of July; and on the 16th the explosion of the magazine at Lerida, at a moment when a considerable force of Spaniards under Eroles was before the fortress, gave him additional anxiety. He returned to Valencia to find some of the relics of Blake's army within a day's march of the city; and on the 21st of July the sails of a British armament were seen off the coast near the mouth of the Xucar, so close to the shore that the forts actually opened fire. To account for its appearance we must glance for a brief moment at Sicily.

225

Sketch
of the
SIEGE OF BURGOS,
1812.

OUTWORKS

HORN
WORK
St. Michel

MUSQUET TRESOR

TRENCH OF COMMUNICATION

TRENCHES

MUSQUET TRENCH

PALLISADED
WORK

SAP

1ST
BREACH

BREACH

2ND PARALLEL

HOLLOW WAY

NAPOLEON BATTERY

White
Church

Castle

UPPER LINE

2ND BREACH

BATTERY

MINE

Cavalier

2ND LINE

St. Roman

1ST. LINE

Suburb of
San Pedro

PORTUGUESE ATTACK
(IGHT OF 22ND.

City of Burgos

Lord William Bentinck, it will be remembered, had divided all his energy in the spring of 1812 between plans for remodelling the government of Sicily and for accomplishing the liberation of Italy, the success of the latter object depending mainly upon the achievement of the former. His progress in the work of constitutional reform was, owing chiefly to his extreme gullibility, remarkably slow; the King, Queen, and Hereditary Prince of Naples contriving each of them to shuffle off their responsibility upon the other and so to delay all concessions, with a dexterity of falsehood which easily eluded the sluggish intelligence of the British envoy.

However, at the beginning of May Bentinck obtained an order for the convocation of the Sicilian Parliament, a pacificatory measure which entitled him to send a part of the British garrison out of the island; and having received at this time an urgent letter from Wellington, pressing for a diversion upon the east coast of Spain, he decided as a provisional arrangement to send thither a force of nearly seven thousand men under General Maitland.

But even so he despatched the armament first to Mahon, where he flattered himself that its appearance would make as effectual a diversion as if it were actually disembarked on the Spanish coast; and he still hoped in his heart to lead it in person to Italy. For Bentinck remained as enthusiastic as ever for a descent upon Italy, or indeed upon any country, other than Spain, where opportunity might offer. Thus upon hearing at the beginning of June that the Montenegrins were in insurrection against the French, he at once sent them twelve hundred men, (35th, 400; Corsicans, Calabrians, Greek L.I., 800. Total, 1200), and twelve vessels of the Sicilian flotilla. Yet at that very moment he was deploring the despatch of Maitland's detachment upon the ground that it was too weak to be of any service in Spain; apparently blind to the fact that a larger force might have been spared had he not chosen to fritter away his strength upon his own petty projects for the enfranchisement of the world at large. There is no more fatal obstacle to human progress than the crude aspirations of ambitious mediocrity. (Bentinck to Sec. of State, W.O., 19th, 20th, 22nd May; 9th, 26th June; F.O., 5th, 6th May; 27th, 30th June 1812).

Maitland sailed on the 7th of June, (see return following), but after long battling with adverse winds, was still at Palermo on the 28th, when at last he was able to pass the straits and make his way to Minorca. From thence he sent word to General Roche at Alicante to join him with his divisions of Spaniards, and to General Whittingham ise to embark his corps, which had been raised for the defence of the Balearic Islands and lay in quarters there. Wellington's design was that Maitland should besiege Tarragona, but there were endless delays before he could leave Minorca; and it should seem that the ships which alarmed Suchet on the 21st were only transports on their way to Alicante to pick up Roche. However, they were assumed to be British by Don Jose O'Donnell, the commander of the Spanish troops about Alicante, who, apparently afraid lest the redcoats should snatch laurels from him, advanced upon Castalla on the same day with twelve thousand men. He was of course hopelessly beaten by half his own number of French with the loss of four thousand killed, wounded and taken, Roche's division alone having shown any firmness in the fight.

★★★★★★

Maitland's Force.		Embarkation return of 25th June :		
20th L.D.,	167 ;	160 horses.	1/10th	935.
Foreign troop	71 ;	75 „	1/58th	871.
R.A. and drivers	177 ;	86 „	1/81st	1274.
Marine Artillery	30		4th Line K.G.L.	750.
R.E.	47		6th „	1064.
Staff Corps	14		det. Roll's	331.
			„ Dillon's	554.
			„ Calabrians	353.

Total : 6638 of all ranks.

★★★★★★

The news of this defeat reached Wellington by the 3rd of August, but was outweighed by that of Maitland's approaching arrival; and he therefore took no notice of it beyond directing General Ross to join Maitland with every man that he could spare of the garrison of Carthagena, and writing to Roche the curt reproof "I request that you may not be defeated again." It was enough for the British commander that Suchet could not detach another man to westward so long as Maitland remained upon the coast; and he ensured that Maitland should remain there by forbidding him—notwithstanding Bentinck's instructions—to quit it without express permission from the British Government. (*Wellington Desp.*, to Roche, 3rd, 5th Aug.; to Ross, 5th Aug.; to Maitland, 16th Aug. 1812).

Reviewing the entire situation Wellington resolved to march on Madrid, and either to bring Joseph to action or to force him to quit the capital. The reasons alleged for this decision were that he could not pursue Clausel further without exposing his rear and communications to an incursion from the Army of the Centre, and also that his presence in King Joseph's capital would have a good effect in Europe. The various aspects of this decision will be better discussed at a later stage; for the present it must suffice barely to record it.

Leaving therefore at Cuellar Anson's brigade of Light Horse, Clinton's division of infantry and the five sickly battalions which had lately joined the army, Wellington marched on the 6th by Carbonero el Mayor, Segovia and San Ildefonso to the pass of the Guadarrama; and on the 11th the advanced guard pushed back the French cavalry and entered Las Rozas, a village within ten miles of Madrid. Here the Heavy Brigade and the 1st Light Battalion of the German Legion, together with two guns of Macdonald's troop of horse artillery, halted; while the four remaining guns and a brigade of Portuguese horse under Colonel d'Urban pushed forward for another three miles to the village of Majadahonda; a party of twenty German dragoons riding ahead of all to preserve contact with the enemy.

Joseph, who had already begun the evacuation of the capital, desiring to gain time, directed General Treilhard to hold back the Allies, and ordered Palombini's Italian cavalry, a brigade of infantry, and four guns to his support.

★★★★★★

Treilhard's division of dragoons consisted of the 13th, 18th, 19th and 22nd, about 1700 of all ranks. The regiments attached to Palombini were the Dragons Napoléon, about 470 of all ranks, and the Lancers of Berg, perhaps 400 men. Chassé's brigade was made up of the 2nd Nassau Infantry and the Spanish regiment La Mancha, about 1450 strong. Treilhard's force, including artillery, was about 4000 men.

★★★★★★

Treilhard accordingly faced about, and the German dragoons hastened back to give the alarm; whereupon D'Urban brought forward his four guns, and, observing Treilhard's leading squadrons to be far in advance of the main body, led his three regiments to the attack.

The Portuguese followed him for a short distance, and then wheeling about galloped away to the rear, leaving the guns to their fate. By great exertion the gunners limbered up their pieces, and began to withdraw them, but the ground was unfavourable for rapid movement. One gun escaped; but two others were overturned, and, the carriage of a third being broken, all three fell into the enemy's hands. Meanwhile, the French dragoons thundered on, and bursting into Las Rozas on the heels of the flying Portuguese caught the Germans unprepared. These last had unsaddled for the first time for three days, and the men were in their shirt-sleeves, washing themselves and leading their horses to water, when at about five o'clock the trumpet sounded the alarm.

Two companies of the Light Battalion hastily formed in advance of the village, and with two small bodies of dragoons, collected in a hurry by their captains, checked the first onslaught of the enemy. Thus time was gained for the rest of the battalion to form in the market-place, and for four squadrons of the German dragoons to be mounted and arrayed. The Portuguese rallied and came forward; and the enemy was borne back to Majadahonda, where being reinforced by men and guns they resumed the offensive. Thereupon the Portuguese for the second time turned tail, and the German dragoons were obliged to retire once more to Las Rozas, with the loss of their brigadier, de Jon-cquières, and a few men captured.

By this time, however, the Light Battalion had established itself in a house from which the men were able to open a telling fire upon the French. Two squadrons of the dragoons charged the enemy with con-siderable effect; and, upon the approach of Ponsonby's brigade of cav-alry and of another light battalion of the Legion, Treilhard drew off his troops, abandoning the three captured cannon. The loss of the Allies amounted to fifty-three of all ranks killed, ninety-eight wounded, and forty-five taken, as well as eighty-one horses; and it must be regret-fully confessed that the mishap, which Wellington described as "a devil of an affair," was entirely due to the misconduct of the Portuguese. One point of interest in the action is that it went near to destroy the reputation of Wellington as a commander who had never lost a gun. Another point, which has not heretofore been noticed, was that the French casualties must have been appreciable, for in the five regiments of cavalry engaged, one officer was killed and fifteen wounded, mak-ing the total loss of officers exactly the same as that of the Allies. From this it is reasonable to conclude that at least one hundred and fifty of the French rank and file must have fallen. (The best account of this skirmish is that given by Schwertfeger, i.)

Meanwhile Joseph was painfully retreating, encumbered by a huge convoy of two thousand vehicles and a mass of ten thousand fugitives from Madrid, amid disgraceful scenes of plunder and indiscipline. On the 12th he halted at Valdemoro; on the 13th he pushed his vast and unwieldy charge over the Tagus at Aranjuez; and advancing amid sti-fling heat through Albacete and Chinchilla, he arrived on the 31st at

Valencia. The march was distressing beyond description. The inhabitants, who had been shamefully ill-treated by Montbrun's troops on their return from Alicante, had carried off their cattle and destroyed their ovens and mills; so that neither meat nor flour were obtainable. The rivulets were dried up, and the wells were soon exhausted by the multitude of the thirsty; and the troops, receiving neither regular rations nor water, took leave of all order and discipline. Soldiers and private servants went marauding together, but few ever returned; for the guerillas hung upon the flanks and rear of the column, and slaughtered all stragglers without mercy. Joseph's Spanish troops deserted almost to a man to join these bloodthirsty bands; and yet such was the misery and hardship of the journey that many Spanish civilians turned back, preferring to risk their lives rather than endure such extremity of suffering.

On the 12th Wellington entered Madrid amidst scenes of wild enthusiasm, ladies even throwing down their shawls for his horse to tread on, while others clung to his stirrup and kissed his boots. There was, however, a garrison of some two thousand men besides invalids, left in a retrenched post which had been fortified round the palace of the Retiro. The interior work consisted of a large square building, originally a porcelain factory, and hence called La China, with an octagonal star fort about it, and the exterior defences of an irregular bastioned enclosure of nine fronts. Though strong enough to form a protection against guerillas, these fortifications could not resist a regular attack; and Joseph could only excuse himself for leaving troops in them by pleading that, without a guard, the invalids might have been murdered by the populace. He made, however, the further mistake of providing a garrison insufficient to defend the exterior lines, and too large to be contained in the octagon; besides which he gave orders, a copy of which was found by the British, that if seriously assailed the garrison were to withdraw at once into the interior *enceinte*.

Accordingly after a feint attack on the night of the 13th, heavy guns were brought to batter La China and the inner defences, and preparations were made to storm the exterior works, when the commandant, knowing the weakness of the post, surrendered. Over two thousand effective officers and men, and over four hundred and thirty sick in hospital, were thereby made prisoners of war, and upwards of one hundred and eighty guns, twenty thousand muskets, a large supply of stores and munitions of war, together with two eagles, all became prize of the victors. Then followed a general sweeping in of small

French detachments.

Tordesillas with about two hundred and fifty men had already surrendered to Santocildes on the 5th; Guadalajara with seven hundred men yielded to the *Empecinado* on the 15th; Astorga with twelve hundred men, (3rd and 4th batts. of the 25th Light), capitulated on the 18th; and on the 25th the guerilla chief Villacampa captured three hundred men of a force which was escorting the garrison of Cuenca to Valencia. It seems extraordinary that so many unfortunate French troops, beginning with those in the forts of Salamanca, should have been thus uselessly sacrificed. Poor Clausel, after such a defeat as that of Salamanca, may perhaps be pardoned for not summoning the garrisons of Zamora, Toro and Tordesillas to meet him at Valladolid; but Joseph might easily have called in that of Guadalajara, and it was against all military advice that he had left two thousand men in the Retiro.

Jourdan explains that the king was afraid of the outcry that might be raised at Paris if he evacuated the capital absolutely; and it seems probable that both Joseph and Marmont were afraid to abandon works which had been built by Napoleon's command, hoping perhaps to relieve them from the pressure of the Allies before they should fall, and to pay court to His Majesty by flattering allusions to the Imperial wisdom and forethought which had ordained their construction. This was part of the base sycophancy which characterised the later years of the empire, and was not a little encouraged by the emperor's habit of reasoning from things not as they were but as he wished them to be. Yet in justice to Napoleon it must be admitted that he pardoned any fault more readily than downright stupidity. Meanwhile Clausel, upon hearing of Wellington's march to Madrid, decided to make an effort to rescue the detachments at Zamora, Toro and Astorga.

Owing to the exhausted condition of the country the disorder among his troops had been very great, but he had tried and shot over fifty marauders and made some stern examples among his officers; and by these means he had succeeded in collecting and reorganising an army of some twenty-four thousand men with fifty guns. He therefore bore down upon Valladolid with his whole force, his advanced guard being sighted by the British patrols twenty miles north-east of that city on the 13th. Wellington, anticipating some such movement, had advised Santocildes to fall back to the Esla if he thought himself too weak to oppose the enemy, and now ordered Clinton to march from Cuellar to Olmedo as if to cross the Douro at Valladolid. Santocildes retired accordingly, but Clinton, far from making the movement prescribed to him, fell back to Arevalo; whereupon Clausel, entering Valladolid without alarm on the 16th, despatched Foy westward with two divisions and a thousand cavalry to rescue the posts on the river and at Astorga.

On the 17th Foy reached Toro, and withdrew the garrison and stores. Turning thence north-westward to Benavente, he overthrew the Spanish rear-guard which disputed the passage of the Esla, and on the 20th reached La Bañeza, where he learned to his dismay that Astorga had surrendered thirty-six hours before. He therefore wheeled to the south and advanced upon Carvajales, hoping to annihilate a detachment of four thousand Portuguese militia under Silveira, which was in that quarter. This operation, however, miscarried, the French cavalry showing culpable lack of enterprise; and Silveira safely effected his retreat across the Portuguese frontier. Much disgusted, Foy continued his march to Zamora, which he entered on the 25th and occupied until the 29th, when upon the summons of Clausel he returned—taking the garrison with him—to Tordesillas, to rejoin the main army. (Girod de l'Ain. *Vie militaire du General Foy*).

Wellington for his part professed not only in difference as to the relief of the French garrisons, but a positive desire that, in some way or another, they should be taken off his hands, he wrote to his brother:—

Anything is better than that I should have to attack and carry these places.

For he grudged the time and the lives that would be spent in a series of little sieges. On the 16th, 17th and 18th he transferred the whole of his force, except the Third and Light Divisions and Alten's brigade of cavalry, from Madrid to the Escorial; and towards the end of the month he ordered the First, Fifth and Seventh Divisions, Pack's and Bradford's brigades of Portuguese, Ponsonby's brigade of light cavalry and Bock's of heavy dragoons to march to Arevalo. Himself leaving Madrid on the 1st of September, he reached Arevalo on the 3rd, and on the 4th led his army upon Valladolid. On the 18th of August Clausel had driven Anson's cavalry after a sharp skirmish to the south bank of the Douro, but had not followed him further; and on the day of Wellington's march the French general occupied Tordesillas and Valladolid in force, keeping a thousand men at Simancas, where he had ruined the bridge over the Pisuerga.

On the 6th of September the Allied Army passed the Douro by the fords of Herrera de Duero, and found the French in position at

Arroyo de la Cisterniga; but in the night Clausel withdrew his troops and, having blown up the bridge at Simancas at noon of the 7th, fell back up the right bank of the Pisuerga to Dueñas, the cavalry of the Allies marching parallel with him on the opposite side of the stream. On the 8th Wellington halted, being anxious for the arrival of Santocildes whom he had summoned to him with the Army of Galicia, (*Wellington Desp.* To Santocildes, 12th Sept. 1812); but that general did not appear; and on the 9th the leading division of the Allies crossed the Pisuerga at Cabezon, while the rear moved to the same place from Valladolid. Clausel therefore withdrew quietly from Dueñas on the 10th; and continued to retire in a leisurely fashion to Magaz and Torquemada, where on the 12th he crossed the Pisuerga and took the road to Burgos.

Anson on this day missed an opportunity of inflicting some loss upon the enemy's rear-guard; and Clausel pursued his unhasting way up the valley of Arlanzon, little pressed by his opponents, until on the 16th he took up a position to cover Burgos. On that day, however, Castaños with over eleven thousand men joined the Allies, and Wellington made dispositions for an attack; but Clausel was too cunning to be caught, and manoeuvring with great skill, retreated again with no more than trifling loss to his rear-guard. On the night of the 17th he withdrew his troops through Burgos, leaving a garrison of two thousand men under General Dubreton in the castle, and fell back north-eastward to Briviesca and Pancorbo.

This retrograde march of Clausel has received great commendation from the pen of Napier, who alleges that he offered battle in nine different positions, and was only dislodged by flanking movements on the part of Wellington. There is, however, no trace of any such manoeuvres to be found in the journals of Tomkinson and Burgoyne, who took part in the pursuit; and the slowness of Wellington's advance, which is admitted by all authorities including himself was due wholly to the erratic movements of Santocildes, who did not reach Valladolid until a week later than had been expected of him. (*Wellington Desp.* To Santocildes, 12th Sept. 1812).

More relevant is Napier's comment that if Wellington had marched straight upon Valladolid from Segovia, he might have cut off Foy from Clausel; and that, if he had taken with him another division and pressed due north upon Burgos by the route of the Somosierra and Aranda de Duero, he would have threatened the flank of Clausel's line of retreat, while Clinton and the Spaniards closed upon his rear.

The historian's conjecture is that want of money and of transport prevented the British general from taking the inhospitable route over the Somosierra, and this may well have been so; but it is more likely, in my opinion, that Wellington felt unable to trust Clinton and Santocildes any longer in independent command, and, as was so often the case, took upon himself the work of a divisional leader as well as that of commander-in-chief.

However, he was now before the fortress which, if captured, might serve to cover the territory which his victories had gained for him; and by this time he was fairly well apprised of the progress of affairs in other parts of the Peninsula. Maitland after long delays had sailed with his detachment and some two thousand of Whittingham's Spaniards from Catalonia, and had appeared before Palamos on the 31st of July. After discussion with the Spanish commander, however, it was decided that the siege of Tarragona was too hazardous an operation for the Allied forces at disposal; and Maitland proceeded towards Valencia, but changed his mind in mid voyage and bore up for Alicante, where he landed on the 9th of August. The French troops stationed to the south of the Jucar at the moment did not exceed five or six thousand, which were lying about Alcoy and Castalla; but before Maitland could collect supplies and transport, Suchet had shifted this detachment northward to San Felipe, and reinforced it considerably.

None the less the British general advanced as far as Elda, about eighteen miles north and west of Alicante, where on the 17th he heard of the junction of the Army of the Centre with that of Valencia, and perforce fell back to his starting-point. Including the Sixty-Seventh and Watteville's, which he found at Alicante on his arrival, Maitland had now some eight thousand British troops, besides the Spanish divisions of Roche and Whittingham, which amounted to as many more; but being out of health, much troubled by the difficulty of feeding his Spaniards and disturbed by a rumour that Soult also was moving upon Valencia, he was reduced to rather an abject state of nervousness, and began to hint at a re-embarkation.

Wellington would not hear of anything of the kind. He had received authority from England to take Maitland's detachment under his command; and he ordered that general positively to stay where he was, heartening him with the assurance that he needed only to stand his ground with firmness in order to gain not only security but honour. Sixteen thousand men, with transports riding on the sea at their backs, were a force that Joseph could not dare to leave behind him unless carefully watched by a considerable number of troops. (*W.O. Corres.* Maitland to Sec. of State, 24th July, 30th Aug., 19th Sept. 1812. *Wellington Desp.* To Maitland, 29th, 30th Aug., 20th Sept. 1812).

All therefore was satisfactory so far as Suchet's army was concerned: as regards Soult's proceedings Wellington was for some time in doubt. Even on the 18th of August he wrote of his intentions to invade Andalusia in September; but a week later he heard credible reports that Soult was contemplating a general movement, probably towards Granada and Valencia; and by the 8th of September he had received definite information that the siege of Cadiz had been raised. As a matter of fact Soult had not received the king's order for the evacuation of Andalusia in any very friendly spirit. Upon the 8th of August on the first rumours of the defeat of Salamanca, he had urged Joseph to bring the Army of the Centre and part of the Army of Portugal by the pass of Despeña Perros into Andalusia; to employ the most demoralised and least efficient of them in holding the necessary posts in the province; and to liberate the Army of the South thus augmented to fifty-five or sixty thousand men for active operations.

★★★★★★

Soult, it must be mentioned, always grossly exaggerated the numbers of Hill, when urging this plan. In his letters of 8th Aug. he ascribes to Hill 10 regiments (not battalions) of British infantry; and 7 (instead of 6) regiments of British cavalry; and gives reports of 10,000 more British infantry and some Italian cavalry as about to join him.

★★★★★★

Soult reckoned that in six weeks all would be ready for entry upon this new campaign.

On the 12th of August, after receiving Joseph's instructions to evacuate Andalusia, he urged the same point with still greater eagerness. The king, he said, should lead to Andalusia all the troops that he could collect of the Armies of the Centre, of Portugal and of Aragon, even at the sacrifice of evacuating Valencia. From the moment when seventy or eighty thousand French should be concentrated in the south, the theatre of war would be changed, and the Army of Portugal would be free. Then it could either return to the Tagus, or hold Burgos and the left bank of the Ebro until reinforcements should arrive from France; for, even if the Allies were masters of the country between the Ebro and the Sierra Morena, they would be little the better for it. On the other hand the loss of Andalusia and the raising of the siege of Cadiz were events that would make themselves felt all over Europe. (Soult to Joseph, 8th Aug. (*Archives de la Guerre*); 12th Aug. 1812. Ducasse, ix).

The great English historian of the war has blamed Joseph severely for not appreciating the grandeur and vigour of Soult's conception. And yet it must be confessed that the plan was extremely vague. There appears in Soult's despatches a breezy indifference whether the force withdrawn from the centre and north of Spain to the south should include the entire Armies of Aragon and Portugal, or one of them only, or parts of both, or the whole of one and part of the other. The great point made by the marshal was that Madrid and even Valencia were not worth holding in comparison with Andalusia; and that the abandonment of the country between the Ebro and the Sierra Morena to the Allies was, relatively speaking, an unimportant matter.

This may have been a sound contention; but Soult never directly faced the question whether communication with France was or was not to be sacrificed; nor was he clear as to the various stations in Aragon and Central Spain which were to be maintained. He specified by name the Retiro, Toledo, and the pass of the Guadarrama—all three of them indefensible—as posts that should be occupied in sufficient strength; and he certainly intended to keep up all existing garrisons in Andalusia as well as to continue the blockade of Cadiz. (Napier—in what purports to be a quotation from Soult's despatches—assumes that the line of communications by the east coast, a very circuitous route from France to Seville, was to be maintained. I can find no sign of this in any of Soult's letters.) But these various places were rendered safe not by the troops which actually held them, but by mobile columns which could revictual them and hurry at any time to their assistance. Did he intend to leave these isolated detachments to the tender mercies of the guerilla-bands? In that case they must without exception have fallen within three months; and the French host in Spain would have been very seriously weakened. Or did he purpose still to retain a surplus of troops for petty expeditions? In that case his army for the field must have been considerably reduced.

What after all was the whole design of Wellington's operations? Simply to force the French to concentrate, so as to give free opportunities to the guerilla-bands. Soult therefore in assembling sixty or eighty thousand, or one hundred and twenty thousand men, (this last figure is Napier's, not Soult's; the marshal never presuming to reckon the field-army at more than eighty thousand), in the south was merely playing the game of the Allies, unless he could be sure of expelling the

British from the Peninsula. How could he feel sure of any such thing? Western Andalusia is certainly dangerously close to Portugal when observed on the map; but the portion of Portugal that really was of importance to Wellington was Lisbon. Now, the lower Tagus being unbridged, and the command of the sea in the hands of the Allies, Lisbon could only be approached by a French Army—no matter what its starting-point—from the north.

How Soult would have made his way to the decisive battlefield at the gate of Lisbon must remain a matter of conjecture; but it is certain that he must have forced the lines of Torres Vedras, a feat which he could not have accomplished without heavy artillery. Nor is it easy to see how he could have brought forward such artillery, together with ammunition sufficient for a siege, without a bridge either over the Guadiana or over the Tagus. But, assuming that he had made himself master of the bridges of Badajoz and Abrantes, his line of communication with Seville from, say, Santarem, would have been over two hundred and fifty miles long, which could not have been properly and safely guarded without diminution of the fighting troops actually at the front.

Meanwhile Wellington, having brought all his force, British, Portuguese regulars, and Portuguese militia, within the lines, would have had more than enough men to repel any army that Soult could by any possibility lead against him; and the experiences of Massena in the winter of 1810-1811 would have been repeated with, probably, additional difficulties for Soult. For while the offensive movements of the French were confined to the small space between the Lower Tagus and the sea, the guerillas would have wrought havoc among such isolated posts of the enemy as remained, eating up a large proportion of them piecemeal. Lastly, if upon Soult's ultimate retreat Wellington had sent a British force by sea to Huelva, he might have captured Seville, and left the marshal without any magazine of warlike stores nearer than Burgos and Barcelona. It seems to me therefore that Soult's plan, though it would undoubtedly have brought Wellington back to Portugal, could only have ended in failure, and, if he had ventured on an assault upon Torres Vedras, most probably in disaster.

In the days that followed the receipt of Joseph's letter Soult pushed forward the siege-works before Cadiz with the utmost vigour, maintaining always a sharp cannonade. In reply to his protests Joseph wrote to him on the 17th of August a second letter calling upon him to obey orders or resign his command; but it is probable that the missive did not reach the marshal before he had himself made preparations to evacuate Andalusia. Meanwhile in pursuance of Wellington's desire that a diversion should be made to alarm the force besieging Cadiz, General Cooke had on the 9th of August embarked eighteen hundred British and Portuguese under Skerrett at Cadiz, (det. 2nd Hussars K.G.L.; det. R.A.; det. 3/1st Guards; det. 2/87th; det. 2/95th; det. 20th Portuguese. Total, 69 officers, 1730 N.C.O. and men), to join twice that number of Spaniards under General La Cruz Murgeon in an attack from the side of Huelva.

Skerrett landed at Huelva on the 12th; and the troops prepared to attack the Castle of Niebla, which, however, was evacuated and blown up by the French on the same evening. The expedition seems then to have been delayed for some days, probably to collect transport; for on the 22nd Murgeon had advanced no further than to Manzanilla. On the 24th Skerrett with a detachment of British and Spanish drove out a French advanced post from San Lucar la Mayor, twelve miles west of Seville; and on the night of the 26th, hearing that the French had raised the siege of Cadiz on the 24th and were preparing to withdraw, Murgeon decided to move on at once to Seville.

Early on the morning of the 27th his force engaged the rearguard of the enemy outside the western suburbs, entered the streets after some smart skirmishing, and made a rush for the bridge over the Guadalquivir, which was carried by the grenadiers of the British Guards before the French could destroy it. The enemy, who appear to have numbered some three thousand, were taken by surprise, and evidently gave way to panic; for they were driven out of the city after a very poor resistance with the loss of several killed and wounded, besides two hundred prisoners and two guns captured. The casualties of Skerrett's detachment did not exceed sixteen killed and wounded. (Skerrett's report and a few words from Gough, Rait, i., tell us all that we know of this affair). That the speedy evacuation of Seville was unlocked for is evident from the fact that two hundred and forty-two pieces of ordnance in good order were taken in the foundry, besides large quantities of merchandise and of victuals, and the private baggage of four French generals. (Return in Arteche, xii.)

Meanwhile, Soult had withdrawn from before Cadiz, leaving in his batteries two hundred and eighty-one pieces of various calibres, for the most part disabled for immediate service, though reparable. He had been on the point of marching for Toledo, which had been abandoned by the French and occupied by a party of guerillas, when he received through D'Erlon the intelligence that Joseph had retired to Valencia. He therefore took the route by Granada and Murcia, still, however, professing to credit a report that Wellington was sending a strong detachment into Andalusia by the pass of Despeña Perros. (*Arch, de la Guerre.* Soult to Joseph, 26th Aug. 1812).

On the 8th of September Wellington, though not yet quite satisfied as to Soult's true direction, sent orders to Hill to pass the Tagus at Al-maraz. The letter, as we have seen, reached Sir Rowland on the 13th, his headquarters being then at Villanueva de la Serena. He at once marched for Medellin, where he crossed the Guadiana, and proceeding thence by Miajadas, Truxillo, and Jaraicejo, reached Almaraz on the 20th, Talavera on the 27th, and Toledo on the 30th, finally halting at Aranjuez in the first days of October. During this interval Skerrett, after driving the French rear-guard from Seville, had halted at Al-cala, whither Cooke brought up additional British troops from Cadiz, equipping them for service in expectation of Wellington's orders.

On the 28th of September these orders arrived, and Skerrett was directed to lead some forty-five hundred men to Truxillo, while Cooke retained command of over four thousand more, besides the detachment at Carthagena, which were assigned as garrisons for Cadiz and Tarifa. (See list following). Thus all measures had been taken Sept. to assemble every possible man of the Allies in Central Spain; and Wellington, who had been advanced to the dignity first of an earl and then of a marquis for his successes since the beginning of the year, was free to take in hand the siege of Burgos.

✶✶✶✶✶✶

Skerrett's detachment : det. 2nd Hussars K.G.L. ; 2 cos. R.A. ; 3/1st Guards ; det. 2/47th ; 2/87th ; det. 2/95th ; 20th Portuguese ; Staff Corps. *Total,* 154 officers, 4348 N.C.O. and men fit for duty ; 422 sick.

Cooke's command (Cadiz) : det. R.A. ; 5 cos. Wattevilles ; 2 cos. Chasseurs Brittanniques. 32 officers, 1358 N.C.O. and men.

Isla (Cadiz) : det. 2nd Hussars K.G.L. (dismounted) ; dets. R.E., R.A. ; 2/59th ; det. batt. for foreign recruits. *Total,* 65 officers, 1710 N.C.O. and men.

Tarifa : det. R.E. and R.A. ; det. batt. for foreign recruits. *Total,* 7 officers, 179 N.C.O. and men.

Carthagena : dets. R.E. and R.A. ; 2/67th ; 5 cos. Wattevilles. *Total,* 45 officers, 1189 N.C.O. and men. 2/59th had landed at Cadiz from England on the 7th of Sept. Cooke to Sec. of State, 7th, 28th Sept., 25th Oct. 1812. *Wellington Desp.,* to Cooke, 9th Sept. 1812.

✶✶✶✶✶✶

The country about the upper waters of the Arlanzon consists of chalk downs naturally escarped; and it is upon a chalk hill, rising high and abruptly from the north side of the river that the Castle of Burgos stands, with the town spread out at its foot. Its defences were limited to a triple *enceinte*, about twelve hundred yards in extreme length by seven hundred in extreme width. The first or outermost of these was composed of a mediaeval scarp-wall, improved by an earthen parapet, and strengthened by flanking works of ingenious contrivance. The second line was to all purposes a field-work, well palisaded. The third or innermost line was of like nature with the second, but revetted and covered by a ditch thirty feet wide, while within and at the summit of the hill were a building called the White Church, of little defensive value, and the ancient keep, converted by the French into an interior retrenchment with a new casemated battery bearing the name of Napoleon.

Thus the fortress was not formidable, and it was the less so inasmuch as it was commanded towards the north-east at a range of three hundred yards by a spur of another chalk ridge, called the heights of St. Michael, which rises one hundred and fifty feet above it, and is separated from it by a deep combe. (Seen from the horn-work the castle appears not better than 100 yards distant; seen from the castle the horn-work seems more nearly at its true distance—a singular optical illusion). Napoleon had ordered the fortification of these heights by a horn-work containing nearly as much ground as the castle itself, but this was still incomplete. The scarp was steep and high, but the counter-scarp was of less than half its altitude, the branches were imperfect, and the rear had only recently been closed by an exceedingly strong palisade. Nevertheless the interior was commanded by the guns of the Napoleon battery, and its branches were well flanked by the guns of the castle.

On the 19th of September Burgos was invested by the First, Fifth, Sixth, and Seventh Divisions of infantry, aided by the two independent Portuguese brigades of Pack and McMahon; the Sixth Division taking up ground on the left bank of the Arlanzon, while the remainder forded the river, and ascending the heights of St. Michael drove the enemy from three *flèches* in advance of the horn-work. The rest of the army was then posted astride of the road to France at Monasterio de Rodilla, some nine miles to the north-east; and the engineers laid their plans for the siege. The south-western end of the castle was the point selected for the attack, partly because the eastern and southern sides were covered by the town, partly because in that particular quarter the front was smaller and the lines weaker than elsewhere, while the fall of the ground was so rapid that the guns above could not be sufficiently depressed to sweep it.

It was resolved that on the first night the horn-work should be stormed and that a battery should be erected under cover of a knoll just outside the western angle, from whence the guns could play upon the castle under shelter from the fire of Fort Napoleon. The southwestern face was then to be approached by sap, and the scarp of each *enceinte* in succession was to be blown up by mines, and assaulted under fire of the battery near the horn-work.

The only discouraging circumstance was that the siege-train counted but three eighteen-pounder cannon and five twenty-four-pounder howitzers, the latter being short brass guns, very useless for a siege and most inaccurate in their fire; whereas the garrison had nine heavy guns, eleven field-pieces, and six mortars or howitzers mounted in batteries, with all the reserve artillery of the Army of Portugal to replace them if disabled.

However, no time was lost in preparing for the assault on the horn-work; and it was arranged that two storming parties should fall upon the salient angles of the two demi-bastions, and enter the ditch at the point where the counter-scarp was low. A firing party of one hundred and fifty men of the Forty-Second was at the same time to move straight upon the front of the work, halt at the edge of the ditch, and fire upon the garrison so as to enable the storming parties to plant their ladders at the scarp and carry the work by escalade. Pack offered his Portuguese brigade for the chief attack, and was permitted to undertake it.

At the same time the light companies of the Guards and of Stirling's brigade under Major Somers Cocks, supported by the Forty-Second, were directed to move round the rear of the work, so as to prevent the arrival of reinforcements, and, if feasible, to break into the gorge. At eight o'clock the assault was delivered, but with many faults in the execution.

★★★★★★

Stirling of the Forty-Second had succeeded Wheatley in the command of the 2nd brigade of the 1st division on the 11th Sept. 1/26th had been sent back to garrison in Lisbon, so that the brigade now consisted of 2/24th, 1/42nd, 1/79th. The 2nd batt. of the 42nd had been drafted into the 1st, and the cadre sent home.

Major Somers Cocks had been recently promoted from the Sixteenth Light Dragoons into the Seventy-Ninth.

Eight o'clock was the hour fixed by Wellington; French accounts call it 8.30.

★★★★★★

The firing party being at once discovered by the enemy was greeted by a heavy discharge of musketry; whereupon the stormers, contrary to orders, returned answering volleys which they continued to the edge of the counterscarp, with the result that before they could reach the ditch they were almost annihilated.

Meanwhile a body of Highlanders, who carried the ladders for the Portuguese, planted them against the scarp and led the way to the summit; but the Portuguese would not follow, and the escalade was a total failure. Cocks, however, led his party to the gorge, under a fire from the castle which laid low nearly half of his men, climbed the palisades, and drove his opponents to join their comrades, who were all of them in the ditch. Separating his men into two divisions, he left one to guard the sally-port into the ditch, and advanced with the other to the eastern demi-bastion, where his fire speedily put an end to resistance. In desperation the French made a rush by the sally-port, overthrew by sheer weight the weak force that was stationed there, and swarmed into the interior of the work. But Cocks, charging with the bayonet, drove them headlong through the gorge with the loss of nearly two hundred killed, wounded, and taken. The entire credit of this success belonged to Cocks, who, if properly supported, would have captured every soul of the garrison.

The Allies suffered heavily, their casualties numbering four hundred and twenty killed, wounded, and missing, of whom two hundred and five belonged to the Forty-Second. Altogether, except to Cocks's detachment, it was not a creditable affair; and the only excuse that Wellington could find for it was the inexperience of the Forty-Second Highlanders. (I have followed chiefly Tomkinson's account (*Diary of a Cavalry Officer*), supplemented by the narratives of Jones and Napier. The story given in *Personal Narrative of a Private in the 42nd* is worthless).

Upon reconnoitring the castle from the heights of St. Michael Wellington did not conceal his misgivings that the means at his command were inadequate to the capture of the fortress. Indeed his first sight of Burgos had greatly astonished and disappointed him, for he

1 been led to expect that it was an insignificant place with slight
 ..mporary works. (Sir F. Ponsonby's MS. Journal. He was at the outposts when Wellington first examined Burgos through his field-glass).
His only hope lay in the facts that the supply of water was deficient,
and that the magazines of provisions were in a situation which might
enable him to set them on fire.

It was disquieting also to learn that a draft of seven thousand men
had reached the Army of Portugal from France, and that more were
expected. However, a lodgement was at once made in the body of
the horn-work, despite the fire from the castle; and on the night of
the 20th the construction of a first battery as also of its trenches of
communication to rear was begun just to westward of the gorge. The
enemy kept up a perpetual cannonade upon these works, but with
small results, owing to the protection afforded by the ground. On the
night of the 22nd two eighteen-pounders and three field howitzers
were mounted in the First Battery; and the building of a second was
commenced in the actual gorge of the horn-work.

At midnight an attempt was made to escalade the outermost line
of the western front, where the wall, though twenty-three to twenty-
five feet high, was unflanked; a Portuguese battalion being appointed
at the same time to assault at a weak point of the southern front which
was defended only by a small guard. Four hundred men drawn from
all the battalions of the First Division were to form in a hollow road
within sixty yards of the ditch, where half of them were to line the
bank and keep down the fire of the defenders, while the remainder
should ascend the scarp by five ladders.

The attempt was a complete failure. The Portuguese would not
face the bullets even of the feeble French guard opposed to them;
the firing party through some mistake or confusion rushed with the
stormers into the ditch; the brave officers and men who led the escalade were easily overcome; those behind them suffered heavily from
combustibles and explosives rolled down by the enemy upon them;
and in fifteen minutes the four hundred fell back with the loss of
half their numbers. This again was an ill-managed affair, which discouraged the Allies and heartened the enemy. (Wellington ascribed
the mishap to neglect of his orders by the officer in command of
the attack, who made no dispositions but rushed on like a common
soldier, and was killed. Moreover, as the plan of attack was found by
the enemy in his pocket, it could not be repeated. *Wellington Desp.* To
Liverpool, 23rd Nov.)

Burgoyne was of opinion that the attack would have succeeded if the Portuguese had behaved as was expected of them; but the compilation of so small a body as four hundred men from several different battalions was in itself a great blunder; for the men, not knowing each other nor the officers, could not work with the unity and confidence that would have inspired the like numbers drawn from a single battalion. The enemy's casualties did not exceed twenty-two killed and wounded. Forty-eight hours having been thus lost to no purpose, reversion was made to the original plan of mining the outer line of defence. The hollow road already mentioned was converted into a parallel on the night of the 23rd, and a communication with it was traced from the suburb of San Pedro.

Heavy rain, which began early in the night, concealed the new work until daylight of the 24th, when the enemy, by stationing marksmen behind a projecting palisade, did great execution among the besiegers; and the inaccuracy of the British heavy howitzers was such that in a whole hour's firing not a single shot or shell touched the shelter wherein the sharpshooters were ensconced. These howitzers had now been moved into the First Battery, the eighteen-pounders having been transferred to the Second; but by this time the ammunition of the Allies was growing scanty, and Wellington was obliged to apply to Sir Home Popham at Santander for powder.

However, two galleries for two mines about sixty yards apart were begun on the western front, and zigzags were carried down from the horn-work towards a ledge of the hill below, where a trench was dug to give protection for a line of infantry. But the enemy were not idle, and by throwing stones, hand-grenades, and small shells into the advanced sap they annoyed the working parties greatly, while their artillery swept away the parapet of the new musketry-trench and rendered it useless.

At last, after much delay owing to the idleness of the British working parties and the skilful resistance of the French, one of the mines on the western face was completed and charged; and the night of the 29th was appointed for the assault. Three hundred men were told off for the storming party, with a forlorn hope of an officer and twenty men. The mine was sprung at midnight; and the French were so much panic-stricken by the explosion that the foremost of the forlorn hope a sergeant and four men reached the top of the parapet unopposed. But, owing to the mortality among officers of engineers, not one could be spared to guide the main body to the breach. The leader took his men too far to the west, and, finding the wall uninjured, returned to report that the mine had been a failure.

The storming party was therefore recalled; and by the time that the sergeant aforesaid could arrive to tell his story, the French had been so much reinforced at the threatened point that any further effort was hopeless. The Allies, having no ammunition to enable their artillery to play upon the breach, the French succeeded in retrenching it before daylight; and thus many days' work was wholly thrown away.

Discouragement now seized upon the besieging force. Heavy rain increased the discomfort of the dangerous duty in the trenches; the working parties, excepting those of the Guards, grew more than ever evasive and careless; and discipline at large became sensibly relaxed. A new battery, the Third, which had been constructed off the western face for the reception of Wellington's three solitary cannon, was knocked to pieces and one of the guns was disabled before they could even open fire. Another battery, thrown up during the night a little to the north of the first, suffered the same fate; the plunging shot from the castle being too heavy for the parapet, and the enemy's gunners too well protected to be touched by musketry.

On the following night, which was very wet and stormy, the whole of the working parties—officers and men—except those of the Guards, absented themselves from duty, and provoked Wellington to issue a severe rebuke in general orders. The two remaining eighteen-pounders were now brought back to their original place in the First Battery; and on the 4th of October they and three howitzers reopened the breach made by the explosion of the mine on the night of the 29th. Simultaneously the second mine a little to west of it was completed and charged. At five o'clock this mine was sprung, blowing many of the enemy into the air and making an extensive gap, which was promptly stormed by a party of the Twenty-Fourth under Captain Hedderwick, while another detachment of the same regiment at the same moment carried the old breach.

In a few minutes they had driven the garrison within the second line of defence, suffering no further loss than thirty-seven killed and two hundred and thirteen, including nine officers, wounded or missing. Sixty-eight of the casualties fell upon the Twenty-Fourth, the remainder being divided among eighteen different corps besides the Portuguese. Among the wounded was Lieutenant-Colonel John Jones, who is still remembered for his history of the sieges during this war.

Approaches were now opened towards the second line, the British howitzers being directed upon the palisades and the cannon upon a re-entrant angle in the northern face. By the evening of the 7th a good part of the parapet had been battered down; but the enemy fired briskly, disabling one of the two British guns, and rolling down shells upon the lodgement in the outer wall, which lay too low for the extreme angle of depression of their guns. Torrents of rain made work in the trenches extremely difficult, and at two o'clock on the morning of the 8th the garrison by a sudden sortie drove away the guard from the outermost wall, and had levelled all the works and carried off the tools before the British troops, re-forming, chased them in turn back within the second line.

Over two hundred of the besiegers fell in this affair, chief among them Colonel Charles Somers Cocks, who was shot dead in the act of rallying his men. On the following morning Wellington came, as was his habit during the siege, into General Frederick Ponsonby's room; but, instead of addressing him, he walked up and down for some minutes in silence, then went to the door, said abruptly, "Cocks was killed last night," and walked out. The dead officer was buried with full military honours in compliment to his distinguished bravery; and the expression of pain upon Wellington's face during the ceremony was so strongly marked that no one present, excepting D' Urban, presumed to approach him. Three times only in the course of his long life did men see the Iron Duke give way to tears; but it is evident that he had a struggle to conceal his grief over the grave of Somers Cocks, he said at last after a long silence:—

> D'Urban, had Cocks outlived these campaigns, which from the way he exposed himself was morally impossible, he would have become one of the first generals in England.

Not until 1855 was some hint of Cocks's great services given to his countrymen in a short pamphlet published by one who, as a subaltern, had served with him in the Sixteenth Light Dragoons. (Hugh Owen, later of the 7th and 18th Hussars, and afterwards of the Portuguese Army, the pamphlet is reprinted entire by Tomkinson; Wellington *Supp. Desp.* vii.) Not until 1895 was the full excellence of that service revealed by the publication of the journal of his own subaltern and close friend, Tomkinson, of the same regiment. With his memory thus embalmed alike by the testimony of his subordinates and by the praise of his great captain, who was even more chary of sentiment than of commendation, we may leave Somers Cocks to his rest beneath the walls of Burgos.

By this time the supply of musket-ammunition had fallen so low, owing to the perpetual fusillade maintained by the besieging infantry to supplement the want of artillery-fire, that the cannonade of the breach was discontinued, an assault being impossible until more cartridges should arrive. The guns were therefore employed in pouring red-hot shot upon the magazine; but the effect after three days' experiment was found to be small, the roof of the building being never really kindled and the flames easily quenched. On the 10th the shot for the howitzers was almost exhausted, and that for the cannon would have been equally scarce had not fallen French projectiles been collected which more or less fitted the bore. However, powder arrived from Popham's squadron, and a new gallery was begun near the eastern angle of the southern front towards the church of St. Roman which, though external to the defence, was maintained as a storehouse by the garrison.

On the 11th October the cannonade from the batteries of the Allies practically ceased; and the French took advantage of the circumstance to retrench the breach made in the second line. At last on the 15th fire was reopened from the Second Battery from one sound and two damaged eighteen-pounders and from one howitzer, the object being to demolish the wall of the keep on which stood the Napoleon battery; but within three-quarters of an hour these pieces were silenced by the heavier metal of the castle. They were therefore turned once more upon the original breach in the second line, and with results so favourable that, had the stock of ammunition permitted, the gap would speedily have been made practicable for an assault.

In the evening a supply of cannon-shot arrived from Ciudad Rodrigo; but the British batteries were so much damaged by heavy rain during the night that the artillery was useless for offensive purposes throughout the whole of the next day. However, the gallery under St. Roman's Church, having been pushed as far as was thought safe, was charged with nine hundred pounds of powder; on the 17th and 18th the British ordnance, scanty and crippled though it was, swept away the retrenchments raised by the French behind the breach; and on the afternoon of the latter day Wellington issued his orders for the assault.

At half-past four the mine under St. Roman's Church was to be sprung, and the gap thus created was to be entered by a party of Spaniards and Portuguese under Colonel Brown. At the signal of the explosion two hundred of the Guards were to rush through the more easterly breach of the first line and escalade the second line; while two hundred of the German Legion under Major Wurmb were to assault the breach of the second line; both parties moving by fifties. The mine being duly sprung at a quarter to five made a large opening which was occupied by Brown's people in spite of the explosion of a counter-mine by the French. The Guards then advanced, escaladed the parapet and formed on the other side of it; while Wurmb with one hundred men gallantly broke into the second line at the first assault. But the Germans instead of turning to their left to clear a stockade upon their flank, as they had been ordered, extended to their right to join the Guards.

A few brave men of both parties actually entered the innermost line, where they were killed; but the second hundred of the Germans never came forward, and the whole attack was inadequately support-ed. Dubreton at once threw his reserves upon the front and flank of the stormers, who were swept back to the first line, leaving more than half of their numbers killed and wounded behind them. No troops in the world could have behaved better, and Wellington in his despatch did full justice to their conduct, for they were cruelly cut up. The Coldstreams lost sixty killed and wounded, including four officers; the Scots Guards twenty-five, including two officers; and the Germans seventy-five, including seven officers. Wurmb, who had distinguished himself by skill and bravery on many occasions, was among the killed.

Altogether it was a disastrous little affair, which practically put an end to the siege. During the night teams were sent out to bring up two heavy cannon from Santander; but this was only a blind, for on the 20th Wellington directed all the ordnance to be withdrawn from the batteries, and quitted the lines to take personal command of the covering army, leaving Pack with from two to three thousand men to maintain the blockade. On the 21st he ordered all stores and guns that could not be removed to be destroyed; and accordingly the three eighteen-pounders were disabled and left upon the road. Early on the morning of the 22nd the troops raised the siege. It had cost the Brit-ish ninety-two officers and nineteen hundred and seventy-two men, a full third of whom were killed outright. The loss of the garrison did not exceed six hundred and seven, of whom one-half were killed or died of their wounds.

Beyond all question this abortive siege of Burgos was the most unsatisfactory operation on Wellington's part during the whole of the Peninsular War. The advance upon Madrid in 1809 had been hazardous, perhaps unduly rash; yet it had at least been undertaken with confidence and executed with vigour. But the attack upon Burgos was initiated with misgiving and pursued with instability both of design and of purpose. To an army properly equipped with heavy artillery and trained engineers and sappers the capture of Burgos would have been a trifling episode; but to one owning no more than the parody of a train—three heavy cannon with scanty ammunition, which had accompanied Wellington from Salamanca—it was a far more serious matter.

Could he have brought forward more guns? Napier hints that he might have obtained some, not only (as he ultimately did) from Popham, but also from Madrid. Sir Edward Pakenham in fact pledged himself to borrow harness and animals of the officers in the capital and to send up some excellent guns from the Retiro. Pakenham's offer, however, was rejected; and it may have been distrust of his brother-in-law's enthusiasm which caused Wellington to report to Lord Liverpool that he could not find the means of moving even one gun from Madrid. (*Wellington Desp.* To Liverpool, 23rd Nov. 1812).

What, then, was Wellington's actual intention? Many years later he declared that, having snatched away more than one Indian fortress by escalade, he hoped to do the like with Burgos, but was foiled by the skill and resource of Dubreton. Yet at the outset he resolved, as we have seen, to make his breaches by mining—a method condemned by one of his best officers—and only attempted an escalade as a variant upon this procedure. Moreover, although he had adopted in great measure what may be termed the Indian system both at Ciudad Rodrigo and Badajoz, he shrank from hurling really strong and massive columns against Burgos, and seemed content to tap at the ramparts with little driblets of thirty and fifty men, and refused to listen to any remonstrance from his engineer, he said to Burgoyne:—

> Why expose more men than can ascend the ladders or enter the work at one time, when by this mode the support is ordered to be up in time to follow the tail of the preceding party close?

Yet it is only too certain that on more than one occasion the supports did not back the storming party closely, and that the failure of the assault was due precisely to this cause. Evidently the terrible losses at Badajoz had so deeply impressed Wellington's mind that he feared to incur them again. Hence his operations were a bad compound of scientific and unscientific measures. First he opened a battery in a very good position to break down the interior lines of the castle as soon as the outer lines should be carried, and decided to breach the outer lines by mining. But to save time he made an attempt to carry the first line by an escalade, which failed owing to bad management. Next, he fell back on mining in earnest, and endeavoured to keep down the enemy's cannonade by musketry, an expedient which proved to be alike costly and futile.

After this failure, he sprang the first mine, but to no purpose, for the storming party never found its way to the breach. Then he brought his cannon down from the summit of St. Michael's heights to the low ground, in order to batter a new breach; with no result but the absolute destruction of one piece and some damage to the other two. Thereupon he replaced the cannon on the top of the hill, and resumed mining operations; sprang the second mine; and successfully mastered the outermost line of defences.

But no impression whatever was made upon the enemy's batteries; and the working parties, unprotected by the fire of artillery from their own side, idled and shirked in a disgraceful fashion. The Guards alone could be trusted to toil in the trenches bravely, cheerfully, and efficiently. After suffering heavy loss from Dubreton's sortie, Wellington resorted to red-hot shot to kindle the French magazines; and, finally, after the springing of a third mine and the miscarriage of another assault, he abandoned the siege. Probably if he had launched a whole division in any one of the assaults he would have captured the place without greater loss of life than that which he actually suffered.

He excused himself in part by blaming his instruments. Thus he ascribed, doubtless with justice, his heavy loss in the storm of the hornwork to the inexperience of the Forty-Second; and he proceeded to say that he had neither trustworthy officers nor good troops, having left them (meaning the Third and Light Divisions) behind him at Madrid. Moreover, he noticed with surprise and dismay that, whether from want of pay or from some other cause, the Portuguese soldiers had greatly deteriorated. (*Wellington Desp.*, to Bathurst, 21st Sept.; to Beresford, 22nd Sept., 5th Oct. 1812). We shall in the course of another year encounter a recurrence of this complaint, that only the Third and Light Divisions understood how to assault a breach; but in the present instance it seems to me probable that the lack of keenness in the troops was due to two principal causes.

The first was that the men were what is called stale, which means that they had had enough for the present of hardship, privation, and danger, and needed rest. They had been strenuously at work since January. In the course of six months they had delivered two assaults, the first very sharp and the second very bloody, and had fought one severe general action. The Light Division, after bearing the brunt at Ciudad Rodrigo, had suffered terribly at Badajoz; and the Sixth not less terribly at Salamanca. The Third Division had lost large numbers in all three affairs, and the Fourth and Fifth in two of them, to say nothing of the fact that in both of the two last divisions their commanders, Cole and Leith, had been disabled by wounds.

Drafts and reinforcements had indeed been received from both England and Gibraltar; but Wellington complained that all of them were very sickly, (*Wellington Desp.* To Bathurst, 27th Sept. 1812), and absolutely untrained in marching. Practically therefore he had no fresh troops; and it is well known to all military men that, when soldiers are wearied out with work, they become demoralised; and that such demoralisation, being contagious, spreads very rapidly through an army. Moreover, the misery of the camp and trenches before Burgos under the deluge of the autumn rains was exceptional even in Spain. In the last days of the siege General Edward Paget arrived to take command of the First Division, bringing with him on his staff Colonel James Stanhope, the friend of Moore. Stanhope wrote in his journal:—

> The First Division is halted or rather bogged between the castle and Villa Toro. . . . I visited the trenches. They are the very devil, for if one is not drowned or choked in mud at the first bayou, one is nearly sure of being shot in the first line if above five feet high. I never saw anything like it. If you held up a cap, you had two or three balls through it at once.

It was this state of things that the Allied troops endured for thirty-three days; and, although the excellence of Dubreton's marksmen cannot be over-praised, yet it must be borne in mind that their advantages in respect of shelter, position, and immunity from fire of cannon were such as to make the contest very unfair, and therefore very discouraging to the besiegers.

In the second place Wellington's misgivings, not only as to the success of the siege, but as to the general situation and the whole course of his movements since the Battle of Salamanca, undoubtedly reacted upon the spirit and morale of his troops. He may be pardoned if, on the evening of the victory, he found himself somewhat at a loss, for he was placed suddenly in a new and strange situation. Since the close of 1809 his army had acted as a moveable force to defend first Lisbon and then Portugal; and the recapture of Ciudad Rodrigo and Badajoz, brilliant achievements though they were, were of importance chiefly in that they thrust back the French advanced bases from the Portuguese frontier. He was able of course to convert these fortresses into advanced bases for his own operations; but what solid enterprise could he, with the force at his disposal, undertake? Was it possible for him to do more than compel the French armies in the north to concentrate, so as to give full play to the guerillas, and then to retire before them to his old position on the Portuguese frontier?

As we have seen, he had actually sent back his heavy artillery and baggage towards Ciudad Rodrigo when Marmont (as Frederick Ponsonby said) outmanoeuvred himself on the plain of the Arapiles, and enabled Wellington to strike a telling blow which put the Army of Portugal for a time out of action. What was then the best thing to be done? The decision was not easy, excepting in the obvious matter of severing communications between the Army of Portugal and the Army of the Centre. Could Wellington by any possibility hold Old Castile? The only chance of doing so was to weaken the Army of Portugal still further by an active pursuit, and to capture Burgos before its fortifications had been repaired and while the discouragement and demoralisation of the retreat were still potent among the enemy. But would he have attained his object even then? It seems to me extremely doubtful; for how would he have supported himself? His line of supply from his bases at Oporto and Coruña would have lain over three hundred miles of bad road, and he could hardly have opened a fresh base at Santander, with a line of communication parallel to the enemy's front.

Burgos itself was no stronghold; and if the Armies of the North and Centre, joined with the best troops of the Army of Portugal, had advanced against him, the fortress would have been of little value or protection. It seems to me therefore that Wellington deliberately abandoned all hope of solid military profit from his victory, and decided to content himself with its moral advantages.

To this end he moved upon Madrid, the capture of which to some extent satisfied his aspirations. It is probable that, if he had followed up Joseph's retreat, he might have made that retreat even more miserable than it was, and possibly have ruined the Army of the Centre; but it must be remembered that the want of water would have been as distressing to the pursuers as to the pursued, and would have rendered the pursuit very costly. A march to Alicante to pick up Maitland's force and operate against Joseph and Suchet, would have involved the detachment of a strong body of troops in the north to hold the Army of Portugal in check, and was therefore out of the question. From a strictly military point of view, therefore, he gained only the capture of the garrison and of the stores in the Retiro, which was beyond question appreciable as a diminution of the resources of the enemy for future campaigns. The immediate moral and political influence of the movement was likewise not to be despised, for Napoleon's march into Russia had so far been triumphant; and the disaffected, who were disposed to rebel against his rule during his absence, needed encouragement.

Moreover, and this was a most important point, the news that Madrid was in British hands might well cause the Americans to think better of their recent hasty declaration of war. Lastly, it was reasonable to expect that the expulsion of the intrusive king from his capital might hearten the Spaniards of all ranks to new and enthusiastic effort. But, the Spaniards and the Spanish Government being such as they were, was it not somewhat presumptuous to count upon the continued occupation of Madrid; and, unless that occupation could be permanent, was it not a mistake to raise false hopes by leading British troops, or at any rate the headquarters of the British Army, into Madrid at all? Was such a course not a repetition of Napoleon's mistake in assuming that the seizure of the capital carried with it the mastery of the kingdom?

Again to what military projects was the capture of Madrid likely to inspire the enemy's commander-in-chief? It was of course impossible for the British general to divine; but it was clear that he expected and hoped that, for the sake of Spain, it would lead to the evacuation of Andalusia either through some direct advance of his own forces upon the province or, as actually happened, by the withdrawal of Soult's entire army to Valencia. This last movement, Wellington declared, would be the fulfilment of his wishes; yet he failed not to realise that the concentration of Soult's, Joseph's, and Suchet's armies against him must have unpleasant consequences for himself. (*Wellington Desp.* To H. Wellesley, 16th Aug. 1812).

★★★★★★

He wrote later with clear insight: "I have always been of opinion that, as far as the Allied British and Portuguese Army was concerned, the discontinuance of the blockade of Cadiz and the evacuation of Andalusia would be misfortunes, however important as political events." To Bathurst, 28th Oct. 1812.

★★★★★★

In the midst of his doubts came Clausel's raid upon his communications in the second week of August, which gave him another opportunity for dealing a heavy blow at the Army of Portugal, so as to disable it for at least some months and drive it beyond the Ebro.

After a second victory Burgos, albeit already repaired and strengthened, might have fallen in a few days, though it is still more than doubtful whether it could have been held. A captured French officer, whom James Stanhope met at Salamanca on his way to Burgos, said:—

Believe me, believe me, you are too far forward, and will not winter on the Ebro.

As we have seen already, Wellington, whether to bring up the Galician Army or from what motive soever, pressed Clausel backward in the gentlest and most leisurely fashion, and then laying siege to Burgos was completely, almost ignominiously, foiled.

The conclusion would seem to be that Wellington was fairly bewildered by the possibilities that seemed to lie open to him after the victory of Salamanca, and that for a moment he lost his hold upon facts. His army was so weak in comparison with the united force of the enemy that its function was still rather to prevent the French from establishing their hold upon the Peninsula than to attempt to drive them from it. The more they were dispersed, the more they played into his hands; wherefore there seems to have been no great object in compelling them to evacuate Andalusia unless by a general action which would wreck the Army of the South.

The longer that Soult frittered his troops away in the blockades of Cadiz and in the occupation of a district measuring at least three hundred miles by one hundred, the better for the Allies. If in spite of everything the French commander-in-chief decided to assemble the Armies of the Centre, East, and South-east in one body, then the only course for Wellington was to attempt to fall upon some one of them before they were united; but to this end it was essential that the Army of Portugal should be first thoroughly disabled. And, judging with the wisdom that comes after the event, it should seem that Wellington ought never to have rested after the brilliant action of the Arapiles until Clausel had been crippled beyond all remedy.

If he had followed that general up vigorously, leaving a division at Valladolid, it is doubtful whether Joseph would have ventured to advance upon that place where Santocildes and Amarante were already in position and Castaños might join them upon any day from Astorga.

Or again, as has been suggested by the Spanish historian, General Arteche, if Wellington had taken up a central position, say at Aranda de Duero, Joseph could not have suffered him to remain for an indefinite time across his communications, and, not being strong enough to drive away the Allies single-handed, must have summoned to his aid one or other of the armies.

Any attempt at a concerted movement with Clausel would infallibly have led to the defeat of one of the two bodies in detail; wherefore Joseph must either have called Suchet's army to him from Valencia, leaving Maitland and O'Donnell free to work havoc in that quarter; or he must have abandoned Madrid and betaken himself to Valencia or Andalusia. In that case the object of Wellington's march to Madrid would equally have been gained; and, if circumstances should have compelled the ultimate dereliction of the capital again to the enemy, the departure of a guerilla-band after a few weeks of occupation would have been a very different matter from the commander-in-chief's humiliating retreat after a somewhat ostentatiously victorious entry.

All this, it must be repeated, is wisdom after the event; nor is it possible for us to view the situation as it presented itself to Wellington at the time. Yet it seems certain that the advance of the main army upon Madrid was a mistake from which issued all the subsequent troubles of the campaign. Wellington had endeavoured to embrace more territory than he had the force to protect.

Appendix 1

Wellington's Army at Salamanca: Composition and Strength
N.B.—Strength according to the morning state of July 15, 1812.
The fighting strength on July 22, owing to losses at Castrejon and
Castrillo, and to weary men falling out during the retreat, may have
been perhaps 1000 less. (From Oman's *Peninsular War*, v.)

I. BRITISH TROOPS

CAVALRY (Stapleton Cotton).		Officers.	Strength. Men.	Total.
Le Mar-	3rd Dragoons	17	322	339
chant's	4th Dragoons	22	336	358
Brigade	5th Dragoon Guards	22	313	325
G. Anson's	11th Light Dragoons	30	361	391
Brigade	12th Light Dragoons	19	321	340
	16th Light Dragoons	14	259	273
V. Alten's	14th Light Dragoons	23	324	347
Brigade	1st Hussars K.G.L.	23	376	399
Bock's	1st Dragoons K.G.L.	25	339	364
Brigade	2nd Dragoons K.G.L.	23	384	407
Total British Cavalry		218	3335	3543

INFANTRY.
First Division (H. Campbell).

Fermor's Brigade	1st Coldstream Guards	26	928	954
	1st Third Guards	23	938	961
	1 Company 5/60th Foot	1	56	57
Wheatley's Brigade	2/24th Foot	23	398	421
	1/42nd Foot	40	1039	1079
	2/58th Foot [1]	31	369	400
	1/79th Foot	40	634	674
	1 Company 5/60th	1	53	54

[1] The 2/58th, though properly belonging to the Fifth Division, appears to have
acted on this day with the First Division.

		Officers.	Strength. Men.	Total.
Löwe's Brigade	1st Line Battalion K.G.L.	26	615	641
	2nd Line Battalion K.G.L.	26	601	627
	5th Line Battalion K.G.L.	30	525	555
Total First Division		267	6156	6423

Third Division (Pakenham).

		Officers.	Men.	Total.
Wallace's Brigade	1/45th Foot	26	416	442
	74th Foot	23	420	443
	1/88th Foot	21	642	663
	3 Companies 5/60th Foot	11	243	254
J. Campbell's Brigade	1/5th Foot	32	870	902
	2/5th Foot	19	289	308
	2/83rd Foot	24	295	319
	94th Foot	24	323	347
Total Third Division		180	3498	3678

Fourth Division (Lowry Cole).

		Officers.	Men.	Total.
W. Anson's Brigade	3/27th Foot	19	614	633
	1/40th Foot	24	558	582
	1 Company 5/60th	2	44	46
Ellis's Brigade	1/7th Foot	24	471	495
	1/23rd Foot	19	427	446
	1/48th Foot	22	404	426
	1 Company Brunswick Oels	1	53	54
Total Fourth Division		111	2571	2682

Fifth Division (Leith).

		Officers.	Men.	Total.
Greville's Brigade	3/1st Foot	32	729	761
	1/9th Foot	31	635	666
	1/38th Foot [1]	36	764	800
	2/38th Foot	20	281	301
	1 Company Brunswick Oels	2	76	78

[1] This battalion only joined the division on the battle-morning.

		Officers.	Strength. Men.	Total.
Pringle's Brigade	1/4th Foot	36	421	457
	2/4th Foot	27	627	654
	2/30th Foot	20	329	349
	2/44th Foot	20	231	251
	1 Company Brunswick Oels	3	66	69
	Total Fifth Division	227	4159	4386

Sixth Division (Clinton).

		Officers.	Men.	Total.
Hulse's Brigade	1/11th Foot	31	485	516
	2/53rd Foot	25	316	341
	1/61st Foot	29	517	546
	1 Company 5/60th	2	59	61
Hinde's Brigade	2nd Foot	27	381	408
	1/32nd Foot	33	576	609
	1/36th Foot	29	400	429
	Total Sixth Division	176	2734	2910

Seventh Division (Hope).

		Officers.	Men.	Total.
Halkett's Brigade	1st Light Batt. K.G.L.	25	544	569
	2nd Light Batt. K.G.L.	21	473	494
	Brunswick Oels (9 Companies)	23	573	596
De Berne-witz's Brigade	51st Foot	27	280	307
	68th Foot	21	317	338
	Chasseurs Brittanniques	27	686	713
	Total Seventh Division	144	2873	3017

Light Division (Chas. Alten).

		Officers.	Men.	Total.
Barnard's Brigade	1/43rd Foot	30	718	748
	Detachments 2/95th and 3/95th Rifles	19	373	392
Vandeleur's Brigade	1/52nd Foot	28	771	799
	8 Companies 1/95th	27	515	542
	Total Light Division	104	2377	2481

	Officers.	Strength. Men.	Total.
Royal Horse Artillery (troops of Ross, Macdonald, and Bull, and drivers)	18	403	421
Field Artillery (companies of Lawson, Gardiner, Greene, Douglas, May, and drivers)	35	650	685
King's German Legion Artillery (battery of Sympher) . . .	5	75	80
Artillery Total . . .	58	1128	1186
ENGINEERS	12	9	21
STAFF CORPS	5	81	86
WAGON TRAIN	24	115	139

BRITISH TOTAL

	Officers.	Strength. Men.	Total.
Infantry	1,209	24,368	25,577
Cavalry	218	3,335	3,553
Artillery	58	1,128	1,186
Engineers	12	9	21
Staff Corps	5	81	86
Train	24	115	139
General Staff	?	?	?
Total . . .	1,526	29,036	30,562

II. PORTUGUESE TROOPS

CAVALRY.

	Officers.	Strength. Men.	Total.
D'Urban's Brigade : 1st and 11th Dragoons (12th Dragoons absent) [1]	32	450	482

INFANTRY.

	Officers.	Strength. Men.	Total.
Power's Brigade, Third Division : 9th and 21st Line, 12th Caçadores .	90	2,107	2,197
Stubb's Brigade, Fourth Division : 11th and 23rd Line, 7th Caçadores .	137	2,417	2,554
Spry's Brigade, Fifth Division : 3rd and 15th Line, 8th Caçadores . .	156	2,149	2,305

[1] The 12th Dragoons were marching to the rear in charge of the baggage-train.

	Officers.	Strength. Men.	Total.
Rezende's Brigade, Sixth Division : 8th and 12th Line, 9th Caçadores .	134	2,497	2,631
Collins's Brigade, Seventh Division : 7th and 19th Line, 2nd Caçadores .	132	2,036	2,168
Pack's Independent Brigade : 1st and 16th Line, 4th Caçadores . .	85	2,520	2,605
Bradford's Independent Brigade : 13th and 14th Line, 5th Caçadores .	112	1,782	1,894
Attached to Light Division : 1st and 3rd Caçadores	30	1,037	1,067
ARTILLERY.			
Arriaga's battery	4	110	114
Total . . .	912	17,105	18,017

III. SPANISH TROOPS

	Officers.	Strength. Men.	Total.
Carlos de España's Division : 2nd of Princesa, Tiradores de Castilla, 2nd of Jaen, 3rd of 1st Seville, Caçadores de Castilla, Lanceros de Castilla .	160	3,200	3,360

GENERAL TOTAL

	Officers.	Strength. Men.	Total.
BRITISH	1,526	29,036	30,562
PORTUGUESE	912	17,105	18,017
SPANISH	160	3,200	3,360
Total . . .	2,598	49,341	51,939

Appendix 2

The figures represent the men *présens sous les armes* (from the *Situation* in the *Archives de la Guerre*).

			15th July. Officers.	Men.	1st August. Officers.	Men.
FIRST DIVISION (FOY).						
First Brigade Chemineau	6th Leg. 1	. .	22	551	20	333
	2	. .	14	504	11	351
	69th Line 1	. .	27	706	24	662
	2	. .	23	702	23	660
Second Brigade Desgraviers	39th Line 1	. .	31	494	31	460
	2	. .	18	424	18	412
	76th Line 1	. .	29	671	18	313
	2	. .	27	680	27	574
Total Infantry .		.	263	4372	183	3765
3 Companies Artillery .		.	7	207	7	207
Total .		.	270	4579	190	3972
SECOND DIVISION (CLAUSEL).						
First Brigade Berlier	25th Leg. 1	. .	25	500	22	462
	2	. .	15	495	10	396
	3	. .	14	490	11	364
	27th Line 1	. .	22	826	20	636
	2	. .	18	811	15	612
Second Brigade Barbot	50th Line 1	. .	27	575	27	470
	2	. .	14	557	11	398
	3	. .	11	358	8	309
	59th Line 1	. .	34	816	26	683
	2	. .	13	715	22	615
			206	6179	172	4925
3 Companies Artillery .		.	7	219	7	216
Total .		.	213	6398	179	5141

THIRD DIVISION (FEREY).[1]		15th July. Officers.	Men.	1st August. Officers.	Men.
	Staff	9	13	10	13
First Brigade Menne	31st Leg. 1	22	755	20	764
	2	15	591	15	548
	26th Line Staff	9	14	9	16
	1	17	575	17	590
	2	18	556	17	510
Second Brigade ?	47th Line Staff	8	24	7	24
	1	20	611	18	601
	2	20	490	19	474
	3	18	503	19	501
	70th Line Staff	3	10	3	10
	1	19	486	13	595
	2	27	618	20	466
Total Infantry		216	5246	208	5162
4 Companies Artillery		5	302	3	193
Total		221	5548	211	5355

FOURTH DIVISION (SARRUT).		Officers.	Men.	Officers.	Men.
First Brigade Fririon	2nd Leg. 1	34	624	33	590
	2	16	577	19	545
	3	16	571	16	567
	26th Line 1	35	646	36	627
	2	17	463	17	456
	3	17	461	18	431
Second Brigade ?	4th Leg. 1	24	449	24	385
	2	18	365	18	330
	3	21	405	21	271
	130th Line absent [2].	—	—	—	—
Total Infantry		212	4561	216	4302
4 Companies Artillery		5	238	5	214
Total		217	4799	221	4516

[1] Taupin in command of the Division on 1st August.
[2] Bilbao and St. Ander.

		15th July.		1st August.	
FIFTH DIVISION (MAUCUNE).		Officers.	Men.	Officers.	Men.
First Brigade D'Arnauld	15th Line 1 . .	23	523	20	419
	„ „ 2 . .	16	528	13	409
	„ „ 3 . .	13	564	13	401
	66th Line 4 . .	19	539	17	391
	„ „ 5 . .	19	592	17	270
Second Brigade Montfort	82nd Line 4 . .	21	452	20	333
	„ „ 5 . .	20	514	19	396
	86th Line 1 . .	18	605	15	519
	„ „ 2 . .	12	550	13	442
Total Infantry . . .		161	4867	159	3580
Artillery		4	212	4	212
Total . .		165	5079	163	3792

SIXTH DIVISION (BRENNIER).

		15th July.		1st August.	
First Brigade Taupin	17th Leg. 1 . .	26	536	25	450
	2 . .	20	511	17	405
	65th Line 1 . .	29	630	25	539
	2 . .	18	627	16	557
	Detachm't 3 . .	6	31	5	33
	„ 4 . .	6	239	6	173
Second Brigade	4th Etranger . .	9	79	9	79
	22nd Line 1 . .	23	495	21	164
	2 . .	20	500	15	476
	3 . .	18	491	4	76
Total Infantry . .		190	4139	155	2952
3 Companies Artillery . .		4	213	4	213
Total . .		194	4352	159	3165

SEVENTH DIVISION (THOMIÈRES).

First Brigade.		15th July.		1st August.	
	1st Line. Staff .	4	13	4	13
	„ „ 1 .	21	563	20	428
	„ „ 2 .	18	442	18	442
	„ „ 3 .	17	213	17	177
Bonté	„ „ 4 .	20	452	20	394
	62nd Line. Staff .	9	16	9	16
	„ „ 1 .	15	518	12	276
	„ „ 2 .	16	488	11	276
	Detachment 3 .	7	54	13	480

			15th July. Officers.	Men.	1st August. Officers.	Men.
Second Brigade.	23rd Line 3, 4	.	—	—	—	—1
	⌠ 101st Line Staff	.	12	19	8	16
	⎮ 1	.	17	466	10	178
	⎮ 2	.	15	446	6	119
	⎩ 3	.	17	457	5	99
	Total Infantry .	.	194	4347	158	2914
	3 Companies Artillery .	.	5	203	None.	
	Total .	.	199	4550	158	2914

EIGHTH DIVISION (BONNET).

			15th July. Officers.	Men.	1st August. Officers.	Men.
First Brigade.	118th Line. Staff .		4	16	0	10
	⌠ ,, ,, 1	.	16	500	9	306
	⎮ ,, ,, 2	.	18	518	13	323
	⎮ ,, ,, 3	.	16	550	15	385
Gautier	⟨ 119th Line. Staff .		4	7	4	6
	⎮ ,, ,, 1	.	21	403	14	209
	⎮ ,, ,, 2	.	19	435	11	314
	⎩ ,, ,, 3	.	20	420	19	302
Second Brigade.	120th Line. Staff .		4	4	4	3
	⌠ ,, ,, 1	.	20	583	19	391
	⎮ ,, ,, 2	.	19	563	21	379
	⎮ ,, ,, 3	.	20	595	22	379
?	⟨ 122nd Line. Staff .		3	11	2	11
	⎮ ,, ,, 1	.	17	553	14	349
	⎮ ,, ,, 2	.	19	527	14	332
	⎩ ,, ,, 3	.	16	491	10	308
	Total Infantry .	.	236	6186	199	4107
	1 Company Artillery	.	3	107	None.	
	Total .	.	239	6293	·199	4107[2]

CAVALRY DIVISION (CURTO).

			15th July. Officers.	Men.	1st August. Officers.	Men.
First Brigade	⌠ 3rd Hussars (2)[3]	.	17	231	14	185
?	⎮ 22nd Chasseurs (2) .		17	236	18	233
	⎮ 26th Chasseurs (2) .		16	278	18	225
	⎩ 28th Chasseurs (1) .		7	87	3	39

[1] At Astorga, captured by the Spaniards, after the battle of Salamanca.
[2] Should be 4007.
[3] Figures in parentheses show number of squadron.

		15th July. Officers.	Men.	1st August. Officers.	Men.
Second Brigade ?	13th Chasseurs (5) .	20	496	28	426
	14th Chasseurs (4) .	14	308	18	332
	Escadron de marche	11	141	9	52
	Total . .	105	1777	111	1492

Dragoon Division (Boyer).

		15th July. Officers.	Men.	1st August. Officers.	Men.
First Brigade Carrié	6th Dragoons (2) .	19	376	19	332
	11th Dragoons (2) .	19	411	18	359
	19th Dragoons (21)	15	328	16	294
	25th Dragoons .	18	314	18	282
Total Cavalry . . .		79	1429	78	1267
1 Company Heavy Artillery, 1 Company Train Artillery		3	193	3	148
Artillery (not already counted) .		50	1450	22	707
Engineers		17	332	16	345
Gendarmerie Impériale . . .		6	129	6	186
Équipages Militaires (9 Companies)		26	742	22	707
General Staff		54	...	54	...
Total of the whole army . . .		2019	47,980	1714	38,737
Total Troop Horses . . .			4278		3231 [1]
Total Draught Horses . . .			2037		1847
Guns—12 pounders . . .			7		None.
8 pounders . . .			21		18
4 pounders . . .			36		27
3 pounders . . .			1		0
Howitzers . . .			13		13
			78		58

[1] Horses of Équipages Militaires, 15th July, 800; 1st August, 331. This is one of many indications which prove that the return of August 1 includes reinforcements received after the battle. The arithmetic of the French returns is frequently incorrect, though the errors never extend beyond units and tens.

Lightning Source UK Ltd.
Milton Keynes UK
UKHW010816260919
350504UK00001B/74/P